THE LAST OF THE SOUTH TOWN RINKY DINKS
The Extended Volume

E. Don Harpe

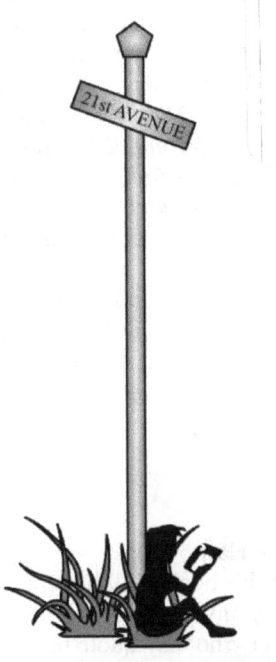

E. DON HARPE

A Note From E. Don Harpe

This is a revised version of the original Rinky Dink book, complete with a newly designed cover, and a couple of new stories.

The book was first published in 2008, and since then I've been asked many, many, rimes to please write another Rinky Dink book. The fact is, I'd love, but I think I told just about all of my old stories in the original edition. However, I did find a few friends who volunteered to compose a story for another book, so I wrote a couple of new ones also, and they are all included in this edition. I felt the new edition could use a new cover, and I liked the picture of my mother and I, so the cover is also newly designed and up to date.

But even more important, since 2008, several of our dear, old friends have passed away and I wanted to be sure to mention them iu this revised version. I want to believe that we will all meet again in a land much better than this one we leave behind, and if we do, I think Heaven will resemble South Town quite a lot. At least, I believe it will resemble South Town as it was in the late 1940s and the early 1950s, which is the time period we recall with such fondness. The friends that I know of that we have lost include John Wesley Wilson, Betty Mayes, Jerome Ellis, Brenda Davidson, Mary Jo Bilyeu, Joe Brown, Patty Summers Evilcizer, Bill Bollinger, Helen Allen, and Ernest Carroll. I've also lost a few friends who weren't Rinky Dinks but who were treasured people to Helen and I. Those include Bill Vaughn, Jim Vaughn, and Tresa Street, all of whom are missed every day.

I hope everyone enjoys the new additions, and enjoys taking the trip back in time to a kinder, gentler, more simple time. I think it will be well worth the time it takes you to read it, and this is me, South Town

This is Rinky Dink Don Harp, wishing all of you a great day, and a great trip down memory lane.

Thanks,

Copyright 1994/2021 Ernest D. Harp
All rights reserved. No part of this book shall be reproduced, stored in a retrieval system or transmitted in any form or by any means without the express written prior approval of the author, except by a reviewer who may quote brief passages in a review to be printed in a newspaper, magazine, or journal.

Second Printing – With Additions
Originally printed as The Last Of The South Town Rinky Dinks and published by Purple Iris Publishing, an imprint of RJ Buckley Publishing

ISBN 10: 0615779638
ISBN 13: 978-0615779638 (Flint River Press)
Published March 2013, BY Flint River Press
Printed in the United States of America

THE LAST OF THE SOUTH TOWN RINKY DINKS
THE EXTENDED VOLUME

DEDICATION
PROLOGUE
CHAPTER 1 INTRODUCING THE RINKY DINKS
CHAPTER 2 GETTING THE LAY OF THE LAND
CHATER 3 SPRINGFIELD, TENNESSEE
CHAPTER 4 RINKY DINK GAMES
POEM: THE CHECKER GAME:
CHAPTER 5 RINKY DINK COWBOYS AND INDIANS
CHAPTER 6 IS THERE A DOCTOR IN THE HOUSE?
CHAPTER 7 1953: LUCILLE COMES HOME
CHAPTER 8 DON LEARNS TO DRIVE
CHAPTER 9 ROSIE THE WITCH WOMAN
CHAPTER 10 A RENOWNED SCOUNDREL
CHAPTER 11 DINNER WITH DAISY
CHAPTER 12 THE RINKY DINKS AND THE LION
CHAPTER 13 FRONT PORCH SWING TO NASHVILLE
CHAPTER 14 WHAT EXACTLY IS A GRAPEFRUIT?
CHAPTER 15 ALONG CAME BUD
CHAPTER 16 THE LONG ARM OF THE LAW
CHAPTER 17 TELEVISON COMES TO TOWN
CHAPTER 18 WAYNE LEARNS TO RIDE A BIKE
CHAPTER 19 WOODLAND STREET SCHOOL
POEM: DADDY:
CHAPTER 20 THE RINKY DINKS TAKE A HOLIDAY
CHAPTER 21 THE WORLD OUTSIDE OF SOUTH TOWN
CHAPER 22 THE TENT MEETING
CHAPTER 23 THE WALKER CLAN
CHAPTER 24 MINNIE AND CLYDE
INTERLUDE
POEM GOD AND MAMA:
CHAPTER 25 MAMA (ONE WORD SAYS IT ALL)
SUPLEMENT 1 THE SOUTH TOWN WOODS
SUPLEMENT 2 THE CARR'S CREEK CRITTER
SUPLEMENT 3 THE KIDS TAKE THE PLUNGE
SOUTH TOWN RINKY DINK HONOR ROLL

THE EXTENDED VOLUME

A RINKY DINKS FIRST LOVE	E. DON HARPE
RECOLLECTIONS OF A RINKY DINK	JAMES A. WALKER
IMPORTED RINKY DINK	CHRISTINE VADEN BROWN
BILYEU SKIES FOR THE RINKY DINKS	WANDA BILYEU KEITH
SPRINGFIELD HIGH SCHOOL DAZE	E. DON HARPE
HONKY TONKS, BEER JOINTS	E. DON HARPE
JOHN WESLEY WILSON	E. DON HARPE

Back in 2008, when we had the first book signing for the Rinky Dinks in Springfield, one of my dearest friends of all came into the store, the same smile on his face, and the same air of confidence that I've seen in him since before we started grade school. Sadly, he won't see this extended version published, because we lost him between then and now. He was one of a kind, a life long friend of the first order, and one of the best men I have ever been honored to know. We shared much of our lives together, and even now it's hard to believe he won't be there the next time I journey back to Springfield. I write this with a heavy heart for his passing but with a heart filled to the brim with the joy of his life, and the true friendship he brought to me and to everyone he knew for so many years. With the highest amount of respect I can give to anyone, I hereby dedicate this volume of the Rinky Dink Book to one of the finest men I have ever known, Lawrence Lee Thaxton. You are missed, my friend, but the world was made better by the life you lived.

LAWRENCE THAXTON

AUGUST 1, 1942   -   AUGUST 26, 2011

DEDICATION

This book is dedicated to every one of Springfield's kids that were ever called South Town Rinky Dinks. The ones who came before me, the ones who lived there when I did, and the ones who live there today. Over the years, they have been judged too harshly.

It is also dedicated to the many thousands of kids all over the country who, simply because of their economic situation, their so-called social class, and especially what part of town they lived in, have been made to feel just a little inferior to those who were lucky enough to be born into more fortunate circumstances.

It is dedicated to the memory of many of our friends who are no longer with us, only a few of which I can name here, but the others are no less forgotten. This book is for Linda Jane White Thaxton, for Jimbo Pearson and Charles Harris. For Jerome Ellis, Brenda Davidson, and Leon Leftrick. It is for Charles Rippy, Donald Ridge, Betty Ann Woody and Faye Leftrick Pentecost. We remember and miss every one of you.

It's dedicated to the memory of Bobby Dean Pentecost, one of my dearest friends of all. Bobby Dean and I shared many good times, and for all of my life I have been thankful that I could call him my friend. We grew up together as South Town Rinky Dinks, and our friendship stood true the test of time. Even though we didn't see each other often in later years, each time we met that friendship was still as strong as it was during the time in our lives when we were inseparable.

I will miss you, old friend, and if I could but say one thing to you it would be that I have thought of you often in these past few years, always with a smile, and always with the idea that one day we would again meet and sit down and talk about the old days, and the trip to Florida, and all of the other happy memories we shared. God rest you well, Bobby Dean, perhaps at some later time we will indeed meet again.

And although I find it almost unbearable to write these next few words, this book is dedicated to the memory of Larry Wayne Wilson. I have had no better friend, will never have a better friend, and could ask for no better friend. Wayne was a man that I was proud of, and was a man that all of Springfield should be proud of, simply because he chose that town to remain in, when he could have done anything or gone anywhere he wanted. Wayne and I laughed together for almost sixty years, playing cards and swapping books, and talking about anything and everything. Wayne loved life, he loved living and he dearly loved his Linda, his wife for so many years. He had a dry sense of humor that Mama loved, and she mentioned it often. Wayne never lost that sense of humor, not even in the face of years of bad health and hard work. I don't know because I wasn't there, but I suspect that on the day he last spoke to his family and friends, he told them not to worry, and I'll bet he was wearing that little grin I remember so well. I truly believe, without a doubt, that we will meet again, somewhere, sometime, and in a better life.

We lost Eva Mai in the early part of 2004, and my stories are dedicated as much to her as to anyone else. I loved her all of my life, and cannot picture her being gone. Perhaps the things I've written here will allow some other people to recall her as I do, and to see what a grand and wonderful person she was. I truly miss her, and I miss not having her to turn to when I have questions, or just when I need to be reassured that everything is really OK.

This book is also dedicated to the memory of Daddy and to all of my heroes; to my uncles and aunts; Jim, Horace, Fred, Willard, Clyde Cannon, Annie Belle & Henry; to the people who influenced me the most, such as John Mayes, and Minnie Cannon, and especially Jewell Bryant "Bud" Bollinger.

It is dedicated to my brother Ray and his wife Pat. To my children Shelly, Jason, Nikki and Derek. To Fay Birdwell and Patty Summers. To honorary Rinky Dinks Ron Rentchler, Edith Scott, Sonny Strickland, Jim Vaughn, Delilah Reed, and John Cassell who read many of these stories as I was working on them and whose input has been invaluable in the making of this book. It's for Sam Traughber, C.C. McCartney, the infamous Rinky Dink Billy Gragg, and to the other family members and friends who acted as my sounding board as I wrote the stories.

It is dedicated to Joe and Christine Brown, and to Charlie Bilyeu, friends all who took an interest and helped me to realize that I needed to go ahead and get this book published now.

THE LAST OF THE SOUTH TOWN RINKY DINKS
THE EXTENDED VOLUME

It is most especially dedicated to my one and only true love, my wife and soul mate of nearly fifty years, Helen Faye Gregory Harp, who has had to live most of our married life in circumstances that she didn't deserve. God knows I wish I could have given her everything I thought she should have had.

She has been the true love of my life, and she has put up with more than she should have as I wrote this story. Many is the time that she has brought me back from the edge of gut wringing emotion as I relived some of these memories. Making this trip, writing this book, sometimes wasn't easy, and without Helen, I probably wouldn't have gotten through it.

I love you.

Did I mention that Helen is a born and bred South Town Rinky Dink herself, so maybe that's why she's so strong, so stubborn, and willing to lend me so much of her own strength.

Of course, first last and always, it is dedicated to Mama. Lena Viola Walker Harp. My inspiration and guide throughout my life. It was from her that I received the gift of loving to read, which in turn led me to loving to write.

Make no mistake about it; although it was a skinny, middle- aged South Town Rinky Dink who finally managed to write these words on paper, it was Mama who first wrote them in my heart.

And my whole heart thanks go out to Rebecca Buckley of Buckley Publishing who took a shot on this book when it was just an idea. She's helped the Rinky Dinks more that she can know, and I think it's time she became an Honorary South Town Rinky Dink. So, here's to you Rebecca. HSTRD *extraordinaire*.

PROLOGUE

In every small town in the rural South, and I suspect in most other parts of the country as well, there is a dividing line, a distinct geographical something that serves to determine the social structure of the town. A boundary line, if you will, that the people of the town use to judge who's who. Which side of the line you live on makes a very big difference in how you are perceived by the people of the town. Not only in the present but also for the rest of your life. Regardless of how many years pass, or how successful or how desperate you may become, you're still known in your hometown by which side of the line you grew up on.

In some towns, the dividing line is the river.

I don't know, but I guess maybe they call the people who live on the wrong bank River Rats.

In other towns it may be a mountain.

I can't even guess at what they'd call those people. Hillbillies, or perhaps Mountain Goats, or some other equally mean and petty little homegrown name. But in the long run, it doesn't really matter what name is used, they all mean the same thing. The names are badges, and while they aren't visible outside your clothing, they serve the same purpose. They are a means whereby the more fortunate people can describe the less fortunate ones, without resorting to actual bigotry. With that in mind, it will come as no surprise to learn that the names are almost always used in a negative sense.

In Springfield, Tennessee, the small country town where I grew up, the dividing line was the railroad tracks. There was the wrong side of the tracks and the right side, the North Side and the South Side. In this case, the wrong side of the tracks was known as South Town, and you can bet the folks who lived on the North side of the tracks had a name for those who lived on the South.

The "wrong side of the tracks" is a catch phrase, an all encompassing term that has come to mean a place where nothing good comes from, where criminals are born, bred, and harbored, and where everyone is poor and either uneducated or undereducated. But most importantly, it means that the people who live there are somehow inferior to those who, through an accident of birth, are fortunate enough to have been born a few miles, or even a few feet, on the other side of the line.

This book is about the people, mostly the kid's that came from the wrong side of the tracks in this run of the mill, quite ordinary small country town where I grew up.

Most of the stories take place in the late forties and throughout the fifties with maybe one or two in the early sixties. A few of them may have happened in the thirties, but regardless of the time frame, the common thread lies in the almost childlike innocence of the times. Innocent, at least, when compared to today.

Springfield is in Northern middle Tennessee, at the top of the famous highland rim, almost directly in the middle of the state, some fifteen miles from the Kentucky state line, and about thirty miles to the north of Nashville.

It was mostly a farming town back then, claiming to be the home of the world's finest dark fired tobacco, a tradition that some folks would like to see carried on today. It's a fact that the dark black dirt in and around Robertson County is some of the richest dirt in the world. You can grow anything there, and over the years, almost everything has been grown there.

There wasn't a lot of industry nor a lot of factory jobs in Springfield back in those days, and a lot of Springfield people drove the twenty-five or thirty miles South into Nashville every day to work. There were only a few jobs in Springfield, outside of farming, and none of them paid very much in the way of wages.

Undoubtedly, it will come as no surprise that most of the people who lived in South Town didn't earn much money. Nor will you be surprised to learn that the kids who lived there were never handed anything on a silver platter. Unless, or course, you count heartaches and hard times, for their legacy was filled with these. Had there even been a platter, however, it would more than likely been made of cheap pink depression glass rather than silver.

But we got by.

In fact, we got pretty good at getting by back then, and it was a habit that some never managed to lose. It wasn't easy then, and for those who couldn't or wouldn't make a change, it still isn't.

Anyway, this book is about those times, and those people, and mostly about the kids that lived there. Some of the stories take place in the years during and following what was called The Great Depression, when times were the hardest our county has ever seen them. Life was different back then, much different.

Some of the stories happened during the Great War. That's World War II, of course, for those of you who have never heard that phrase before.

But most of the stories take place in the Fifties, when I and the other kids of South Town were first beginning to learn about the world and about ourselves. For the most part they're stories about the kids of Springfield. The kids from the wrong side of the tracks. The kids everyone on the other side of town looked down on, the kids who had a special name.

Exactly what did they call those kids, you might ask.

Are you ready for this?

They called those kids the South Town Rinky Dinks.

Kids like me.

I was one of the Rinky Dinks, and if you want the truth, I still am.

You know what? I'm pretty proud of it.

One thing's for sure. You won't read any apologies in these pages about where I came from, or how I grew up. And if I know the rest of the kids that grew up there, you won't get very many apologies from them either. There wasn't a single one of the Rinky Dinks that wasn't tough as a hickory nut when we were kids, and most grew up the same way. They used to say that we didn't have a pot to pee in, or a window to throw it out of, and maybe that's right, but the key is, we didn't know it. We were tough, we were proud, and we still are.

It's a fact that almost every one of us turned out to be pretty good adults. We don't rob people, we don't cheat on business deals, and we don't take advantage of our friends. Add to that the fact that most of us haven't spent any time in jail, and you'll see that being a Rinky Dink might have not been so bad after all. Sure, of course I'm aware that there were a few exceptions, there always are, but there weren't that many.

I think the single most important thing about those kids is that we're all still friends. That's saying a lot. After fifty plus years of knowing each other, we're still friends.

We don't see each other as much as we'd like, in fact, mostly now when we meet it's at a funeral, but at those times, you can count on one thing. When a Rinky Dink meets another Rinky Dink on the street or anywhere else, we don't avoid one another, and we sure as heck don't pretend we're from somewhere we're not. We're more than happy to talk about the old days, back when it was always summer, the sky was a lot bluer than it is now, we had the field to play in, and we had each other.

So here then is my Rinky Dink book.

A collection of stories about a lifestyle very much unlike our life is today, yet hauntingly familiar to many of us. The stories will be familiar to anyone who was born and raised during that period in time, and especially familiar to those of you who grew up poor, on the wrong side of the tracks, and had to put up with other people who thought they were better than you. These are the stories of the Last of the South Town Rinky Dinks. The last kids who grew up on 21st. Avenue, before they tore down all the old houses and built the projects there.

Sometime, I guess it was 1957 or '58, they came in with bulldozers and trucks and pushed and rammed down all of the small, red brick sided houses on 21st Avenue and Carter Street and Cherry Street, and even a lot of those on Park Street, and they brought in progress.

Progress they called the Projects.

Of course, looking back, we all know the many wonderful and strange happenings that life in the Projects brought, and how much better off everyone became because of that progress. Not only in my hometown, but in hometown's all across the country. Sure.

So yes, we were the last of the South Town Rinky Dinks. The original ones. And this book is dedicated to those of us still living who will read these words and remember, and to those of us who have passed on, who will look down, or up, as the case may be, and laugh when they see the looks on the faces of the Rinky Dinks as they're taken back in time.

THE LAST OF THE SOUTH TOWN RINKY DINKS
THE EXTENDED VOLUME

There is one thing I want you to understand and remember as you read these pages. I'm writing this book from the viewpoint of a young boy, somewhere between ten and fifteen years old. I want it to reflect the innocence of the times, and I felt that too much research, or too many so called "true facts" might take away from the books real feeling. If any of you lived there during that time and these stories are not exactly as you remember them, I apologize. I'm writing what I was told as a kid, what I remember from those times, and I'm trying to put myself back inside the head of the kid I was then, and not let too much of the man I've become influence the stories.

Perhaps there will be a book two of the South Town Rinky Dinks stories, and if so, I'd welcome any input you may have. But until then, I hope you enjoy what I've written, because even though the way I tell the stories may not be exactly the way you remember them all, I'll bet you remember your version of every page.

E. DON HARPE

1

INTRODUCING THE RINKY DINKS

Sure enough, kids are coming into the front yard from all up and down the street. It doesn't take much imagination to know that the nine or ten tow headed boys and girls standing there waiting for me to come out are the backbone of the Rinky Dinks.

Like I said, I was kind of the ringleader. I guess you could say that.

Or maybe not, I don't know. Maybe we didn't even have a ringleader, and I was just the one who kept suggesting things to do. If no one had any better ideas, then we did whatever it was that I suggested. If they wanted to play something else, then I didn't have a problem with that. Just so long as we did something all of the time. None of us wanted to let any grass grow under us.

I suspect that even back then I had the knack of knowing what most of the kids wanted to do, and then suggesting it before anyone else did. However, in the purest sense of the word, that may be all there is to leadership anyway. Of course it's not like there were a lot of choices anyway. Some kind of ball game, bike riding, reading funny books, or shooting marbles was about it. It didn't really require a lot of leadership.

Anyway, the first two kids in the yard are brothers, John Wesley and Larry Wayne Wilson. Wesley was the older, about two years older than me and Wayne, but he went along with whatever we wanted to do most of the time. For a good reason. We were all he had. Wesley probably had more good old plain horse sense than the rest of us combined, and later turned out to be a very successful businessman. At the time though, he was just one of us.

Wesley and I later worked together, ran around and drinks together, and dated the same girl, and we have remained close friends since our earliest days. I took my drivers license test in Wesley's 55 Plymouth, he got me a job at Phillipps and Buttorff in Nashville, and we still see each other every now and then. Mostly at a funeral or at the Springfield Wal-Mart, which for some reason we used to seem to visit at the same time once or twice a year.

I've been telling Wesley that I was writing this book, and I guess he just didn't quite believe it. We'd bump into each other, talk a while, and then I'd say " Hey, I'm still working on the Rinky Dink book, got some good stuff in there." Then he'd say; "Aw, Donald, you've been working on that for years, you ain't never gonna get it finished."

Well, it's true I have worked on it for years, for it is truly an ever-changing story. I've let some of the old gang read parts of it, and they've all been very supportive. I've been encouraged by a couple of folks to keep on writing, keep on letting the stories come out.

Mary Alley and Lola May Bollinger read parts of the book, and the tears in their eyes when they told me how much it meant to them makes all of the effort worthwhile. Billy Gregg has one of the original copies, and his support meant a lot in the fact that this is yet another revision. And I have to admit that Wesley Wilson played a part in my finishing it too, just by being his suspicious self, and for even thinking that I might not keep working on this project, regardless of what else may fall by the wayside. Hard to believe we've passed that seventy-year mark, ain't it, Wesley, old boy, but we have. Course, you're a lot older than me, and I was always better looking.

I sent Wesley a copy of the manuscript a year or so ago after Wayne died, and he said he enjoyed reading about the old days. That makes the book a success, that's all I ever wanted it to do.

Wesley and I have known each other, and most of the others as well, for over half a century, plus ten. Seems unbelievable, doesn't it, but it's true. There was a time, in fact many years of times, when we "boys" wouldn't have been able to tell each other that we loved them, it just wouldn't have come out of our mouths. But that time is past, and the fact is that we do. We were all more like brothers than friends, and time hasn't changed very much at all.

Hang on a minute and let me get myself out of yet another of the frequent times when I simply could not make myself write anymore, not till the emotions were brought back under control and my fingers knew their way around the keyboard again.

Back to the story. Back to the story.

Wayne Wilson had a heart condition, and had to go to the doctor in Nashville every so often. Most of the time his mother would take him there on a Greyhound bus, at least I think that's how they got there, but I know for sure that he always had to take a lot of medicine. But heart condition or not, Wayne played just as hard as any of us. Which was pretty hard. Full speed was the only speed we had. That and full stop.

The only thing Wayne and I liked as much as playing outside was going inside and reading our funny books. Most every day we'd take an hour or so time out and go inside either my house or his, get out our stack of well worn old funny books, stretch out in the floor, and let Superman or Batman or The Doll Man or The Green Lantern take us off to worlds that no one else even knew existed.

The comics, or funny books, as they were called back then, were as adventurous as any television program is today. Probably even more so, because imagination is much more real to a kid than a television show can ever be. At least, it always was to me.

We had another friend named Carl who shared our love of comic books, and I've also spent many lazy afternoons lying in Carl's house or he in mine. Carl lived around the corner on what everybody called "Short 21st." Carl was one of the Rinky Dinks too, but that's another story, maybe for another book.

On some days, Jerry Mantlo would be hanging around, and maybe Charles Rippy or Ray and Charles Harris.

Of course, Goober was always there. Goober was the nickname of my nephew, William Ray Harp, and in the course of the rest of this book, you'll read plenty about him. The story is that he was nicknamed "Goober" after a country singer called "Goober and the Kentuckians." His mother, Eva Mai, heard the band singing the "Hadacol" theme song one night, held her baby up, and said to no one in particular, "Here's my little Goober." And of course the name stuck. Those kind always do. Goober, being a few years younger than us, usually played with Wayne Birdwell, Danny Woody and Charles Lee Hutton, who were also a little younger.

Thomas Lee Birdwell was usually there, and you could count on finding little Roger Dale Hutton running up and down the street. Roger was even younger than Goober and Wayne, and mostly just ran around in the yards behind the houses playing with whoever or whatever he could find to play with.

Then there was Melvin Tanner. Melvin lived two blocks over, on Blair Street, and wasn't on 21st every single day, but he was there often enough to be one of the inside gang.

And then there's Wesley Dean Birdwell.

Wesley was a freckled faced kid, and more than a little self conscious about it. He'd bristle up in a minute if anyone mentioned his freckles, and over the years had more fights than he did freckles.

One of my sidekicks was a kid who lived down on South Main Street, next to the tobacco factory. Later, as we grew older and went to high school, he became one of my very best friends of all. His name was Bobby Dean Pentecost, and we shared many wonderful adventures together, including a trip to Daytona Beach Florida in the fall of 1958 that led to one of our first experiences in the world outside of South Town. More on that a little later.

Now and then, actually more often than not, one or two of the girls would also be at my house. Although they never played marbles, and almost never played in any of the various ball games we had, they were as much Rinky Dink as any of us.

Mostly though when they decided they wanted to play with us, the girls played "Dale Evans" to our "Roy Rogers," or sat on the porch and sang songs.

The ones that hung around the most were Faye Birdwell, Wanda Thaxton, and Joyce Woody.

A couple of years later Mary Lee Harp could be found hanging around with us quite a lot, but even though she had the same last name as me, we never thought we were kin.

Mary Lee later married one of my best friends of all time, a young man named Billy Johnson. Billy and I had some great times, too many to talk about here, but there are some stories I could tell.

Billy passed away in the fall of 2006, and I hadn't seen him in about ten years. This was another of those times when I wished I'd gone back home at least once and contacted some of the old gang. I wrote this in February of 2007, and just the week before I read in the Springfield paper that Mary Lee had died. Strange how some people don't last that long once one of them goes, isn't it?

I spent a lot of time with one of my cousins, Betty Blanche Mayes, when she was living in Springfield, but she didn't live there all the time.

My best buddy back then among the girls was always Faye Birdwell. She was Wesley and Wayne's sister, and was a cute little brown haired girl with great big dark eyes. Most of the time, Faye didn't have a lot to say, which was a truly endearing trait to the boys on the street. Now and then she'd get mad and either tell us off, or threaten to tell on us, for one thing or another, so we kind of stayed on our toes when we played with Faye.

I remember once, when we were about thirteen or fourteen, I walked into Margaret's kitchen, (Margaret was Faye's mother) and I saw Faye mixing up some pimento cheese spread. She was standing there at the table, with her hands deep in a bowl filled with creamy yellow Velveeta cheese, little pieces of bright red pimento, and a gob of white mayonnaise. She was working the mixture, kneading it with her hands, squishing it until it oozed out between her fingers, and as I stood there watching, transfixed, she asked me a simple little innocent question.

Here, Donald, want a bite of my pimento cheese?

Naw, Faye, I don't think I do.

Aw, c'mon. It's good.

Naw, I don't think so. I don't like that stuff.

Now I didn't take a bite that day. In fact, and I don't think I've ever told Faye this, I didn't take a bite of pimento cheese spread until I was about thirty years old. I think that was because I'd also seen Faye work up a mud pie or two between those same ten fingers. Anyway, I just couldn't stand the thought of eating something that was made by squishing it between your fingers like that.

Remember now, I never claimed I was the smartest Rinky Dink in South Town, and I was always really curious about what I ate. Still am. To this day, Faye remains one of my fondest memories from those days, and one of my dearest friends, although we very seldom see each other. But you know, I don't have to see Faye every day, or even every year, to love her. And I wouldn't hesitate to say that she loves me. Back then it wasn't a boy/girl love, and it never turned into a man/woman love. It's just been fifty plus years of friendship love. Faye married one of the finest men I know, and raised a family anyone would be proud of, and every time we run into each other, whether it's at a super market or a funeral, our eyes meet and that same old feeling is there. We have the same roots, and they run deep and strong, and I've always been glad of that. Oh well, enough already, I'm getting a little too sentimental. Hang on, here we go again.

When all of us gathered each day, right in the middle of the bunch you would always find Lawrence Lee Thaxton. Lawrence was a little younger than me, but by the time he was eight or nine, he was bigger than any of us. And that boy dearly loved to fight.

Occasionally two of three of us would jump on him and get the best of him, but I don't recall a single time when any of us could have held our own in a fight with Lawrence if we'd had to fight him by ourselves.

Lawrence's Daddy sold home-brew from his house on 21st, and was also known to like a good fight, but he was one of those men that all little kids just like by instinct. Morris was a big man, with dark curly hair and a loud, ready laugh, and loved children. And all of the kids loved him.

Let me stop for just a minute and explain exactly what I mean when I talk about a fight between the Rinky Dinks.

Kids fighting back then wasn't anything at all like kids fighting today. For one thing, most of the time we weren't mad at each other, and weren't trying to hurt each other at all. We were just scuffling around or throwing a few punches, and in thirty or forty minutes we were all back playing ball or marbles or whatever. Our fights weren't serious things, and there was never any question about not being friends just because we had a fight.

The fact is, we were probably better friends because of the fights. I know one thing for sure. All the fights we had as kids worked as a kind of common bond that seemed to make our friendship stronger as we grew older. I don't remember a single fight that resulted in a permanent break in any of our friendships. The other thing is, most of the fights don't stand out in my memory as single events, only as collective things. Things that happened in our natural, normal, everyday run of the mill existence, and weren't notable enough to be really important.

THE LAST OF THE SOUTH TOWN RINKY DINKS
THE EXTENDED VOLUME

It's not like there were a lot of fights anyway. Two or three a day sometimes, or maybe a few more, and that's all. Most days, anyway.

But I don't want you thinking that all the Rinky Dinks did was fight. That's not all we did. Most of the time we played marbles or baseball, hide and go seek or kick the can. Kids today don't have any idea how satisfying the sound of a good marble shot can be. They're too immersed in the electronic sound of video games, and the head throbbing sound of what they insist on calling music.

Let me tell you about a sound that could decide the fate of a kid for the next two or three weeks. It was the hard click of a marble striking another marble, in a game of "keeps," and whoever won the daily game knew he'd have to defend that win every day for weeks, or until the others won back their marbles.

We played a lot of games back then, some great and others greater. We had to make up a lot of what we played, and I think that's what made them so great.

The Rinky Dinks didn't know we were so inventive, but if we hadn't been, all we'd ever have done was sit on our hands and watched grass grow.

Come to think of it, I'm not so sure we didn't do that too, at least part of the time.

2

GETTING THE LAY OF THE LAND

It won't take long for you to read these stories, but I hope the few minutes you spend inside the pages they let you become lost in the magic of yesterday. I hope they let you return to a street that existed in a simpler time, a street that lives on in the memory of every kid that ever walked down it.

For a while, sit back, relax, and let these pages take you to that street.

It was called 21st. Avenue, and of course you may have already guessed that's where I lived.

It's easy to find. All you have to do is let your memory or your imagination lead you slowly South of the railroad tracks along Batts Boulevard. Bear right on Woodland Street until you get to Mrs. Gragg's store, and then turn right onto 21st Avenue.

Half a block down on the left, on the corner of Carter Street, you'll find 401 21st Avenue South. That address was home base for my generation of Rinky Dinks, and maybe for the generation that came before mine.

401 21st Avenue.

That was where I lived.

If you'll tag along for a while, I'll try and give you the layout of the few blocks where most of these stories take place.

On the right hand corner of Woodland Street and 21st Avenue, as I've already noted, is a neighborhood grocery store owned and operated by a fine lady named Mrs. Gragg. Of course Mrs. Gragg had a first name, but in all of my hundreds or thousands of times in her store, I don't know if I ever heard anyone use it.

Mrs. Gragg had several children, but the one I remember best was a boy named Billy. Billy was several years older than me and my generation of Rinky Dinks, so we didn't see too much of him hanging around the street. Billy already had other, grander ideas forming in his head, and even then he had enough determination and guts to go after his goals full force. And while there's no denying that he met or exceeded most of his goals as he grew older, even now when I have the occasion to talk to him, I get the feeling that somehow he still might be in hot pursuit of yet another dream. If so, there's no doubt in my mind that he'll catch up with it. After all, Billy was a Rinky Dink too, and I've never heard him deny it. And if you say too much to him about it, especially if you say anything bad about those days and those kids, you're probably gonna get an answer you won't particularly care for.

On Woodland Street, beside Mrs. Gragg's store, stood a white frame house where two sisters lived, Elizabeth and Edna Blackburn. I don't remember a lot about the Blackburn sisters, except that Elizabeth grew up and married Tooter Geezley. I honestly don't know what ever happened to Edna.

After you turn the corner on 21st Avenue, if my memory serves me well, I think the first house on the right was where the Pooles lived, and next to them was where Mrs. Burchie Fryer lived. Mrs. Burchie lived there with her husband, Goodloe Fryer, and her sister, Mrs. Carrie Yates, and Burchie and Carrie's father, a Mister Yates.

Burchie had a grown son named Charles Fryer, who also lived there. Charles was an epileptic and used to scare us to death when he had one of his "fits." He was a big, strong boy, quite a few years older than most of us, and sometimes when he had a fit, as everyone called his seizures, it took two or three grown men to hold him down until the doctor arrived.

Mrs. Burchie and Mr. Goodloe had a very pretty daughter named Marjorie, who had married and moved out of South Town in the 50s, but she came to visit often, and I remember most about Marjorie was her smile. She had a beautiful smile for just about everyone, and even though we didn't see her every day, I have fond memories of her.

Next door to Mrs. Burchie was where Oscar and Nora Hutton lived with all of their kids. And there were a lot of them. There was Charles and Roger and Anita and a whole passel whose names I simply can't remember. Oscar and Nora were good, kind people who worked hard and lived about as straight a life as anyone I ever knew.

I always had a lot of respect for Oscar Hutton, and I believe everyone in South Town did too. Oscar worked at Fort Campbell, Kentucky, as a carpenter and drywall finisher, and Daddy told me on more than one occasion that Oscar was just about as good as you can get when it came to finishing sheet rock. I took that as gospel, because my Daddy just didn't hand out compliments every day of the week. Especially about anything to do with building houses. If Daddy said Oscar was good, then that was all there was to it.

Oscar's wife was named Nora, and I remember her well. She was a pretty, blonde lady who always made all of us kids feel at home in her house.

Her mother was named Pearl Woody, and I also remember her as being a gracious woman. She had a son named Junior Woody who was one of my father's friends, and who sometimes stopped by our house to have a drink or two and maybe play some poker with daddy.

Junior had a older brother named Henry Woody, who was married for a while to a women named Beatrice, and they were the parents of Danny Woody, who was one the younger kids on the street.

Next door to the Huttons lived another family named Harp, namely Jackie Harp and his family, and to tell the truth, I also can't remember the names of all of his kids. I remember Mary Lee, Wanda and Jacqueline, but that's about all.

Jackie was married to Oscar Hutton's sister, Elizabeth, and they had several children, but most of them were younger than me.

Now, while I can close my eyes and still see most of their faces, I just can't put many names on them.

Jackie's parents were Clarence and May Harp, and the story was that we weren't kin to them at all.

There were only three families of Harp's living in the county then, and none claimed kinship with any of the others. I don't know if we really weren't kin, or if it was just that neither family wanted to claim the other.

I don't guess it makes a lot of difference, either way. I know that most folks liked and respected Jackie Harp, and he worked for Austin and Bell Funeral Home for many years.

At this point, I tend to get a little lost remembering who lived where, but I think that Lawrence Thaxton and his family lived in the next house, and a married couple named Rosie and Archie lived in the next one. I don't want to get into any of the many stories about Rosie and Archie at this time, and perhaps not at all. They were a colorful couple, to say the least, and made for some exciting times among the Rinky Dinks.

Lawrence's Mama and Daddy were named Morris and Ethel Thaxton, and Lawrence had two sisters, Betty and Wanda. Lawrence was part of the inside group, if such a thing existed, of the Rinky Dinks. He loved to fight, and didn't much care who with or when. I'll tell you more about Lawrence later, but right now just let me say that he was one of the best football players ever to come out of Springfield High School, and that's saying a lot. Lawrence was chosen High School All American Tackle during his senior year at Springfield High School, and there aren't too many people in the whole country that have had the distinction of achieving that honor. I'm proud to say that Lawrence was a Rinky Dink through and through.

The path to the field was on the left hand side of Lawrence's house, and the field is where we spent most of our time, playing our never ending ball games, or just lying on our backs on the soft green grass watching the big lazy planes pass overhead.

Staying on 21st, the next few houses seemed to have different families living in them much of the time, and I can't remember many of them. I know for a while there was another family of Huttons that lived in one of them, and somewhere on that side of the street may be where the Roland family lived. There was also a pretty little girl named Stella Moss that lived there for a while, but I lost track of her somewhere along the way. Further down the street there was a lady named Rosie Finn living, and next to her was the family of Tommy Casey.

They said Tommy was a little off, or crazy, as most of the people on the street put it, and I think he had to spend a little time in the asylum, but I don't know that for a fact. I do remember the folks on the street always talked about the day Tommy claimed his wife was trying to poison him, and without another word shot and killed her and Rosie as well. Someone told me that he also shot another man that same morning, but I'm not sure.

I don't know what happened to Tommy after that, and I didn't try to find out for this book. I'm sure it would have made a great story, but I'm trying to stick to things that I can recall. And, as I said, I'm not vouching that I'm telling all of them the way they actually happened.

Anyway...

Also on that end of the street lived a man by the name of Allison Starks. His wife was named Ruth Starks, and Ruth was crippled, and spent most of her time in a wheel chair. The unique thing about the Starks was that folks claimed they were bootleggers. They said they sold whiskey from their house to people they knew, and very seldom to anyone they didn't know. Which, of course, if you were indeed a bootlegger, would have been a very good business practice.

They had a son named Donald Starks, who had the nickname "Duck" and who was also a little younger than most of us. That meant Duck played with the smaller kids most of the time. He was a likeable little kid, and always got along just fine with everyone on the street. I lost track of Duck after we were grown, and haven't seen him in years.

At the end of 21st, the street made a 90 degree turn to the right, and just around the corner was the grocery store of Mrs. Thompsie Graves. Mrs. Thompsie had been married several times, and ran her store in the same location for years. Later she moved to a new location on South Main Street, and I think she continued in the business until she died.

Mama kept a running bill at Mrs. Gragg's store for many years, and later she also had a bill with Mrs. Thompsie.

Every afternoon Mama would walk the couple of blocks to the store and pick up a little food for supper. The basic daily items were always the same. A quart of sweet milk, a loaf of light bread, and a package of Old Gold cigarettes. After that would come maybe a pound of baloney, (Yes, I know it's spelled bologna, thank you) but regardless of how you spell it, what the Rinky Dinks ate was baloney.) Maybe we'd get some potato chips, or a can of soup or chili, or perhaps a pound of hot dogs or hamburger meat. And that was what we'd have for supper that night.

My Daddy was a hunter, and a lot of the time we had whatever Daddy had killed that day.

If Daddy went into the woods and killed some kind of critter, you can bet that he was going to have Mama cook it. We called it meat.

Sometimes we had fried chicken, sometimes we had beef roast or pork roast, steak, ham or bacon, and the rest of the time we had meat. I still get a little suspicious when I'm not exactly sure what is on the table before me. There are a lot of things that will fry up crispy brown and tasty looking, but I don't bite into anything until I know for sure what it is.

Over the years, Daddy killed and Mama cooked a large variety of small furry creatures. We had squirrel and rabbit, groundhog and possum, (And yes, I also know that's spelled Opossum. But if you'd ever seen one of the grinning little rascals fried up for supper, you'd also call it just plain old possum, like the rest of us do.) There was also coon and a variety of small birds. Quail and the like.

Daddy wasn't a deer hunter, and now that I'm grown, I sometimes wonder why. Seems like a deer would have provided more meat than a lot of the smaller animals combined.

It sounds strange, but one of Daddy's most favorite foods was squirrel brains and scrambled eggs. Don't ask me how he acquired the taste, or where he got the recipe, or even how he talked Mama into cooking them for him, but for whatever reason he loved to eat that particular dish.

I don't know if Daddy ever went hunting just for the sport of it. I know he used to run his coon dogs just to listen to their "mouths," but I think Daddy did most of his hunting because he was trying to put food on the table.

And that's how it came about that I don't eat "meat." Because I'm still never sure exactly what it might be.

Anyway, every day for years and years, when Mama went to the store, she'd always get me and Ray a Butterfinger candy bar and an R.C. Cola. It never varied. Butterfinger and R.C. Every day. We didn't think to ask for anything different, and neither Mama nor Mrs. Thompsie ever thought to throw a little variety into our afternoon snack. Nope. Just a Butterfinger and an R.C. Seems to me that I should have grown tired of them after the first four or five years, but I don't ever recall a single day when I wasn't there waiting when she got home, anxiously waiting on the soft drink and candy bar. I do recall that when the prices of soft drinks were raised a penny, from 5 cents to 6 cents, our parents said we wouldn't be drinking many more of the dang things.

One of my first half-grown experiences came in Mrs. Thompsie's store. I decided I wanted to buy a pack of cigarettes, but the sale didn't happen exactly the way I'd thought it would.

I started smoking a few cigarettes a day when I was fourteen or fifteen, but I had absolutely no way of getting enough money to buy them for myself. (By the way, it's now been many years since I smoked, but I try not to preach on the subject.)

By this time, I was making the daily trip to the store for Mama two or three times a week. One day, it seemed perfectly natural for me to smile my very sweetest Donald Harp smile, which was ordinarily a pretty good persuader, and politely inform Mrs. Thompsie that Mama wanted to buy two packs of Old Golds today, please, as she had been smoking more lately.

Pretty smart, huh?

Mrs. Thompsie didn't believe a word of it. She refused to let me have the extra pack of cigarettes, and the next day told Mama I'd tried to buy them. I don't rightly remember how I explained myself out of that one, but I know for sure I never tried to buy another pack of cigarettes from Mrs. Thompsie as long as she ran her store.

Bet you didn't know that back then a storekeeper would open a pack of cigarettes and sell them for a penny each. Only had a nickel, buy five cigarettes. That would last for a while anyway.

Let me come back down the other side of 21st, and then I'll try to remember something about some of the other streets.

On the outside corner as we start back down 21st, lived an old man who had a kind of junked up place. I don't remember if he had a real junkyard, or if his yard just looked like that. He didn't allow us to play in his yard, or anywhere around his house, at any time, and as I remember it, most of us didn't like him all that much. But that was probably just because he was so particular about letting us come through his yard.

Next to that house was a house that also had several families move in and out over the years, but to tell the truth I really can't remember any of the folks that lived there.

At one point in time a family named Middleton lived in one of the houses in that row, and Fred Middleton grew up to be a good friend of mine. Fred was a hard worker, and made some pretty good decisions over the years. One of the best ones he ever made was when he married a pretty girl name Becky Sircey. Becky and Fred had three children, Theresa, Jamie, and Jason, and Fred and Becky owned and operated Middleton's Carpet Center in Springfield for many years.

Next to that house lived the Birdwell's. Their house was on the corner of Cherry Street and 21st Avenue. Vernon and Sis Birdwell lived there with their kids, Mary Sue, Thomas Lee, Dorothy, and Beverly Jane. Dorothy has the same birthday as I do, but is two years younger than me. Vernon's father lived with them, and the best I can recall he had seven or eight first names. He was named after not only family, but also after two or three presidents. To use an old country expression, it sure beat all to hear him recite off all his names in a single breath.

Vernon was Eva Mai's brother, and Eva Mai was married to my brother Norman until he died n 1948 from tuberculosis.

Beside the Birdwell's house the old man had laid out a horseshoe pit, and on the weekends a lot of the men on the street would gather and pitch horseshoes. They very seldom let us kids play, although after we got a little older, we all learned the basics of the game. Back then we played with real horseshoes, and not the manufactured kind in use today, but we still learned enough to throw our share of ringers. At the corner of the house was a great big mulberry tree, and when we could get up in it without getting caught, we'd watch the horseshoe games and eat the sweet berries. There's probably never been another taste that enchanted so many kids as a sun warmed mulberry, picked fresh off the tree, and popped into your mouth with even looking to see if it was clean, or had a small spider on it, or anything like that. Who cared? The mulberries were the greatest fruit in the world.

Across Cherry Street and about half a block down, lived Mrs. Nan West. Nan was somehow related to Allison Starks, and often kept Duck Starks at her house. She was also the grandmother to Michael Wayne Hayes, and Michael was also one of the inside group of Rinky Dinks during that period of time. I think Mrs. Nan was the first person in our part of town, or at least anywhere near 21st, to get a television, and every now and then some of us kids would get to go over and watch a few shows.

The only show I actually remember watching there was once when our class at school went to her house and watched the "Howdy Doody Show." I hate to say it, but Howdy didn't really impress me a lot. First off,

I could see the strings that made him move, and it was plain he was made out of wood. I remember somebody said he had more freckles that Wesley Birdwell, and of course that started a fight. Anyway, most of us figured Buffalo Bob had a neat suit, but we didn't think he'd last very long on 21st. dressed like that.

Mister Charlie Gragg lived on the same side of Cherry Street as Mrs. Nan, but closer to 22nd Avenue. His house was at the back of the Woodland Street School ball field, and it took a pretty good swing of a bat to hit a ball all the way to Mister Gragg's house.

Mister Gragg was married to the lady that ran the store on the corner, and they had several children. I've already mentioned Billy, and there was another boy who was named Hershal, or Herthal, or maybe Herthel, and they had a pretty sister named Dimple. I think there was at least one more boy in the family, but I can't remember his name. It may have been Charlie, but I'm just not sure. And I think there might have been another girl, but I can't recall very much about her.

Mister Gragg had a team of mules, or one mule, or maybe they were horses, I don't remember which, but he was called on to do most of the plowing around South Town. He plowed up the gardens of just about everyone around, and he and his mule could lay down as straight a furrow as any you're ever going to find done with a modern day tractor.

I might also note that it's a fact that the vegetables that came from a back yard garden tasted better than they do from the best of today's fancy produce isles.

On the other corner of Cherry Street and 21st. was the little Baptist mission. A lot of us went to church there, even when we didn't know exactly what a church was. But with the help of wonderful people like Mrs. Burchie Fryer, the Reverend Elmer Mason, and a man named Mr. "Pat" Patterson, we got our first taste of religion.

Let me also mention Mister Henry Bollinger.

He was one of those kind of men that took an interest in people and in kids, and even in entire neighborhoods, and it was probably because of Mister Henry that a lot of people in South Town ever went to church at all. Mister Henry was a hero, a good and true person, and a man that would be looked up to in any society in any town at any time.

Of course, most of what we learned at church was to pray to Jesus that we would go to heaven, or that we would at least get out of South Town.

I still believe most of the things I learned in my early church days. Although I don't attend church every Sunday morning, I know in my heart that in Jesus rests the salvation of the weary world. When all else fails, even the staunchest disbelievers can find comfort just by calling his name.

I also believe that a lot of good people are going to get into Heaven just as surely as the most devout Christian. There are many different ways to serve God, and to my way of thinking, good deeds are never wasted.

Next door to the mission was where a family named Fulps lived, and this is another family that I don't recall a lot about. I do remember two of the Fulps girls, one named Peggy and one named Josie, and have nothing but the warmest memories of them. Josie married one of my good friends, a boy named Charles Wilson, who was Daisy's son, and then later Peggy married my uncle, Horace Walker, and became my aunt.

Peggy had a daughter named Virginia from a previous marriage, and Horace and Peggy then had six kids together. For the record, their names were James, Josie, Eddie, Thomas, Buford, and Rodney. I grew up close to these kids, probably a little closer than to any of my other relatives, and I hold a lot of affection for them.

Rodney lost his life in a car accident while he was a teenager, and none of the family ever really got over it.

James was probably the most stable of the kids, I suppose that's the best way to say it, and has made a very successful life for himself. James was a good kid, and turned into a good man, but I still have a bit of trouble calling him Jim. (Inside thing.) He may be as educated as anyone in the family, seeing as how after many years he only recently got his Masters degree.

Eddie was a little wild for a few years, but settled down and turned into a real family man. I think Tonya had a lot to do with that.

Buford is now called Jack, and does construction work and plays pool. In fact, he plays pool on a par with a lot of professionals.

Virginia and Josie were married to Paul Wayne Gainous and Ricky Grey respectively, and raised fine families in Robertson County. Paul and Ricky are also good men, who have lived good and productive lives.

That only leaves Tom. Tom. What can I say about Tom? Tom is big, he's loud, he's rough, he'll fight a buzz saw, and most of the time he'll start the fight. He's crazy as a bedbug, apparently having inherited all of the wildest genes of the Walker family, which everyone knows is pretty wild. But if I ever had to have someone at my back, Tom is the one I'd call. I like Tom, and I trust him. And for me that's saying a lot. Course, he knows it. We have a understanding about family, he and I, and we're more alike in some ways than either of us would care to admit.

But now, let's get back to our little tour.

Next to the Fulps lived a family named Rippy. Jack and Fred Rippy. And before our modern day readers read something into the names that isn't there, let me tell you that Fred was the Daddy, and Jack was the Mama, and there was never any doubt about that. If you live to be three hundred you'll never meet a nicer, warmer, funnier woman than Jack Rippy. That woman has fed me more times than I can count. She once gave me the last glass of milk in her house, because I was sick and there wasn't a store open. They just don't come much better than Jack and Fred.

Their son Charles was the first kid I knew that learned to pick a guitar, and that boy could really sing. Charles had a sister named Barbara and an older brother named Jerry Donald. My first memory of Jerry was when he had a job was delivering ice.

What? You don't remember when ice was delivered daily by an old truck, or any of the jokes associated with that occupation? Well, it was, and Jerry Donald was the iceman. Let me tell you about it.

Every day he'd drive the ice delivery truck with its bed filled with chunks of ice and covered with a tarpaulin. He'd roll to a stop, get out of the truck, and very deftly use his ice picks to cut off whatever size piece of ice you needed. Mostly that was a ten, twenty or twenty-five pound chunk, which fit nicely inside the compartment of your old ice box. He'd lift the ice from the truck with a great big pair of iron ice tongs, and bring it in the house and put it in the ice box.

Next to Jack and Fred was where Margaret and Jewell Birdwell lived.

They had three kids, and they were all part of the backbone of the Rinky Dinks.

Wesley Dean was the eldest, next came Faye, or Juanita Faye, to use her full name, and the youngest was named Jewell Wayne.

Over the years, Wesley and me probably got into as much mischief as most of the rest combined. We shot marbles, raced bicycles, played ball, and ran rip roaring up and down 21st Avenue like wild Indians for years. We didn't see much of each other after we got older, and that's a shame, as close as we once were. Wesley went into the Air Force, and when he came back, he got married and moved out of Springfield. I only see him, like many of the others, now at funerals.

Next to the Birdwell's lived Randal and Elizabeth Woody and their kids. His name might have been spelled Ranal, I'm not sure.

The kids name were Betty Ann, Joyce Marie, and David. David was also younger than the main gang, and mostly played with the smaller kids. Joyce hung around with Faye Birdwell and Wanda Thaxton, and I don't remember too much about Betty Ann, except that she married early, left 21st Avenue and South Town behind, and died when she was a very young woman.

Next door to the Woody's lived Eva Mai and Bud Bollinger. Eva Mai is Ray's Mama, and as I've already said she was married to my brother Norman before he died from tuberculosis. Eva lived with us for a few more years, until she met Bud Bollinger and they decided to get married. They moved into the house on the corner of 21st and Carter, just across the street from us. I've got too many stories to tell of Eva and Bud to begin them here. There's a whole chapter devoted to a man who had as much influence on me as anyone in this world ever had. With the exception of Daddy, I possibly thought more of Bud Bollinger than I ever have of any other man in this world. He taught me things, Bud did, and not necessarily the things my parents wanted me to learn. But things that proved to be much better building blocks that anyone would have ever expected. I've had several major heroes in my life. My Mama was the first and the greatest, and my Daddy was another, although he might not have thought so. Ernest Mayes was a hero of mine, and so was Jim Walker. Uncle Clyde Cannon meant as much to me as anyone, and so did John Mayes. There's a later chapter devoted to John, but let me say now that John has been a genuine inspiration, in a lot of ways, and remains that way, even though now it is in memory.

Over the years I had friends and teachers, pastors and professional people whom I admired and emulated, but other than Mama and Daddy, the one man who influenced me the most was Jewell Bryant "Bud" Bollinger.

A lot of people from Springfield and South Town will shake their heads at reading that, but I couldn't care less. Bud was special to me, he was the big brother I desperately needed, and whatever some folks may think of some of the things Bud did, and the way he lived, you'll not hear me saying anything bad about him. Bud was there for this skinny little Rinky Dink every time I ever needed him, and to this day I remember him as a hero. Like I said, there'll be more on Bud later.

But right now let's wind down our tour of the neighborhood, because we've finally reached my house.

The house that sat at 401 21st wasn't much. None of the houses on the street were. Like the others, 401 was a small frame house, the outside covered with red brick siding, and the roof made of gleaming, although slightly rusty, sheet tin roofing. But there are a few things that set 401 apart from the others.

We had four rooms, count em, four rooms in our house, while most of the others were little shotgun houses with only three rooms. And we had two small outside buildings. One was a coal house, where we stored coal each winter, and kept part of the overflow of stuff from inside the house. I'll fill you in on the second little building later.

There's one other thing that set 401 apart from the others. We had running water. No big deal, right?

Wrong.

In the late forties and early fifties, running water was an extremely big deal for most of the poorer people. None of the houses had bathrooms, and many didn't even have electricity. A lot of the Rinky Dinks did all of their homework by the flickering yellow glow of a kerosene lamp.

Also, at that time telephones were rare indeed. The common practice was for the folks who had phones to take messages for the folks who didn't, and send one of the kids running the half block or so needed to tell someone that they had a call. Not very complicated at all, is it? And like most really simple things, the system worked.

I guess that was because everyone on the block was friends, and everyone was interested in what happened to everyone else. Passing along a phone message was as natural as helping each other with a quilt, or watching each others kids, or any one of a dozen things folks took for granted back then.

Nowadays, most of us don't mind taking a phone message for one of our friends and passing it along, at our convenience of course. But it's a fact that not many people today would take messages for all of their neighbors for months or even years at a time, especially without complaining all the time, or trying to charge them for the service. We're much too busy now for that kind of thing, and of course, the way things are now we don't have any friends that want us knowing anything about their business.

I don't think that anybody on the street ever locked their doors. I was out of high school and 21st was only a memory before I remember ever locking a door at night.

Mostly all we had was hooks on the screen doors, and we never used them that much either.

I'm not sure exactly why that was. I know there were folks living in South Town who would steal. I'd like to think that we were so much like a big family that no one would ever think of stealing from anyone else who lived there. I'd like to think that, I really would, but that's not really true. Looking back, however, I can see that the possibility exists that not any of us had even one single possession that anyone else on the street wanted. Add to that the fact that if anyone wanted something, the chances are it would have been given to them, and the very real possibility that anyone who was caught stealing would have met up with a very angry group of 21st Avenue men who wouldn't look all that favorably on the person who did the stealing.

Anyway, back to the running water. I was stretching the truth just a little when I first mentioned that. Not that we didn't have running water, we did, it's just that it wasn't inside the house. The water was in the front yard, and you only had one choice in what kind of water came out of the faucet, cold.

We had one of the only hydrants on the entire street, and most of our neighbors came up to our house once or twice a day and filled their buckets. The same man owned almost all the houses on the street, he paid the water bill, and the water system, just like the telephones, seemed to work just fine.

THE LAST OF THE SOUTH TOWN RINKY DINKS
THE EXTENDED VOLUME

In the winter, we had to wrap the hydrant to keep it from freezing, and all year long we had to keep the little ditch clean. The water trickling out of the faucet ran down beside our front yard, cutting a ditch alongside the fence till it reached a small branch that flowed through the field down below our house. The funny thing is, I never heard Mama or Daddy complain about the water hydrant. It was all just part of living on 21st Avenue.

Truth is, I guess we were pretty lucky. Not only did we have water in the front yard, we also had both electricity and a telephone. But we were the exception rather than the rule.

I don't remember a time when we didn't have electricity, but I think we got the telephone when my Aunt Lucille, Mama's sister, came to stay with us when she got sick with heart trouble.

I guess you've got the picture of 401 21st by now.

Except for the other little building in the back yard that I mentioned.

Of course, that little building was the toilet.

Like everybody else on the street, our toilet was in the backyard. And we always called it a toilet, never an outhouse. Beats me why that was, but anyway, ours was down in the left hand corner of our big back yard, close to an open field, and for those of you who know what I'm talking about, we had a two holer.

Gotta admit that we were living good back then. We had electricity, a telephone, water in our front yard, and a two hole toilet. What else could a family want?

When you walk into our front yard, you'll notice three things. There's a Chinese elm tree planted pretty close to the water hydrant, an old brick walk that leads almost all the way to the street, and a large rose bush growing on the right side of the yard. There's also a wooden swing on the left side of the front porch, and it won't take much imagination to smell the morning glories Mama kept planted by the side of the house.

There are two front doors in our house, but you can quickly see that we use the one on the right. Open the screen and walk on inside.

There's a small, single bed on the right just inside the door. That's where Daddy slept.

In the right hand back corner of the front room is the double bed where Mama and me and Goober slept.

At the foot of Mama's bed, resting against the wall, there's a little table with a big old Sylvania radio on it. We used to listen to the 10:00 news every night before we went to sleep, which is a habit I've kept all my life. I can't count the times I've lain awake on Saturday night and listened to the wonderful sound of the Grand Ole Opry pouring in from Nashville. I remember thinking that Nashville must be a million miles away from Springfield. I also remember Mama telling me when I was about seven or eight that one day we'd all have radios that had a moving picture on them that we could watch what was happening. Fancy that.

On the left side of the room, there's a coal-burning grate, with a mantle over it. For years that was pretty much all the heat we had.

Walk through the door in the back of the room and you'll find yourself in the kitchen. Mama cooked on a wood stove, and had the reputation as being a great cook, and I'll write more on that later.

You can almost taste the ice water in the big bucket that sits on the small white table by the door. Help yourself to a dipper full, and then we'll head outside to the front yard. I think the Rinky Dinks are gathering for our first adventure of the day.

SPRINGFIELD, TENNESSEE
(HOME SWEET HOME)

This book is actually written about the people of South Town, and not about the entire town of Springfield, but, after talking with a few people about the idea behind the book, I can see that there are some interesting things about the town that should also be mentioned. A little background, perhaps, that should be set in place so that the stories are taken in the proper context.

Some of the folks I spoke with almost demanded that I write about how the town itself was back then, but many of them wanted me to write about it the way they remembered it. I really couldn't do that. I had to write what I recalled, and sometimes my memories are not exactly the same as the other folks. I make no apologies about that, I simply state that these are my memories, and that right or wrong, fact, fiction, or half-truth, they are what I recall about Springfield.

It's funny, but I'll almost bet that some of the folks who asked me to write this chapter will probably be the ones that disagree the strongest with what I've written. So be it.

I even ran into one lady that told me she had lived in Springfield her entire life and had never heard anyone referred to as "South Town Rinky Dinks." I won't dispute her word, but I can tell you it's a million to one that she didn't grow up or live South of the railroad tracks. If she had lived there, she would be as familiar with the term as the rest of us are.

Of course, in this day of "political correctness," it's possible that there are those folks who wouldn't want to admit that such sentiments ever existed. Actually, with "out of sight, out of mind," and "what's done is done" as their theme, it's more than possible, it's a certainty. Well, the world may be more politically correct now, but back then, it was a different story. South Town was Springfield's slum district, and we sure enough were called Rinky Dinks.

There were also names for certain other communities in Springfield then, but I would guess that due to PC and age most of them have been conveniently forgotten as well.

But anyway...

It won't be hard to picture the Springfield I'm writing about. It's exactly like any one of a thousand other little towns around the country. The town has grown a lot since then. It's more cosmopolitan now, becoming more of a small city rather than a country town, and much more than the backwoods wide spot in the road it was when I grew up here.

To me it's lost a lot of its charm and appeal.

Like the houses in South Town, the charm and appeal of Springfield fell by the wayside in the name of progress. There is a lot more industry now, and I suppose that's good. The schools are bigger now, with many more children, and they don't even teach the same things they did back then. The Lord's Prayer and the Pledge of Allegiance were standard fare every day, and I don't recall ever seeing a gun at school. My point is that I don't personally think the schools are necessarily better now, but I know there are those who would argue that point. I think the kids are a lot smarter now than we were at the same age, but anyone who looks inside their own mind can see the real truth. The fact that kids are smarter today is due more to exposure to the internet and to television and programs like Sesame Street than exposure to the school system.

Moving on.

There are a lot more people in Springfield now and there are bigger department stores, bigger grocery stores, more fast food franchises than you can shake a stick at, and it seems as if there's a gas station or car lot on almost every corner in town.

Back then the streets were narrower and not paved nearly so well as they are now, and the houses weren't as expensive. Of course, as in many small towns, there were quite a few older homes that were large and beautiful, but they were mostly on the streets North and West of the town square, with a few being in the section called Eastland Heights. There weren't any sub-divisions back then, and for the most part that was before developers started naming the communities inside the city limits.

But back then you could walk down the narrow, poorly paved streets in safety, and you knew almost everyone you met. Folks would come out to talk to you as you passed, and you could spend a few minutes just enjoying the company of a friend. That doesn't happen so much now.

While I'm at it, let me make it plain that I don't consider jogging or pulling around a little would be dog on a leash an evening walk.

I would wager that there are many people in Springfield now that don't know who their neighbors are, and probably don't care. A little afternoon visiting is a thing of the past, and now almost everyone needs an invitation and a reason to come over. Ladies don't talk over the clothesline like they did back then, and for a good reason. Most of them don't have a clothesline. In fact, a lot of them probably don't even know what a clothesline is.

There are still some folks who use one of the several public laundries in town, but for the most part they don't start a lot of conversations with the other patrons. I guess there are several reasons for that. Number one, they probably don't know the other folks there, number two, they probably don't want to know them, and number three, it's almost certainly a fact that they don't trust them.

Yeah, we had narrow little streets, lined with trees and flowers, where folks sat on their front porch and spoke to other folks that passed by. We had small neighborhood schools that taught kids things like reading, writing, and arithmetic, and how to get along with each other. We didn't have a lot of industry and there was very little to do most of the time. We mostly just stayed at home and tried our best to raise our families and get along with our neighbors.

Shucks, folks, isn't it a good thing that progress finally caught up with Springfield? (And all of the other little towns all over the country.)

Yes, it was different then, and to tell the truth I don't really want things to be the way they were, but wouldn't it be nice if we could somehow have managed to maintain part of the way things were, and combine those things with the many advantages that have come along since?

Look up one horse country town in the encyclopedia and you might very well find a picture of Springfield's courthouse square. But even though Springfield could have been the poster town for country in the forties and fifties, the seeds had already been planted that would bring Springfield, and little towns like it all over the country, kicking and screaming into the future.

America was no stranger to hard times during the thirties, and Springfield fared little better than the rest of the country. Actually, small towns all across the country and especially in South were mirror images of each other. The Great Depression left a lot of folks hungry, a lot of folks out of a job, and a lot of folks looking for cheap housing.

It's a fact that most towns wound up with neighborhoods where these folks lived.

Cheap rent and neighborhood schools looked very good to poor folks back then, and regardless of the fact that in many of the houses there were no utilities and no bathrooms, living conditions were still better than they might have been.

The forties brought war, and saw a lot of boys head off to countries many people in Springfield had never heard of.

There were also a lot of folks that left the South to go to Northern cities that many of them had only read about before. A lot of the ones who were too old, or too sick, or failed to pass the Army entrance exam for some reason, left the Tennessee tobacco fields and headed north to work in the defense factories. "They also serve who sit and wait" became a familiar slogan during those years, and patriotism ran high among those who remained at home.

In 1945, on an island half a world away, the war ended with the biggest bang anyone had ever heard or seen, and it wasn't long before some of the boys who had marched away came marching home.

Some, but not all.

Sadly, many thousands never returned. I had a brother and an uncle who were counted among those who gave their life so that the world might be a better place for everyone else. I'm proud of that, I'm proud of them, and there is no doubt in my mind that the everyday fruits we enjoy today were paid for in part with their blood.

Some of the folks who had headed north also came home, but again, a lot of them didn't return to the south.

Many of them chose to remain in cities like Chicago, Milwaukee, and Detroit, raising their families in the new abundance they had discovered outside of the South.

The fifties brought new problems. There was another war, this one called a "Police Action," in a country called Korea, and once again our boys were called on.

Once again they answered.

The fifties also saw the birth of another evil.

An evil so overpowering that parents throughout America were certain the downfall of civilization was at hand.

And maybe it was.

Preachers stood in their pulpits and called on the American people, with a little help from God, to cast out the demon, but it didn't happen. The demon was here to stay. Looking back, perhaps our elders were wiser than even they knew.

The Demon had a name.

It was called Rock and Roll, and it turned the kids of America, and the world, upside down, inside out, and every which way but loose. (I just had to say that.)

Rock and roll came to the cities and it came to the country towns, and eventually it made its way to Springfield.

Eventually we felt its effect the same as the rest of the country. But to tell the truth, during the first years there was still a lot of the time when rock and roll took a back seat in Springfield, and many other little towns across the South, to country music.

You see, country folks were bound and determined to listen to Hank Williams, Webb Pierce, and Lefty Frizzell, and no wild hip gyrations and by a bunch of side burned youngsters was going to change that. At least, not very quickly.

Folks in country towns have never been very much given to change, whether it be good, bad, or indifferent, and Springfield was no different. But after a while, all of the towns across the nation gave up the ghost, so to speak, and rock and roll was here to stay.

The fifties also brought a new generation of South Town kids into their teenage years, and little did we know that these would be the most innocent years of our lives, years that brought an end to the world of our parents, and a beginning of the wild and scary world we were going to have to make for ourselves.

It's been said over and over, but I feel it's important to keep in mind that in those years things really were a lot different than now, and as you read these stories, remember that they can't be looked at from a viewpoint of political correctness, nor as being either right or wrong. The stories are simply a window to a time that was nothing at all like today, and to a town that was probably not so different from a thousand other small towns around the country.

This then is the Springfield I knew, the town I grew up in. I was proud of it then, and for the most part I've remained proud of it.

LIFE IN THE COUNTRY

Farmers poured into town every Saturday to stock up on dry-goods, groceries' and gossip.

The men stood around on the street and talked, or went into the Midway Cafe for a cold beer, while the women walked into almost every store in town, "just lookin'," and the kids wandered up and down the street, watching everything that went on.

It was a simple town, like most are, where everybody knew almost everybody else, and most everyone in town were friends.

But it wasn't only the farmers who went to town each Saturday.

Almost everybody in the county came to town, including the Rinky Dinks and their parents. Mama and Daddy took me and my nephew Ray into town just about every weekend.

Once a month Mama would go to the Commerce Union Bank to cash her check, or just to do whatever business she might have. The bank was on the right side of the street, heading North on Main Street, and what I remember most was that it had a big, fancy lobby. There were large ropes, covered with dark red velvet, dividing off certain sections of the main lobby, and tellers with green eye-shades sitting behind their counters. (That part about the green eye-shades may have come from a movie I once saw, I'm not really certain, but it paints a great picture, doesn't it?) Everyone always smiled, and the banker spoke to every person that came in, calling them by their first name. (Actually, I'm not even really sure about that. See my last note:) But I am sure that it was a friendly place, home grown and home owned, and between it and the First National Bank, they had most, if not all, of the banking business in town.

Mama and Daddy received a small insurance check from the government, from when my brother Carlos was killed in World War II, and that's the check Mama took in each month to cash. It wasn't much money, but it pulled us through many a tough spot.

Most of the time Daddy would join some of his friends in the Midway Cafe for a couple of ice cold beers. He'd have a Pabst Blue Ribbon™ or two, or maybe a frosty Carling Black Label™, and just sit and talk for a while. The men who visited the Midway were farmers, carpenters, and factory hands, and they worked hard and long, fifty or sixty or even more hours a week, and nobody thought anything was wrong with a couple of hours on a hot Saturday afternoon spent with friends over a few cold beers.

The Midway was owned by a man named Boots McAdams, and his wife was called Mrs. Mac. I thought they had the best chili in town, and that's where we ate sometimes on Saturday. The waitress, usually Mrs. Mac herself, would bring your steaming hot bowl of homemade chili to the table, together with a handful of small crackers. They were called soup crackers, or oyster crackers, I have since learned, and I loved to put a handful in the bowl of chili and watch them float. It usually took a few minutes for the crackers to begin to soften up, and I always tried to eat mine while they were still crunchy. Of course this meant that the chili was hot enough to burn the inside of my mouth, but that never made any difference at all.

We didn't always eat at the Midway Cafe. If Daddy was in the mood for a fish sandwich, then it was back toward South Town to the railroad tracks, take a right on 10th. Avenue and stop at the restaurant just across from the train depot. A man named Carl Draper ran the cafe, and had the best fish sandwiches anywhere in the county. Bill Wingo also ran a restaurant somewhere in the same vicinity, and Bill later moved to Memorial Boulevard, after they finished building the new highway. Memorial Boulevard was finished in 1956, and sometime after that Bill opened the Rainbow Grill. For many years afterward, Bill Wingo had one of the finest restaurants anywhere in the county, if not in the whole state of Tennessee. Later, my wife worked for Bill at the Rainbow, and he and I became friends. Bill was a nice person, and never failed to take the time to stop and talk to this Rinky Dink whenever the opportunity came along.

If we wanted Bar-B-Cue, which Mama and Daddy did a lot of the time, it was on out 13th. Avenue, past the cemetery, to a little place called the Chew And Chat. The Chew And Chat was operated and maybe owned by a black man, and to this day it's hard to find real, authentic southern Bar-B-Cue that even comes close to what they served at that tiny little place.

There was a man named Mister Craig and his wife Bertie who ran a small restaurant on the little alley that led from Willow Street to Main Street. The alley was across from the jail, and that restaurant was the first place I ever saw the small, Krystal™ style hamburgers. I always heard that they mixed the hamburger meat with meal in order to stretch it out, but I don't know if that's true or not. I know they had a distinct taste, and we used to go there every now and then.

The rest of the time (which was most of the time) we ate at home, and we ate chicken, beef, pork, or meat. Remember me mentioning what "meat" was a little way back?

In the mid-fifties, most of the kids in South Town went to the picture show on Saturday afternoons. Notice I said picture show and not movie, or theater. Back then, we went to the picture show to see a movie. Or maybe we went to the picture show to see a picture show. Depends on what you said at the time. Either way, everyone knew what we meant. Well, to be a little more truthful, we went, sure enough, but only when we could scrape together enough money.

Actually, there were two theaters in town at the time.

The Capital Theater, on Main Street, was operated by a man named Mister Hancock. (Of course, his first name wasn't really Mister, but that's all I ever heard him called.)

The Princess Theater was around the corner on 5th. Avenue, across from the Court House, and they usually had a double feature on Saturday. I don't remember who ran the Princess, but I do recall that I once saw cowboy movie star Sunset Carson there in person.

The other thing I remember about the two movie houses is that the seating was segregated back then in both of them, but I mention it here only as another indicator of the times. I've already stated that I will not, I cannot, pass judgment on the ways things were back then. All I can do is write things as I remember them, knowing that the world has made much forward progress in the years following the ones I grew up in.

Seeing as how I've mentioned 5th Avenue, I recall that the big hill on 5th Avenue that led into Springfield from the East was called "Pull Tight Hill," because it was so steep that many cars had to change gears to get up it. Occasionally, a car had to back up the hill to make it. I think it may have been called "Pull Tight" hill for another reason as well. When anyone was taking a team of wagon and mules down the hill, they had to "pull tight" on the reins to hold the team steady.

Sometimes when we had a little time to kill before or after the picture show, we'd go to one of the two ten cent stores in town. We'd buy popcorn, or look at the funny books, or just look at all of the toys on the shelves.

There was a Ben Franklin Five and Dime on the corner of Main Street and Seventh Avenue, but I can't remember the name of the other one. A Mister Gregg owned and ran one of them, but again, I don't know who ran the other. Oh yes, another thing that I recall is that we called them "The Ten Cent Store," not the Dime Store or the Five and Dime as I wrote above.

Once, when I was in the eleventh grade, Mama went to Paul's Men's Store and gave $25.00 dollars for a white sports coat for me. It was made of soft wool, and was the first really good sports coat I ever owned. If you can remember back then, you'll know that $25.00 dollars was a lot of money, and once you know that, you'll know how much that coat meant to me, and what it meant for Mama to spend that much money on it. I have a picture of a rather handsome young man of perhaps sixteen, wearing a white shirt, a tie with tiny checks in it, and the most beautiful white sports coat you've ever seen. I don't hesitate to call the boy in the picture handsome, because I'm sure if you could see the picture, you'd agree.

Maybe in this chapter, more than any other place in the book, I need to once again remind folks that I'm telling the stories about the times and the people as I remember them. I've asked a few people to refresh my memory, but I don't claim that this book is the be all and end all chronicle of life in Springfield, Tennessee, during this period of time. I don't intend for it to be that.

There are probably some books already written on Springfield that are much more detailed than this one. For those of you who want to say that the way I've written these things are not exactly how they happened, I will tell you now that you are more than likely right. I know there are stories I'm leaving out, things I'm getting wrong, things I don't remember, some additional things some people would like to read about, and I'm sorry that I can't include all of them here. There are a lot of people who remember much more about life in Springfield during this time than I do, and may rightly take exception with what I've written as either being wrong or not in enough detail. To them I not only apologize, I also say, in my most polite manner and tone, why not write your own book?

I hope most of you, however, read these remembrances and take them as they are intended. Stories from the memory of a boy who grew up here, and is proud of it, and has taken the time to write down a lot of little odds and ends simply for the joy of writing them and for the enjoyment of those who read them.

Now that that's over with ... back to our shopping.

I remember the first time I spent more than ten dollars on a pair of tennis shoes. They were all called tennis shoes then, not sneakers or any of the other fancy names. They were mostly high top, black canvas shoes, with a big white ball on the outside ankle of each shoe.

I went to Brantley's Shoe Store one Saturday afternoon, in need of a new pair of tennis shoes, and saw a pair of low top, white leather shoes. They were Red Ball Jets™, if I remember right, and they cost $10.99.

I had never dreamed of paying that much money for a pair of tennis shoes. Most of the time we didn't even pay that much for dress shoes. Back then we didn't pay $11.00 at a time for food. I knew Daddy would have a fit when he found out how much the shoes cost, but I had worked and saved my money for most of the summer, and I went ahead and bought the shoes anyway. I was glad when Daddy didn't have any comment about the purchase, and a little surprised. He gave me that look though, and I knew exactly what he thought. I think the same thing now when one of my kids say they want a pair of sneakers that cost $60 or $70 or more.

The same thing runs through my mind that must have run through his.

THE LAST OF THE SOUTH TOWN RINKY DINKS
THE EXTENDED VOLUME

Tennis shoes? Tennis shoes? You gave how much for that pair of tenn ...

There were several drug stores in town, (ok, ok, pharmacies) and they were pretty popular with us, especially after we became teenagers, started going to high school, and began walking home from school with girls.

McCord and Harris was on the northeast corner of Main Street and 7th. Avenue, and sometimes we stopped there, and Shannon's Drug Store was a little farther North on Main, closer to the Court House.

We spent many afternoons at Shannon's, sharing a cherry coke or having a grilled cheese sandwich. Shannon's had the old-fashioned ice cream furniture. You know the kind I mean, wrought iron chairs and small round tables, usually painted black or white. I think Shannon's chairs and tables were painted black, and they weren't the most comfortable chairs in the world.

But somehow, when you're sharing a coke with your best girl, sipping slowly through two straws, and staring into the most dreamy eyes you've ever seen, what kind of chair you're sitting on doesn't really make a lot of difference.

But the drug store where the Rinky Dinks spent most of our time was down by the railroad tracks, on South Main Street, and was called the Southside Drug Store. A pharmacist named Dr. Maxwell owned and operated Southside, and he didn't care if we kids hung around the store, drinking cokes and reading the latest funny books. Dr. Maxwell had the first automatically opening doors in the county installed at the Southside Drug Store sometime in the mid to late fifties. I know because Daddy was the one who installed them. They were the kind of doors that open when you step on a rubber mat in front of the door. Dr. Maxwell had seen the doors somewhere, and had bought a set, and called Daddy to see if he could figure out how to install them. The doors had to be hung in the frames, but first the floor panels had to be set. After the doors were installed, we all got a big kick out of standing and watching people walk up on the rubber mats and then jump back as the doors began to automatically open.

Dr. Maxwell used to cut half of the top off the front cover of all of the comic books that he hadn't sold for a dime, and then sell the cut off copies for a nickel. Daddy did so much work for him though, he gave me a lot of the comics free.

In the late fifties, a man named Jesse Holman Jones gave Springfield a few acres on the corner of Brown Street and 5th. Avenue to build a new hospital. There was an old Southern style house, almost a mansion, on the property that had to be torn town before the hospital could be built.

I don't recall the name of the man who contracted to tear down the old house, but Daddy was one of the men who were hired to actually do the work, and oversee some of the workers. Daddy was working there when a set of stairs collapsed under him, sending him to the hospital with a couple of broken ribs.

But, in time they got the old house torn down, and a brand new hospital built. I don't know for sure what year they opened Jesse Holman Jones Memorial Hospital, but I do know that it served the town and the county well for many years.

Let me complete the story of the hospital in a rather unique fashion.

In 1995, another new hospital was finished and dedicated in Springfield, this one on a highway south of town that was nothing more than an empty field when they built Jesse Holman Jones Hospital.

The day they shut down Jesse Holman Jones hospital, moving patients, doctors, nurses, and equipment across town, was the end of an era.

As it happened, someone in charge at the new hospital did something that is strangely familiar, especially to those of us who were called South Town Rinky Dinks. They named the new hospital "NorthCrest" even though it is on the Southern border of the town, on the "other side of the tracks" and well inside Rinky Dink territory.

I may be the only person to ever wonder if there could be some of that same old mentality still hanging round after all these years. I get the feeling that there were still some people in town who just couldn't bear the thought of calling it "SouthCrest." Funny how that relates back to the basic ideas I wrote at the first of the book, isn't it?

Oh well, on with the show...

I once bought a beautiful, shiny black 1956 Pontiac from Bill Shannon, who had a small car showroom on North Main, across from the

Colonial Hotel. Somewhere in one of my many boxes of "stuff," I still have the title to that old car. The old fashioned kind of title which was a small card, black with white writing on it.

Next door to Shannon's Car lot was a building that housed Jack Browning's Cafe. Jack Browning sold good food and cold beer, and after he remodeled his building in the late fifties, which by the way, Daddy did the work, Mama's brother, Harry Odell Walker, opened up a barbershop in one side of Jack's building.

Uncle Odell was a good barber, and a haircut only cost a quarter. He gave me my first store bought haircut, probably along about the time I started school, and he continued to cut my hair up until the early sixties.

Odell was a one legged man, having lost a leg while hopping a freight train. He was probably drinking at the time, as Odell did quite a good job of putting down the whiskey, but he would have probably hopped the train even if he'd been cold sober.

Odell Walker was a jolly, heavy-set man, with a loud, ready laugh, and a joke on his lips for all of his customers. He laughed a lot and loved living, but everyone who knew him knew he was not a man to fool with. He was mean when he wanted to be or had to be, especially when he was drinking, and he carried a small hideaway gun in his shirt pocket. He always said that only having one leg meant he had to have a little advantage of some kind. He also carried a sharp knife, and maybe even a straight razor, being as he was a barber, you know.

I have a cousin named Billy Walker, who is Willard's son, who has always reminded me of Uncle Odell.

Billy was a rough tough old country boy, just as Odell was, and I'm pretty sure he could be as mean as he needed to be in a given situation. But I think it was his attitude that made me think of Odell, more than anything else. I don't think either of them, Odell or Billy, ever gave a dang about much of anything, other than family, and I'm not so sure that isn't a good way to approach life. They'd just laugh and get on with what they were doing, and the heck with the consequences. They'd worry about those later.

Actually, most of the Walker men were that way. They'd hug you or fight you, and it didn't make a lot of difference which one they did.

Daddy remodeled the old Jack Browning building in the summer of

1957 or 1958, and it was so hot that the 78 rpm records in the jukebox half melted and were all ruined.

A Mister Felts and Daddy were the ones who contracted to remodel the building, and I helped out as many hours as I could. Mister Felts had a son that everyone called "Payday" and he also worked on the job.

I recall that while we were working on the back part of the building, we had pulled the jukebox to the front of the cafe, and it stood in the direct sun most of that day. The large black records were bent and folded in half by the end of the day, and had to be thrown away.

Not long after the re-modeling was finished, a city garbage truck turned into the alley, hit the corner of the building and knocked down most of one wall. Daddy and Mister Felts went down and rebuilt it again.

Main Street School was on the corner of North Main and 4th. Avenue, and that's where the kids in North Town went to grade school. After the sixth grade, of course, all of us started to high school. At some point in time they built the new Cheatham Park Elementary School, across from the Main Street School.

The high school was on West Fifth Avenue, and it's interesting to note that we didn't go to middle school then, just through the sixth grade at the elementary school and then directly into high school.

Springfield High School has a long and rich tradition as a school where kids got a good education, and through the years turned out some of the best high school football teams that Tennessee has ever seen.

Friday night in the fall was football night in Springfield. Almost all of the stores in town hung gold and white streamers on tall poles outside on the street every Friday night during the fall, and the football field was almost always filled.

Many years Springfield had one of the best high school football teams in the state, and maybe in the country as well.

Coach Boyce Smith was one of the most beloved men who ever lived in Springfield, and for a lot of good reasons. He probably had more influence on more young men in the town than anyone before or since.

He was almost always simply called Coach, and he was Coach at Springfield High School for over forty years. At one time he was the winning-est high school football coach in the country, and was one of the first coaches, if not the very first, to be elected into the High School Coaches Hall of Fame. Or the High School Football Hall of Fame. Whichever. It doesn't really matter which Hall of Fame so much as it does that Coach was elected to it.

Everybody always said that Coach Smith must have had a secret way of winning football games. Well, that's for sure. But it wasn't a very well kept secret. His secret to winning football games was to get the very best out of all of the players on his teams. And how did he do that, you ask? Well, he loved his job, he loved the game of football, and most of all, I think he loved every boy that ever played any sport for him. That love showed in his win/loss record, it showed in the respect the town had for him, but most of all it showed in the lives of every boy who ever played on one of his teams. He got the best out of his boys by demanding that they give their best at all times, and accepting nothing less. It showed in their level of sports play, and it always carried over into their everyday lives.

I was lucky enough to play basketball at Springfield High School in the late fifties for Coach Smith and for Coach Jimmy Suter, and I know for a fact that two finer men never walked the streets of Springfield, or taught in the Robertson County School system.

The leading jewelry stores in Springfield gave little gold or silver charms to each graduate of Springfield High during that time. I don't know if that practice is still being followed or not, but it should be. I still have a small charm that bears the engraving, "Springfield High School, 1959," that I got for graduation, and one of the stores gave a silver chain and a small silver football or basketball to every kid on either team. I still have that too.

The jewelry stores were Downey and Jones Jewelers and Williams Jewelers, and Springfield was lucky indeed to have such store owners as these. I don't know if this tradition still lives, but it would be a shame if there were no store left in town with enough public spirit to carry it on.

The radio station was upstairs in a building close to the Commerce Union bank, and across the street from that was the Bell Building. I think the Bell Building was the only building in town with an elevator, as well as an elevator operator. There were several doctors and dentists who had offices in the Bell Building, and Mama took me there a few times.

Of course, there were a lot of other stores in Springfield, and I know I'm probably missing some of the important ones.

You can't talk about industry in Springfield without mentioning the Springfield Woolen Mills, which made woolen blankets that were famous around the world for their workmanship and high quality.

I could go on but I think you get the picture. Springfield was nothing more, nor nothing less, than a typical, small country town. And like most little country towns, the folks who lived there were hard working, God-fearing people. Springfield was a good town to grow up in, and I'm proud of where I was born and raised.

And I know, deep in my heart, that Springfield should be, and probably is, proud of all of her kids, even the ones they called the South Town Rinky Dinks.

THERE ARE GAMES, AND THEN THERE ARE RINKY DINK GAMES

The Rinky Dinks played a lot of games when we were growing up that kids today would laugh at, but I expect we had as much fun as they ever dreamed of, and probably a lot more. We often found fun in the smallest things, and could make a game out of just about anything.

Take the empty tin cans we found lying around on the street, for instance.

Just thinking about it, there doesn't seem to be a lot one could do with empty tin cans, does there? Kids today would smash them, throw them into large plastic garbage bags, and take them to the nearest recycling center.

But not the Rinky Dinks. No way. Tin cans were wonderful things.

We used to play ball with empty tin cans and broom sticks. I can't count the hours we've passed just batting an empty can around. If you think it's easy to hit a tin can someone throws at you, you should try it. Especially with a really small broom stick.

If you don't know what a broom stick is, let me explain it in real simple terms. Get an old broom, break off the broom part and toss it aside, and what you have left is a broom stick. That's all there is to it. They're great to use as ball bats, swords, stick horses and a dozen other things. All you need is a worn out old broom and a lot of P.T.I. (That's Pre-Television Imagination. The kind kids used to have.)

Of course, everyone knows you can tie a string between two tin cans and make a handy dandy telephone, and we did that now and then, but the Rinky Dinks had a way of using tin cans to their fullest potential.

Tin cans can be used for targets as well as they can for balls. You can sit them in a row on fence posts and throw rocks at them, which we also did for hours at a time, or you can shoot 'em with your B B gun. Which we also did for hours at a time.

Right here, let me take a few lines and tell you why I keep saying we did things "for hours at a time." It's literally because we did. Once we started playing a game, we played it until we were too tired to go on, or until we had worn out whatever it was that we were playing with. From the time we got up in the morning, until we went to bed at night, all we had was "hours at a time." Time doesn't mean a thing when you're twelve years old and have nothing at all to do except play.

Anyway, it's a lot of fun to hear the tinny plink of a B B when it strikes the can, but it's a lot more challenging to try to hit a can with a rock from forty or fifty feet away. I'd like to say that we could hit the can five of six times out of ten, but that would be a lie. Maybe five or six times out of a hundred. The thing is, it was fun to try to hit the cans, and that's all a game is supposed to be, isn't it? Fun? And the hours of practice throwing at tin cans sure helped once we started playing real baseball. We made very few wild throws to first base or when someone was trying to steal home. Throwing rocks at tin cans did that for us.

Tin cans also make a dandy first alert warning system. You tie a lot of cans to the clothesline, or to the fence, or maybe you place them around in the back yard where anyone who is trying to break into your house will step on the cans and you'll hear them before they can get to your back door. This is one jewel of a warning system. Unless of course your Daddy gets up in the middle of the night and heads down through the backyard for the toilet. Daddies don't like to step on empty tin cans. Especially if it's summertime and they don't have on any shoes. I suppose it's conceivable that a tin can warning system might stop a burglar from coming up to your house and hurting somebody, but it's a fact that if your Dad steps on an empty tin can in the back yard, he's going to limp into the house, cussing very loudly, and paddle somebody's rear end. Guess whose rear end?

And of course, that burglar thing was another instance of where the kids were using that old magic P.T.I. We didn't have any burglars on 21st Avenue. I've already said that nobody on the street ever locked their doors, and I don't think any of us had anything anyone else wanted to steal.

Back to the game playing.

As a general rule, the softball games at Woodland Street School were always over by nine or ten o'clock at night, and once we got home from the ball field we'd all gather round the street light in front of my house to play kick the can.

The streetlight was a dim, yellow bulb on a tall pole in the front corner of our yard, and was the center of all our night time games. The harsh glow was a beacon that drew us together and it's hard to tell if its attraction was greater for the dozen or so kids that always skittered about on the ground, or the million or so hovering, darting bugs that were drawn to the light to feed.

For the bugs, it was a nightly ritual of kill or be killed, eat or be eaten, survive or perish. For the Rinky Dinks, kick the can was much the same. We might not have actually been quite that competitive, but most of the time we were in that same category.

Kick the can wasn't a hard game to play, there were only a few rules, and it just might have been the favorite nighttime game of the Rinky Dinks. We played almost every night, and for some reason, we never seemed to tire of the game.

We'd set a can down in the middle of the street, under the light where everyone could see it, and then one of us would be chosen to be "IT." Everyone who was playing, except "IT" of course, would get to hide. Whoever "IT" was had to hide their eyes and count to a hundred, usually by fives ... something like this.

Five, ten, fifteen, twenty... eighty-five, ninety, ninety-five, a hundred... here I come...

"IT" would then try to find where everyone was hiding, without straying too far from the can of course. "IT" would spot a hiding kid, run to the can, which was home base, put his foot on the can, and holler...

I see Jerry, hiding in the grass by the fence. You're out.

Jerry would have to come and stand by the pole, or sit in the dirt, or lay in the grass, or something like that, while "IT" tried to catch the rest of the kids.

Kick the can would have been a pretty simple game, if that's all there was too it, but of course, like all of the really great games, there's more.

There's the can kicking part.

All of the kids would be trying to run up and kick the can, which would let everyone hide again while "IT" ran and got the can and set it back in the street, and started over.

It can be pretty frustrating to catch eight out of the ten kids that were playing, and have the ninth kick the can thirty feet away.

Five, ten, fifteen, twenty... over and over, till everyone was caught, or we had to go inside for the night.

Probably the most stupid game we played with empty tin cans involved stomping them with our feet until they bent up around our shoes, and then running up and down the street seeing who could make the most noise. The greatest danger in this game arose when someone's Dad got tired of hearing the clomp, clomp, clomp of our tin canned shoes and came outside and whipped a little Rinky Dink tail or two. Talk about noise.

I never said these games were smart, just that they were fun. And remember, we didn't have video games back then. Of course, it wouldn't have done us any good even if we'd had video games, come to think of it. None of us had a television set, and like I said before, some of us didn't even have electricity.

There were other games, of course, that didn't involve empty cans. We played "King on the Mountain" sometimes, but that game usually ended up in a fight. And we played "Hide and go Seek" a lot. We'd pick an "IT" and everyone else would go hide and "IT" would have to find everyone else. "Hide and Go Seek" wasn't exactly like "Kick the Can" but it was close. The biggest difference was that in "Hide and Go Seek", you didn't get to kick a can.

Me and Wayne have gone inside and read funny books for hours while "IT" tried to find us. Once we looked for one of the guys for two days before we found out his family had moved.

We made kites out of newspaper and glue out of water and flour, and used straight weeds for sticks. We'd tie on a tail made of socks or strips of worn out bed sheets, and run around in the yard for hours trying to get it to fly. And if we stayed with it long enough, and if a good strong breeze came up, we'd get the homemade toy in the air.

More than once I made wings out of big sheets of cardboard and tried to fly. I tried to fly off the coal house, and out of the sugar maple tree, and I tried to fly across the little branch down behind the house, but every time I only got off the ground for a couple of seconds at a time. If I climbed up on the coal house, took a good running start, and jumped as far as I could, I could fly just exactly as far as I could jump. When the jump force wore off, so did the flight. At that point, I usually flew straight down. Very quickly, I might add.

Once I made a great big kite and took it over to a hill in the South Town woods. This was a huge kite, made of the sides of a cardboard refrigerator box and some strong pieces of scrap wood I'd found. I tied a short piece of rope to the cross members of the kite, and held on for dear life. When I felt the wind kick up and began to blow, I picked up the kite, positioned it over my head, and started running down the hill as fast as I could. When I felt the wind lift the kite, I leaped into the air as high as my twelve year old legs would propel me. Sure enough, I flew downhill for maybe twenty or thirty feet before the kite buckled from the combination of my weight and the strong wind. When I picked myself up and found that no bones were broken, I knew then that flying with a kite was possible. It was only a matter of the right material, the right wind conditions, and something a little higher to jump off of. I also decided to try again. The problem was getting a big cardboard box. It was rare that anyone in South Town got a new refrigerator, so I didn't have a lot of natural resources. In fact, I never did try it again. Of course, a lot of other people did. And they proved it works. Sometimes I still wonder what would have happened if the kite had been a little stronger and I'd have caught a really good updraft. Actually I know what would have happened. I'd have killed my dang fool self. There would have been Rinky Dink splattered all over the South Town woods.

The Rinky Dinks were introduced to gambling in a game of marbles. We'd draw a big circle in the dirt, each boy would line up five of his own marbles on a line drawn in the center of the circle, and we'd take turns shooting until all the marbles had been knocked out of the circle. You got to keep every marble you could knock out. It was that simple. Or that hard. Marble games were mostly warm up periods for the fight that was sure to follow. Let your shooting hand slip an inch across the line, and you knew somebody was going to call you on it. That was called fudging and it just wasn't allowed. We called this variation of marbles "Keeps" and that's what we played for.

There were other marble games, some of which we played now and then, but "Keeps" was by far the most popular of them all. All of us carried a little sack full of marbles around with us, and would play most anytime. "Keeps" was the chief contributor to aching thumbs, scuffed up shoe toes, and worn out blue jean knees.

But hands down, of course, the game we played the most was ball.

Baseball, softball, football, basketball, any kind of ball. Every single day we played ball. We used real balls, when we had 'em, and home made balls when real ones weren't available. We played with rubber balls, hard balls and balls made from socks rolled up and sewed together.

Wesley and Wayne Wilson's Mama used to make a lot of the balls we played with. She really knew how to make a ball. She'd roll up a lot of old socks or rags and stitch up the ends, and they would last for two or three days sometimes. And that's saying a lot, cause we played hard, and when it came to playing ball, we really did play hour after hour.

From early March or April, as soon as the weather began to get a little warmer, we started throwing a ball around.

There was hardly any traffic on 21st, so we stood in the street and played catch much of the time. Back and forth, in the air or on the ground. Throw the ball, catch the ball, throw the ball, catch the ball. Whether it was a hard horsehide baseball or a soft rubber bouncy ball, the end result was the same. We played catch. Every day. If it rained softly, we played catch in the rain and got wet. If it was pouring down rain, we played catch in the rain and got soaked. Didn't matter. Nothing stopped us from playing ball.

If there were no one else around, we'd throw the ball against the house and catch it on the bounce. Or throw it straight up in the air and catch it when it came down. I've thrown the ball up on the roof of the house and caught it when it rolled off so many times I used to be able to close my eyes and catch the ball just from the sound it made as it rolled down the tin roof. If that sounds unbelievable, maybe it is. The best I can remember, I could do that. I think I could do that. I tell my kids I used to be able to do that. Actually, it's not all that hard. It's easy to tell where the ball is coming, from the way it clanks and bounces on the tin. All you have to do is stick out your glove and you'll either catch the ball or miss it. Or it'll hit you on the head. Missing the ball and getting hit in the head are what happens most, but now and then the ball hits your glove and you catch it. I've done that, many times. Remember, I used to do that "for hours at a time."

But usually there were plenty of kids around that wanted to play. Down the street, behind the little row of shotgun houses on the right, was a good sized field where most of our ball games were held, and just as we gathered around the street light at night, every day we gathered in the field. It was a ritual of sorts, I guess, to meet every day in the field and choose up sides for the day.

Choosing sides was mostly for that day's ball game, but sometimes we kept the same sides all day long regardless of what we played.

Let me assure you, there's an art to choosing up sides. It ain't as simple as it sounds. There's a lot of psychology involved, especially when you're trying to decide whom to pick first.

Whatever you're using for a ball bat that day is what you use to decide who gets first pick. Somebody will say something like;

Donald and Wesley, y'all choose up sides.

One of us will grab the bat, pitch it to the other one, and the process begins.

You try to catch the bat as close to the top as you can without missing it. If you miss, the other one automatically gets first pick. Wherever you catch the bat, you hold it there and kinda shove it out toward the other kid. He places his hand around the bat, directly above yours, and then you place your other hand on the bat, directly above his. This process continues until you reach the top of the bat. the last one who can get hold of the bat and not drop it wins the right to pick the first player.

For this example, let's assume I get to pick first. Not fair, you say. Well, the fact is, a lot of the time I did get to pick first, and the other thing is, it's me who's writing this account, so I'll pick first if I want to.

I pick my first team member, taking into consideration a lot things. First of course, is how well they play ball. All kids are not created equal, at least not where playing ball is concerned. Some are much better than others. The eight or ten really good players always go first when you're choosing up sides. Next, you have to know if anyone get hurt yesterday bad enough that he won't be able to play very well today? Then, you have to check and see if any of the kids have a real ball. You always try to pick a kid who has a real ball if you can.

And you can forget about that old stuff of a kid getting mad and saying, "Well, I'll just take my ball and go home." Uh, uh. Not when you're playing with the Rinky Dinks. It doesn't matter whose ball it is, once you bring it to the field, it stays there until we're through playing with it, or it gets lost. Oh, and there was one other hazard we always had to take into account anytime we played with a rubber ball.

My nephew, Ray Harp, (remember Goober?) ate rubber balls. We never did know why, but for some strange reason, he liked to eat rubber. He'd nibble on the rubber around a cars window, and pencil erasers had a very short life span.

But his favorite of all was eating rubber balls.

He was the best outfielder we had, and always got picked pretty close to the front. He could catch a ball as well or better than anyone I've ever seen, and even as a little kid had a shotgun for a right arm. But whenever we played with a rubber ball, whoever had Goober on their team could be at a distinct disadvantage. The batter would hit the ball in Goober's direction, he'd streak across the field in hot pursuit, (he was fast, fast, fast) but invariably, once he got his hands on the ball, he'd take a bite out of it before he threw it to the infield. A lot of times, this allowed the runner to get an extra base, or a man to come home who might not have scored at all. We've stopped a lot of games to go out into the field and tell him time and time again just to pick up the ball and throw it, not to eat it. We didn't have this problem when we played with a real baseball, or even a sock ball. He didn't like to chew on either of those. But all of us have caught many a ball that he threw in from the outfield with a big chunk bitten out of it, and spit just beginning to dry around the teeth marks.

Then there was the problem of picking the girls.

Oh, you don't think picking a girl should be a problem? Well, it was back then. A big problem, and not one the Rinky Dinks handled very well, I'm afraid. But we had the perfect solution.

Obviously, you tried not to pick a girl. That was our whole strategy. Don't pick one unless you absolutely had no choice. And if just you had to pick one, try to say something that would make her mad enough that she'd leave and not play.

THE LAST OF THE SOUTH TOWN RINKY DINKS
THE EXTENDED VOLUME

Whether you believe it or not, this wasn't sexual discrimination. Fact is, the girls just couldn't play ball as good as the boys, and if you had a couple of girls on your side you usually lost. If there was any discrimination at all during the procedure, it was of a ball game nature. We didn't want to lose, and if that meant the girls couldn't play, that was just the way it was. But sometimes, regardless of what we said to them, they wouldn't go home. They stood out in the middle of the field and insisted on playing. We learned early on that reasoning was out of the question, talking things through did no noticeable good, and once they had their minds made up, there was little we could do to change them. So at times like these, we did the things men always seem to do, we gave in. We let them play ball with us, and usually got the tee total heck beat out of whichever team they were on. But it was a small price to pay for them not telling our parents we wouldn't let them play. Diplomacy can very rewarding and can become a very real part of your life, and that's especially true if you know for a fact that your Dad will whip your butt with a willow switch if you get told on. We knew it. And the worst part was, the girls knew it too.

But in all fairness, later on there were some really great women's softball teams that played at Woodland Street School, and over the years they compiled a super great win-loss record.

Helen Gregory, the girl who later became my wife was a great softball player, and kept playing right up until we had our fourth child.

But still, when we were choosing up sides in the field, the object was to not pick a girl unless you had absolutely had to. So most of the time we didn't. A typical day of activity in the field might sound a little dull, but if you'll hang around a little longer I'll expertly guide you through one of the more exciting aspects of being a Rinky Dink.

I'll let you spend Saturday afternoon with us at the movies.

As you've probably already guessed, Saturday at the movies usually meant we would see our favorite cowboy star draw his six guns and blaze away at the bad guys.

Usually, but not always.

Although the Rinky Dinks were partial to the cowboys, we also had a few other stars we liked almost as much.

There wasn't a kid alive in the early fifties that at one time or another didn't want to climb up into a tree, grab a handy grape vine and swing out across the jungle, screaming the Tarzan yell at the top of our lungs. All of us have mouthed the famous "Me Tarzan, you Jane," line so many times we thought it must actually be true.

But while Tarzan of the Apes was a big favorite with all of us, he wasn't the only star that lived in the forest and fought the villains.

There was also the most famous outlaw that ever roamed the King's forest, Robin Hood and his band of Merry Men. Outwitting the Sheriff of Nottingham at every turn of the trail, and rescuing Maid Marion without fail.

The Rinky Dinks made bows and arrows of any sticks we could find lying around, and for several years we played Robin Hood almost as much as we did cowboys. Many times we've cut and trimmed sticks and went to the branch behind my house and fought the famous Robin Hood, Little John bridge fight. One of us usually managed to fall into the branch and get wet, which was one of the main reasons we liked the game so much. One thing though, even though we liked Robin and Marion, at that time in our lives none of us were quite ready for that kind of relationship. The girls were still playing dolls, and the boys would still much rather ride off into the sunset on our great white stallion.

Anyway, it's time for you to c'mon along for an exciting afternoon at the picture show. We're gonna see the cowboys.

THE LAST OF THE SOUTH TOWN RINKY DINKS
THE EXTENDED VOLUME
THE CHECKER GAME

GEORGE THOMAS GREGORY
September 30, 1900 - January 31, 1978

Dedicated to Helen's dad, George Thomas Gregory. George was a cantankerous, ornery old fellow if one ever lived, but he was a hard working man, a man dedicated to his wife of 57 years, Lena Rodgers Gregory, and to his family. His greatest delight in life was a good, hard fought game of checkers. Physically, George was not a large man, but across a checkerboard he was a giant.

THE CHECKER GAME

He had a shiny railroad pocket watch that he used to tell the time,
And every morning he walked into town, about a quarter after nine.
He'd settle down on the same old bench he'd been sitting on for years,
Lay out his checkerboard, and then he'd ask for volunteers.

There were always one or two young bucks who'd want to call his hand
They couldn't see his wisdom, they just saw a tired old man.
He'd take his time making sure his board was all set up to play
Then he'd say, "Which one o' you boys, will be the first to fall today?"

He was like his checkerboard, faded, old, and gray.
But his hands were steady as a rock, when it was time to play.
His eyes were dimmed with age, but they'd shine like a diamond ring
And he'd grow a little younger, every time they crowned his king.

I was just a kid too young to play but I recall it well.
How one by one they took a seat and one by one they fell
And I can't forget the way he laughed or what he told the crowd,
You can't teach an old dog new tricks, boys, ain't you learned that by now?

They've built a brand new shopping mall where that old park used to be
And the checker games are just a part of my hometown memories.
Old George went home a few years ago to claim his just reward
And I heard nobody ever found his treasured checker board.

He was like his checkerboard, faded, old, and gray
But his hands were steady as a rock, when it was time to play
Well, I'll bet he's sitting down with God,
With that board laid out between
And if I know George, he's just one move away…
From winning one more game.

RINKY DINK COWBOYS AND INDIANS

There was another game that the Rinky Dinks played, and loved, almost as much as we did one of our ball games.

That game was Cowboys.

Back then it usually wasn't Cowboys and Indians, just simply Cowboys.

About the only way I know to set up this particular story is to tell you my version of Saturday afternoon at the movies.

As I've already said, there were two movie theaters in Springfield when we were kids, and we'd all try to make it to one or the other, or both, every Saturday.

There was the Capital, in the exact same location as the current Springfield Cinema, and there was the Princess Theater, located on the North side of the town square. A child's admission ticket at either theater cost ten cents, a bag of popcorn another dime, and a good sized soft drink cost a nickel. All told, we could spend an entire Saturday afternoon at either movie for the grand sum of one quarter.

On some occasions, when there was a little more money at home than usual, we might be given a whole half dollar, which meant we could go to both movies, have two popcorns, two cokes, and spend all Saturday afternoon riding the range with our heroes. Heroes like Roy Rogers, Gene Autry, or John Wayne. There was Rex Allen, Sunset Carson, The Durango Kid, The Cisco Kid, and Billy, the greatest Kid of them all. Or any one of a dozen or a hundred more.

Whatever you do, don't make the mistake of thinking they weren't heroes. They were. In every sense of the word. They were the good guys.

They wore the white hats and rode the great, wonderful stallions. Dream horses with names like Champ, and Coco, and Topper, and of course the greatest of them all, the most amazing horse in the world, the golden palomino with the blonde mane, Trigger the Wonder Horse.

Even the outlaws were heroes.

Gunfighters like Billy the Kid, Jesse and Frank James, and the Dalton Brothers. We loved them all, and to us, even at their worst, they were still heroes.

They rode into town every Saturday, and so did all of the South Town kids.

Three or four or five or more strong, we'd begin gathering about noon every Saturday. With our shirts and trousers starched and ironed, our faces, ears, and hands scrubbed till they shone, and our hair neatly combed, we were ready for the mile walk from 21st. Avenue to the Capital Theater, our first stop of the day.

Actually, only part of that is correct. It is about a mile from 21st to town, but it generally wasn't a walk. We ran, we skipped, we jumped, we hopped, we bolted, dashed, darted, sprinted, raced or otherwise moved along the street, but we seldom, if ever, walked. So it's not surprising that when we finally got to the show we were no longer starched, ironed, clean, or slicked up in any way.

Let me make a little side note right here, if you please.

Back then we didn't call it a movie, or a theater, or a movie theater. We called it a picture show, or more simply, just the show. Oh yeah, from now on, that's what I'm gonna call it in this story. The Show. And was it ever.

On the days when we only had a quarter, we'd usually go to the Capitol, probably because it was about a block and a half closer to 21st., making it the first one we came to when we got to town.

Our little rag tag bunch would arrive, more or less all together, shortly after noon, and usually there was already a line waiting to get in the show. We'd stand in line and fidget and laugh, as excited each Saturday as if it were our first time there. Finally moving up to the window, we'd plop down our dime, grab a ticket stub, and quickly scoot through the big double glass doors in the front of the building. Once inside, we'd all line up again, this time to buy our popcorn and coke.

Sometimes we'd decide on a candy bar instead of popcorn, and back then a ten-cent Butterfinger or Baby Ruth was about as much candy as you can get for a dollar or a dollar and a half today. Sometimes, if we left home a little early and got to town a little quicker, we'd walk down the street to the Ben Franklin 5-10 Store and look around for a while before we went to the show. At the ten cent store, which everybody called it that back then, instead of the Five and Dime it was later called, you could buy a bag of popcorn that was almost twice a large as the bag at the show, and it was only a dime too. The folks who ran the show didn't really care where you bought your popcorn, and would let you bring it inside with you if you wanted to. Every now and then we might even splurge and buy a bag of hot roasted mixed nuts. Umm, ummm.

Anyway, after we'd bought our treats for the day, we'd make our way through the big double doors that opened into the theater at both sides of the lobby, and fumble, stumble feel our way down the dark aisle until we found just exactly the seat we wanted. Of course, our seating arrangements were subject to change each Saturday. Some Saturdays we'd go all the way to the very front row, and sit there with our heads tilted back and our necks almost out of joint while we watched. But most of the time we liked to sit about mid-ways down. That way we could look around and see where everybody else was sitting, and decide if we wanted to move or not.

Once seated, we'd begin digging in the popcorn bag, anxiously waiting for the lights to dim and the show to start.

I don't think they showed the *"EXITS"* back then the way they do now at the start of each feature, and if my memory will let me, I'll try to see if I can come up with the order in which they showed the shorts and the features.

First they showed the *"PREVUES OF COMING ATTRACTIONS."* Not that it actually made that much difference. We were coming back next Saturday anyway. But they always showed them. And back then, they usually showed three different movies each week. They had one feature for Monday, Tuesday and Wednesday, another for Thursday and Friday, and a third, almost always a Western, for Saturday.

And here's a novelty for you folks that don't remember those days. There was never a movie on Sunday. In fact, if I remember it correctly, there weren't many, if any, businesses in town open on Sunday. You bought everything you needed during the week or on Saturday, because if you didn't, you were up the proverbial old creek without the proverbial old paddle. Friday night and Saturday were the busiest days of the week in small towns back then. Mostly Saturday, I guess, because that seemed to be the day when almost everyone came to town. But that's another story. Right now, I've got to get back to the picture show.

After the previews, they usually showed a short *"NEWSREEL"* which allowed people to be able to see some of the events they'd been hearing about on their radios during the last few months.

Next came the *"COMEDY,"* or *"CARTOON,"* whichever they had that day. We'd laugh till our sides hurt at Bugs Bunny, or Porky Pig, or Popeye the Sailor Man, and even more so at the antics of the Three Stooges. Nyuk, nyuk, nyuk.

The *"SERIAL"* was shown next. The serial was a continuing story that featured the likes of Batman, or Superman, or Flash Gordon, or one of the other larger than life heroes. A particular favorite of mine was a character known as Bullet Man. Or maybe his name was Rocket Man. Anyway, he wore a thick, black (brown maybe, after all it was in black and white) leather coat, and a silver, bullet shaped metal helmet on his head. Around his waist was a wide leather belt that held the controls to the fabulous rocket jet pack strapped to his back. He'd take a few short, quick running steps, ending in a mighty jump, and when his feet hit the ground he'd activate the belt control and ZOOM, ZOOM, ZOOM he'd take off and fly into the sky like one of the mighty jet airplanes we'd just seen in the newsreel. I think I liked him the most because deep down I thought that maybe, someday, in someway, somebody might really invent one of those rocket packs and we'd all be streaking around the sky like human bullets, bent on stopping whatever evil might be lurking about. Even back then, I think we knew there was gonna be plenty of evil in the future, and there was going to be a need for a great many real life heroes.

Of course, that was the beauty of the movies back then. The good guys always won. And you always knew who the good guys were. We were the good guys. Always. And we always won.

Occasionally, there was another little short feature that I really liked. It was called "Screen Songs" and the idea was to show the words to a song on the screen as a little bouncing ball bounced along on each syllable and the audience sang along. These were pretty popular with all of us kids, and most of the time we sang along to the top of our lungs.

After the serial came the *"FEATURE MOVIE"* of the day. As I said, most every Saturday there was a western as the feature. I'm not going to try to name all of the western stars, it would take too long and I know I can't remember them all anyway. And another thing, we didn't call them the star, or the featured actor, or anything like that back then. Nope. We always called the star of the show the *"MAIN PLAYER."* Beats me how that got started, but even today I find myself occasionally asking my wife, when she mentions a movie she wants to see, "Who's the main player, honey?" Course, even though she's not as old as me, she knows what I mean, and always tells me who's starring.

Getting to the heart of this story, let me see if I can partially explain why we loved the cowboys.

Really, it's simple now that I stop to think about it. We wanted to be them. We wanted to wear two six guns tied low on our hips, and a great big white hat, and ride one of those beautiful horses. There wasn't a single one of us who wouldn't have climbed on Trigger behind Roy and rode off into the sunset.

It was for that reason that every chance we got, after we got home from the show, or a lot of times even in the middle of the week, we played cowboys.

Almost every one of us would ask for, and get, a set of cap guns for Christmas. They were really pretty, those guns were. White pearl handles, shiny chrome barrels, and they made a great sound when you had fresh caps in them. The gun sets came with belt and holsters, and several little square red boxes of caps. Sometimes we'd get hats and vests and maybe even a set of strap on spurs. The hats always had a little rope lanyard that looped around the crown and down through two holes in the brim, and usually had a wooden bead so that you could pull it up tight under your chin. I don't recall any of us ever getting a real pair of cowboy boots, but we were just as happy to strap our spurs around our regular shoes and get on with the game.

I don't think any of us, at least not the bigger kids, ever played with a stick horse. We just used our imagination for a horse.

At the movie we'd watch carefully the way the cowboys held the reins as they rode, and when we played we pretended we were holding our own reins. We'd bend both elbows till our hands were about collar bone high, make fists like we had something in our hands, and move our bodies as though we were actually riding. We'd prance around on our feet, which I swear we thought were hooves, and we'd roll our shoulders up and down, up and down, up and down as we trotted or galloped around in the yard. Every motion of our bodies was as close as we could get to the motion made by the cowboys as they rode. We tried to imitate them exactly, and to tell the truth, we didn't do such a bad job. And as we rode, we made the horses hooves sound with our mouth. tecup-tecup-tecup-tecup-tecup-tecup

Whoa, Trigger, Whoa, horse.

Of course we all had our favorite characters that we pretended to be. I was almost always Roy Rogers, or maybe Billy the Kid, and Wesley was almost always Gene Autry. The summer Betty stayed with us, she played Dale Evans a lot of the time, but usually the girls just sat and watched us ride around the yard. And, like Roy and Gene, I always took time out to sing a song or two.

Of course, our games reflected the way we actually felt. We rustled each others cattle, ran off sheep herders, and occasionally even knocked each other out with the butt of our six guns during our games. We had gunfights and saloon brawls, and for a while I had a sign on my coal house that read "O.K. CORRAL." (*This was before I knew that I am probably a distant cousin to one of the most famous true old west gunfighters that ever lived, the main man at the OK Corral, Wyatt Earp.*)

I even remember once when I got sick I sent either Wayne or Thomas down the street and told the other kids that I had hoof and mouth disease.

The fact is, like many other kids of that time, many of the values and beliefs that we grew up with we learned from our cowboy heroes.

Right and wrong? The cowboys knew the difference, and so did we.

Family values? If anyone ever exemplified the very best of family values, the cowboys of the fifties did. I think some of that rubbed off on us.

The cowboys showed us a world that poor kids in a little southern town had never seen before, and weren't likely to ever find in reality. Now that I think of it, it's probably for the best that we never really found that world. If we'd seen the real movie cowboy world, it might have shaken our belief in the entire world, so I'm glad it never happened.

THE LAST OF THE SOUTH TOWN RINKY DINKS
THE EXTENDED VOLUME

Because, you see, I still believe in Roy Rogers, Gene Autry, John Wayne, Rex Allen, Hopalong Cassidy, and all the rest.

And I always will.

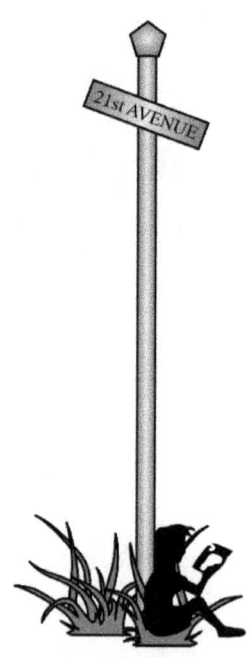

6

IS THERE A DOCTOR IN THE HOUSE?

Our family doctor was Doctor John Wilkison, and Mama, like most of the other citizens of Springfield, thought a lot of him. His office was on the town square, on the South side of the square to be exact, across from the courthouse, and Doctor Wilkison would either make a house call or else Mama would take us to the office whenever we got sick, and she always laughed at how much the Doctor charged. To be more precise, she laughed at the way the Doctor decided how much to charge.

Mama always said Doctor Wilkison could read her mind about how much money she had in her purse. If she went to the doctor with only three dollars and some change in her purse, the conversation went like this;

How much will that be, Doctor, she'd ask?

He'd think for a minute, study the wall or one of his many paintings, and reply;

That'll be three dollars, Honey, he'd say.

Doctor Wilkison called a lot of people Honey.

The next time Mama visited the doctor, she might have six dollars, or maybe just two, but it never seemed to matter. He always seemed to guess within a few cents how much she had with her on that particular day.

Doctor Wilkison, like most doctor's back then, kept quite a lot of medicine at his office. Usually, he wouldn't even write a prescription, he'd just tell his nurse, Thelma, what kind and how much medicine to give each patient.

Once Ray went to see Doctor Wilkison for some illness or the other, and after paying for the office visit, he told the doctor;

Doctor Wilkison, I just don't have enough money to pay for all of the medicine you're giving me today.

How much money do you have, young man, he asked.

I've only got ten dollars left.

Thelma, give this young man ten dollars worth of medicine, the Doctor called out, and Thelma hastened to obey.

Anytime you couldn't manage to fit your money to the medicine, Doctor Wilkison would always manage to fit the medicine to the money.

He was a good man, and a good Doctor, and most of all, he was a good friend to the people of Springfield.

Doctors still made house calls then, and it wasn't unusual to see Doctor Wilkison's shiny car pull up in front of a house on 21st. at any hour of the day or night. He came to take care of sick people, and if we didn't always have his money, he took care of us anyway.

Springfield was known as a marriage mill for years, with folks coming in from all over this part of the country to be married. You could get married in one day in Springfield, and Doctor Wilkison made sure you could get a blood test in about an hour. All you had to do was get a license from the courthouse, head over to the Doc's for your blood test, and then back to the courthouse to be married. Over the years, thousands of marriages have been performed there, and even though they were called quickie marriages, they were as legal, and as lasting as any other kind of marriage.

The science of medicine and being a Doctor has come a long way since then, and none of us would want to go back to the way things were. But I truly believe that today's doctors should take a look at the way it used to be done. It's not that Doctors today don't care for their patients, its just that they almost never seem to reach the personal level doctor's reached back then. And that's a shame.

Then suddenly, before I even knew it, it was 1953, and the whole world started changing.

7

1953: LUCILLE COMES HOME

1953 was a remarkable year in more ways than one. The armistice in Korea was signed, signaling an end to the "conflict," as they called it, Hank Williams passed away in the back seat of his Cadillac on New Years Eve, causing nearly the entire South to go into mourning, Ike was sworn in as our President with "I Like Ike" buttons everywhere, and I turned twelve years old.

Me turning twelve could be called remarkable, I guess, depending on how you look at it. I was into so much, and did so many silly, half dangerous things that a lot of people said it would be remarkable if I ever reached my twelfth birthday. But in spite of all their reservations, I did make to be twelve years old, so I guess 1953 can also be marked by that milestone as well as the others.

1953 was also remarkable in that it was also the year that Aunt Lucille came home to die.

That may sound strange to a lot of folks now, but in 1953 it was perfectly acceptable that people returned to their hometown and their families when they thought they only had a short time to live. The reason I say that Lucille came home to die was because she had an incurable heart condition, and she had no one to take care of her after she became bedridden. Besides that, she was living in Detroit City, and she sure didn't want to spend her last days there.

Lucille's husband, Ernest Mayes, looked after her, but I think she probably wanted to be back in the place she considered home during this trying time. There was never any doubt that Ernest loved Lucille, or that he'd take care of her the best he could. But Ernie was known to take a drink now and then, and also to make an occasional small wager. Lucille didn't hold too much with drinking and gambling, especially when it was

Ernest doing the drinking and gambling, using their small amount of money, so it was that being bedridden with only Ernest to look after her was more or less out of the question.

Of course there was Betty Blanche. Betty was Lucille's only child, and would have taken care of her if she'd only known how really bad the heart condition had become, but Lucille wouldn't tell her. I think at this time that Betty had been married a little less than two years, and her husband John was in the Army. They were stationed in Germany, and still had a couple more years to stay over there.

Lucille didn't want to be any trouble to Betty, especially not to the point of calling her home from Germany, so when she finally realized she was too sick to care for her self, she did the only thing she could have done.

She came home to Mama.

Of course, that's where everyone eventually ended up anyway. Anytime something really terrible happened to one of the family, they always came home to Mama.

Mama and Lucille were sisters, with Mama being the oldest girl in the family, and Lucille being the youngest. There was never any question about where Lucille would spend her last days. Mama was the backbone of the family, the strength and the bedrock.

Mama wasn't a big woman, at least not in physical size, but in all the ways that really counted, Mama was a giant. When strength was needed, Mama stood strong, and when comfort was in order, her shoulder was always available. Her sense of humor was exceeded only by her wisdom. Mama was wise not from formal schooling but from being a very astute student in the school of life. She read book after book and studied people every day of her life, and she had enough common sense for ten people. Mama could always be depended upon for an answer, even when the questions sometimes made very little sense.

But even Mama didn't have an answer to the problem Lucille posed, that summer of 1953 when she lay in her bed in our front room and waited to die.

It had been a bad winter, and everyone was more than ready for a little bit of sunshine when the first pretty days of early spring rolled around in March and April. Ernest had moved Lucille to Tennessee from Detroit around the first of February, and all she talked about for a week was how glad she was to be home with Mama. She hadn't thought she would even live until Christmas, and she'd been afraid she was going to die up North in Detroit, and she didn't want to do that. As it turned out, she did make it through Christmas, and she did make it out of Detroit and back to Tennessee. But the cold days and colder nights dragged by and by the end of February she still wasn't feeling very well. Not only that, but it was becoming plain that even Mama didn't really know what to do.

I remember Mama standing on the front porch one afternoon, telling us kids that she thought two or three days of sunshine would do Lucille a world of good, so a whole bunch of us little Rinky Dink kids spent the first two weeks of March praying for warmer weather.

Sure enough, our prayers were answered.

The third week of March gave us two days in row that were filled with sunshine and sixty degree temperatures. We took that as a sign that Spring was on the way, and that Lucille would soon be up and about. Mama didn't tell us any better, and we never once questioned the fact that Spring might have come anyway, even if we hadn't prayed so diligently.

I said Mama was smart, I never said the rest of us were.

Of course, I was the only one of the kids that really belonged to Mama, except for Goober of course, but all of them thought they did, and all of them hung around our house every day, waiting for a sign that the warm weather was doing its job. We took turns peeking through the window, hoping to catch Lucille out of her bed, dancing around in the floor, listening to "How Much Is That Doggie In The Window" on the radio. But it just didn't happen.

Not right away, anyway.

Lucille was the youngest girl in Mama's family, and maybe the prettiest. She had a big booming laugh, and never seemed to let anything get the best of her. She was still pretty young when she married Ernest Mayes, and they spent most of their time living somewhere other than Springfield. Ernie had lived somewhere up North for a long time, maybe in Ohio, though I don't know what city, and I was never sure what he did for a living. To tell the truth, I'm not so sure that even he knew exactly what he did for a living either. I seem to remember Ernie as being a man of many fortunes. Sometimes he would come to visit with a fist full of money, and other times with nothing but the shirt on his back. And sometimes there was somebody close behind him wanting to take the shirt.

I always thought Ernie might have done a lot of gambling, but I'm not too sure of that either. I know he loved to take a drink, and I know he knew just about every swear word in the book. In several books, more than likely. He may even have written one of the ##@%&***##%@, ##$&^**@#@ books.

Sometimes Ernie and Daddy got along all right, and sometimes they didn't. Daddy also liked to take a drink, and now and then when both of them were in the bottle, they'd have a few words.

I remember once when Daddy and Ernie had a small altercation that turned out a lot different than either of them expected. They had started drinking pretty early in the day, and by sunset they were pretty well drunk, and they were getting louder and more belligerent all the time. At some point, I think it was around seven or eight o'clock that night, the big words finally turned into action.

I'm not sure if either of them actually hit the other. It seems I recall they were mostly pushing and shoving, and of course mouthing off a little more all the time.

The problem was that they had brought the fight inside the house, and that was something both of them knew better than to do.

Fighting in the yard was one thing, fighting in Mama's house was a horse of an entirely different color.

It didn't matter who you were, or how bad or mean you were, or how drunked up you got, you just didn't bring your fight into Mama's house. To start with, Mama's brother's were among the meanest men that ever walked the streets of Springfield, or any other streets, for that matter. Everyone knew that if they ever harmed Mama in any way they would have to answer to Horace or or Willard, or, God help you, maybe even Jim or Odell. Nobody wanted to answer to Odell for anything.

I've seen some of the meanest men that ever drew breath turn into puppies when they came to our house. It was always Yes Ma'am, Miss Lena, Yes Ma'am.

Anyway, this particular night, Daddy and Ernie brought the fight inside the house.

Now Daddy was about five foot eleven inches tall and weighed in at about one eighty-five, and being left handed and a carpenter by trade, Daddy had a left hand that could knock down a mule.

Ernie was smaller, but not by much, and was a mean man in his own right, and neither of them intended to back down on this occasion.

Mama, on the other hand, just barely topped five feet tall, maybe by an inch, and never weighed much over a hundred pounds. So it stands to reason that she wouldn't have stood much chance in the middle of these two drunk, strong, angry men. Right?

Guess again.

Mama was standing watching the fight, telling them time and time again to stop. I seem to remember also being in the room at the time, and I know for sure that at some point in time one of them pushed the other and he fell against the footboard of Mama's bed.

Now Mama didn't have a lot of nice furniture, but what she had she wanted to keep in one piece, and she was dearly proud of her bed. Her three piece walnut bedroom suite was the only really nice thing she had, and when she saw the two men fall against the foot board she suddenly got very quiet.

I remember the looks on the faces of both men, Daddy and Ernie, as they realized what they had done. They had broken Mama's bed.

Both stood up away from the bed, and you could have heard a pin drop as Mama slowly marched across the room. She stopped when she reached the far wall where several tools lay in the floor, ready for Daddy to take to work the next day. Mama stood by the tools for a second, then slowly bent down and picked up a claw hammer.

Turning to Daddy and Ernest, in the quietest voice I'd ever heard, Mama spoke;

If either one of you says another word, or makes another move, I'll beat both of you to death with this hammer.

And she stood there and stared at them until they both sat down in the floor. The fight was over, and they didn't say another word that night.

The next day, Daddy fixed the bed before he went to work, and I don't know if he ever left his tools sitting in the house again.

There's no way of knowing what would have happened if they had not stopped when she told them to. What I do know is that neither of them wanted to find out what might happen if they went against her.

I'm not sure if this incident happened during the time Lucille was sick or not. It may have been then, or it may have been before that, because Ernie and Lucille lived in Springfield, down on South Main Street for a while, and were around the house a lot of the time.

Anyway, the summer of 1953 found Lucille at Mama's house, expecting to die most anytime.

But she didn't.

She didn't get completely well, but she got better.

I don't know if it was the Doctor she had, the fact that she was at home, or the prayers of everyone in South Town, but she did get better.

In fact, she got better enough to move back to Detroit, where she lived for two more years. Or almost two years. Lucille passed away in 1955, and this time when they brought her back home it was to bury her.

Ernie knocked around for several years after Lucille died. He lived in Springfield for a while, and I think he may have lived in Detroit part of the time. He also lived with Betty and John for a long time, either in Chattanooga or Northern Georgia, and I think he worked at an amusement park down there.

To tell the truth, I don't really remember a whole lot about Lucille. I remember her laugh, and I remember how good she cooked, and that's about all. I remember a little more about Ernest, but not a lot. I guess the thing that stands out in my mind is that I never once went and asked Ernie for help with one of my little childhood projects that he didn't take the time to do whatever he could to help me. He listened to me, and he tried to show me how to do things, and that made a lasting impression on me.

I know a lot of people saw Ernie's bad traits, and I guess there were several of them. But I didn't see them. I saw a ready smile, actually it was a little lopsided grin really, and a brown hat set at a rakish angle on his head. And a voice that I can still hear sometimes. In a thick Northern brogue, of course.

Whaddya want, kid?

Not much Ernie, can you help me fix...

Sometime in the fifties, I think it was, Betty and John eventually moved back to the states, and over the years I got to know the man everyone called "Dude."

Folks, in my 70 plus years of life, I've met famous entertainers, I've met big time politicians, even a President or two, and I've met some pretty impressive people.

No single person has ever impressed me more than John Mayes.

DON LEARNS TO DRIVE
THOU SHALT NOT STEAL:
THE GOSPEL ACCORDING TO JOHN

Betty Blanche Mayes was a slender young slip of a girl, pretty as a picture, with blonde hair and the most wonderful eyes. Betty was Lucille's daughter, and had inherited her mother's looks, laughter, and devil may care attitude. Being as Lucille was Mama's sister, Betty was my first cousin, but for years I think we both thought we were brother and sister. One thing's for sure, we wouldn't have been closer if we had been born to the same mother.

In 1955, when the heart condition finally got the best of Lucille, they brought her home for the last time. If I remember it right, we had her funeral there at the house. That was the first time I remember hearing gospel songs sung when someone had passed away.

During this time, I guess I loved Betty more than anyone in the world. She was older than me, but not by much, and my first cousin of course, so it wasn't the boy/girl kind of love, it was the like/adore/admire/believe/ want-to-be-around kind of love. Betty and I played together, and we always had lots of fun. But we were also good friends, besides being just kin.

Mama had a big bed of four-o'clock's planted outside the house, and to this day I remember thinking that Betty was prettier than the flowers. Course, I never told her that. I'm sure she knew she was pretty, and she knew I thought so, so we never discussed it. I do recall that she had a dress that had big flowers on it, and I know for a fact that when she wore that dress, the real flowers came out in second place every time. Like I said, I always loved Betty. Still do, and I'll bet, if you could call her up and ask, she'd tell you she loved me just as much.

And then John Mayes came along. John was a big, good looking fellow that everyone called "Dude," and he and Betty hit it off from the very first. All at once, Betty had a boy friend, and I had a hero. I guess John was my very first role model, although no one had ever heard that term back then. I wanted to do things just like John did. I even thought as much of John as I did the cowboys.

John was in the Army, and had fought in Korea, and he was one heck of a striking figure of a man. He was big, and strong as an ox, and as handsome as a man could get. It was easy to see why Betty fell so head over heels in love with him. And vice versa, I might add. Right from the start it seemed pretty apparent that John worshipped Betty, and always would. If there were ever two people made for each other, it was Betty and John.

Everybody knew John wasn't scared of anything that walks, crawls, flies or otherwise. He'd fight a man at the drop of a hat, and every now and then it'd be John who dropped the hat. Or, at least that's what everybody said. And I believed them.

I'm not exactly sure what year it was that John and Betty got married, but I seem to remember that it might have been a double wedding. John's brother, Tommy Mayes, had also met and fallen in love with a Betty. This pretty young girl was Betty Thaxton. Betty was Lawrence's older sister, and she and Betty Mayes were best friends.

John and Tommy both played the guitar and sang, and Tommy had the most perfect natural tenor voice I've ever heard. I always thought they were good enough to have made a living at it, but I guess they sang mostly for pleasure, and for the enjoyment of everyone who would gather to listen.

Tommy was a farmer, and he and Betty lived in Coopertown, a small community about six miles West of Springfield, out Highway 49. Tommy and Betty were good people, hard to beat both as family and friends. And even though Tommy liked to take a drink now and then, the last time I saw him before he passed away his voice still sounded as crisp and clear as ever.

But back to the story.

I'm being completely honest when I say I was as happy as I could be when John and Betty got married. Being a kid didn't stop me from seeing how they looked at each other, and anyway, it was more like I had gained a big brother than lost a sister.

John was stationed in Germany, and before we knew it they were gone, packed up and moved to Germany for a few years. It was while they were living in Germany that one night I had a dream.

It must have been in February or March, I guess, but I'm not sure at all which year. Just that it was in the early to mid fifties. John or Betty might know what year it was, if they recall the incident at all. Anyway, it was in the early fifties, I was just barely a teenager, and had already begun to do some pretty strange things. Some people would probably say stupid things, but I prefer to think of many of the things I did back then simply as a preview of coming attractions.

Anyway, this particular incident began with the dream.

I dreamed I woke up in the middle of the night and heard a car stop out in front of the house, and got up to see who was coming to call at that time of night. Well, I saw a 1952 Ford (I think it was a 52, I know it was a Ford) come to a stop, and watched as Betty and John got out and walked up on the front porch. The car was dark blue, I think, and had some kind of strange, different looking taillights. Anyway, I only glanced out the window for a minute, and then went back to bed, knowing I'd see them in the morning.

The next morning I got up about eight o'clock and went into the kitchen looking for Betty and John, but found that they weren't there. As far as anyone knew, they were still in Germany. I couldn't believe it was only a dream. It had seemed so real. I described the car and even what Betty was wearing (I don't recall now exactly what it was) but it was no use. They weren't there.

About the middle of the morning, a bunch of us were in the front yard throwing a ball around when we heard a car horn blow. I stood up to look and saw a beautiful, dark Blue 1952 Ford, with strange, different looking taillights pull to a stop in front of the house.

Of course, it was Betty and John. Betty even had on the dress I'd described to Mama. When Mama saw them walk into the house, the first thing she did was wink at me. Mama knew I'd had several little things like that dream happen to me, and she believed in them even though she couldn't explain them.

Anyway, Betty and John were there, blue Ford and all, just like I'd dreamed.

They spent the day just catching up on things, and making plans for their stay in Springfield. Most of the men in our neighborhood liked to hunt, and John was no exception. Rabbit hunting was a favorite sport, as well as being a way to put meat on the table when otherwise there might not have been any.

The next morning all the men decided to go rabbit hunting, including John and Daddy. They all loaded into one or two cars and left the house, and John left his car sitting out front.

I was at just exactly the right age to be thinking of nothing but cars. I wanted to drive more than just about anything in the world. Wesley Birdwell and I were sitting on the porch talking about how great John's car was, and I hollered in the house and asked Betty if we could sit in it for a while.

She said sure, as long as we didn't touch anything, and we in the car faster than a duck on a June bug.

I slid under the wheel and Wesley climbed into the other side and we sat there for a while and talked about how much we'd like to have a car like this one, and how fast it was and all the other things kids talk about when they're talking about cars, and all at once I noticed that John had left the keys in the ignition.

Uh, oh.

The car had an automatic transmission, and although I'd never actually driven a car, I'd sat in Daddy's car a lot of times, going over every detail of driving, until I was sure that I actually knew how to drive.

I can drive this car, I told Wesley.

Naw you can't, you don't know how. Wesley said.

Sure I do, I said. I can drive this car.

Naw you can't, Wesley said.

Back then I was even worse about some things than I am now, if that's possible. For me, to think has always been to act, and I was reaching for the ignition before the words were out of my mouth. Besides, I really needed to show Wesley that I could drive.

Betty heard the engine roar to life, as I gave it twice as much gas as it needed to start, but by the time she was standing on the porch screaming at me, I had the car rolling down 21st Avenue at a pretty good clip. The funny thing is, we didn't meet a single car on the road as we made our way down the street, and I was driving pretty slow and as carefully as I knew how. Wesley said there were three or four people running after us, but I couldn't look back, I was having too much trouble holding the car straight. It was a little tougher than I thought it would be, but nothing I couldn't handle. I did know there were a lot of the folks on the street standing out watching me drive by. I sure wish I could have waved, but I was afraid to take either hand off the steering wheel.

I wasn't driving very fast yet, because I still hadn't got the hang of it. I was going just fast enough to keep whoever was chasing us from catching up. I made the left turn on Cherry Street, and Wesley waved at Michael and some of the other kids as we went by their house. What the heck, I was driving, and I wanted them all to see. I didn't stop at the intersection when I reached 22nd Avenue at the Pet milk factory, but there was nothing coming anyway, and by now I was doing much better. I hung a left on 22nd Avenue and gave her a little more gas. Son. This was getting easier all the time.

I roared past Woodland Street School and the tires screamed as I made the 90 degree curve that put us on Woodland and headed back toward 21st. I looked at the speedometer as I went down the hill, and saw that I was doing sixty, and I remember thinking that was pretty good, especially for my first time behind the wheel. There were cars parked on both sides of the narrow little street, but I was sitting really high up in the seat, and could see all of them, so I just made sure I didn't turn the wheel and hit one of them. I slowed down and made the left that got me back on 21st, and as my foot found the brake and pushed it hard enough to actually stop us in front of my house, it suddenly dawned on me just what I'd done.

I turned off the key, got out of the car, and turned around to look at Wesley. Or at least where Wesley had been. By this time, Wesley was already halfway down the street, headed to his house as fast as he could go. I had to face Mama, and Betty, all alone.

I'm pretty sure I didn't ask them not to tell John I'd driven the car, because I knew he'd find out regardless. Shucks, everybody around the block knew about it, and I was pretty sure somebody would manage to let John know.

Remember I said John was in the Army? Well, not only was he in the Army, but he'd been to war, and he really liked to fight and kill people, and stuff like that. At least, that's all that ran through my mind as I sat in the house and waited for them to come back from rabbit hunting.

I knew John was going to beat the heck out of me, and I knew Daddy was going to let him. I'd be lucky if he didn't just kill me outright. And I wasn't too sure Daddy wouldn't help him do that too.

Of course, Mama wouldn't have went along with them hurting me, but I didn't think about that at the time. Nobody, not even John, ever went against what Mama said. But even she wouldn't have tried to stop the spanking I was sure I was going to get. And in this particular instance, Mama just stood back and didn't say a word. As an after thought, Mama probably could read John better than any of the rest of us could. She was like that, Mama was.

It was the middle of the afternoon when they got home. I stood there looking out the window, and nearly fainted when John got out of the car. He was seven or eight feet tall, and not only that, he had a big shotgun in one hand, and a bunch of bloody rabbits in the other. For a fleeting moment, I wished he'd just shoot me with the big 12 gauge and get it over with.

Betty met John and Daddy in the front yard and I could see her lips moving as she told them the story. I saw Daddy set his jaw, and I knew right then that whatever John decided to do was going to be all right with him. John just stood there looking at Betty, with a strange expression on his face. I remember thinking that was probably the way he looked over there in Korea when he was getting ready to shoot somebody. But this time it was going to be me. Looking back, I don't know if John ever shot anyone in Korea or not, he was never one to talk about stuff like that. But at the time, I was pretty sure he'd already killed five or six hundred men, and I was just a skinny little South Town Rinky Dink that was next in line.

Donald, come on out here, John hollered.

And then Daddy hollered; And do it right now.

THE LAST OF THE SOUTH TOWN RINKY DINKS
THE EXTENDED VOLUME

I walked the ten or twelve miles from the door to the front yard, and all I could think about was that John was going to kill me, maybe even two or three times.

But there was one thing for sure. I'd proven to Wesley that I could drive a car.

John stood there for a moment just looking at me, while I trembled and shook.

Get in the car, boy, John finally said, in a voice that was stern and un-comprising. It was the most serious tone I'd ever heard.

I slid in on the passenger side and he got under the wheel, and we headed down 21st and turned left on Cherry, right on 22nd, and left on Highway 431.

Dang, I thought, he's going to take me out in the country and kill me, and dump my body in Carr's Creek.

We drove three or four miles out in the country, and turned off on a gravel road, and since we'd left the house John still hadn't even spoken to me. Needless to say, I was scared to death.

But I had driven the car. You can bet on that.

John finally pulled the car over to the side of the road and cut the motor. He sat there for a few minutes, still not speaking, like he was trying to figure out exactly how he wanted to finish me off. As he'd left the shotgun at Daddy's house, I figured he was going to strangle me. I grabbed the door handle and braced myself.

Betty tells me you drove my car today, boy, that right?

Yes sir.

You know they call that stealing a car?

No sir, I didn't steal it. I just drove it around the block.

You stole it.

No sir, I just drove it around the block. Are you going to kill me?

He looked at me for a moment before answering, as though considering what I'd said. Then he finally spoke.

Get out of the car, John said, and he opened the door on the driver's side and got out himself.

Come around here, he said, and motioned for me to come around to where he stood waiting.

He still had a funny look on his face, and for a minute I thought about running. I didn't think he could catch me. I was pretty fast. But I knew I'd either have to go back home sometime, or run off and join the circus. And I didn't know nothing about elephants. Besides, he'd probably follow me there anyway. Or Daddy would tell him where I was. Either way, I was in big trouble.

You've probably figured out by now that my Daddy didn't hold for me taking off in somebody's car without permission, and probably thought I deserved to get my little butt whipped.

What could I do? Nothing at all. So got out and walked around the car. I can't really say that I wanted to, but that's what I did. I walked around the car and stood looking up at John.

He was the biggest man I'd ever seen.

He stood beside the open door on the driver's side.

Get in, he said, and motioned for me to get behind the wheel.

Thunderstruck, I almost couldn't move. He wants me to get under the wheel. Why? Why?

As I slowly slid under the wheel, John walked around to the other side of the car and got into the passengers side.

If you're gonna drive my car, he said, I guess you better learn how. Start the engine, he said, and I did. Take off slow, just give it enough gas to make it move. Touch the brake real smooth, he said. It'll stop where you want it to stop. Don't ever stomp down on the brake.

In absolute wonder, I drove around on the country back roads for thirty or forty minutes, with John showing me lots of little things about driving, and explaining that it's always best to ask before using other people's things.

John drove back to my house, and didn't talk very much about the incident ever again. But I still use most of the things he told me that day. Because even though I did a few really dumb things, I was actually a pretty smart kid, and I learned more that day than just a bunch of stuff about driving.

THE LAST OF THE SOUTH TOWN RINKY DINKS
THE EXTENDED VOLUME

When the two of us got out of the car, the brash, barely teenaged Rinky Dink kid and the tough Army Sergeant, I remember looking at John again. You know what I thought?

I thought he was eight or nine feet tall, the biggest man I'd ever seen.

You know what? I still do.

NOTE: John and Betty were married 50 years on December 24, 2001. John passed away the next day from cancer. He served in the US Army for 20 years, from 1950 to 1970, and after retiring he loved to paint, play music, and fish. He loved Betty from the day they met until the day he died, and I think will continue to love her through eternity.

9

ROSIE THE WITCH WOMAN
THE NIGHT CORN FELL FROM THE CEILING

Rosie Slaten was one of the most colorful characters that ever walked the streets of South Town, although the reason for her colorfulness might not have been her fault.

In later days, especially after everyone saw the movie "THE EXORCIST," we might have said that Rosie was possessed, and we might have been right, for if any of the stories are true, that's probably what she was.

Not only possessed, but clairvoyant as well. And physic. And a fortune teller. And a witch. But even with all this going on, everyone said she was a really nice person. At least most of the time.

It's just that Rosie had a lot of strange things happen when she was around. Like tables tapping their legs on the floor, and heavy chest of drawers moving across the room by themselves, and of course there's the story of the night the corn fell from the ceiling in Mama's bedroom.

But, first things first.

Rosie Slayton was married to Leslie Fred Walker, one of Mama's brothers, and for a while they also lived on 21st, a few houses down the street from us, on the other side.

They say that sometimes when Rosie would walk up the street, cats would run from her, and yowl that wild eerie cry that cats let out when they're scared of something. They'd jump over to the side of the road, never taking their yellow eyes off Rosie, and hump up their backs and let out the scream. They said that when you'd hear them hollering like that you'd have thought someone was skinning them. Of course, they do say there's more than one way to skin a cat. If that's true, then it's also true that the folks on 21st knew them all.

Anyway, the cats all acted like they were scared of Rosie, and sometimes a few of the people acted that way too.

But not Mama. Mama was never scared of anybody or anything, least of all her sister-in-law. Not even if a lot of folks thought that particular sister-in-law was a witch.

Sometimes, back before Rosie got too scared of whatever power she thought was inside her, she used to hold séances, and a lot of the time she held them at our house.

A few of the people from the street would gather, and they'd all sit around the living room watching as Rosie strutted her stuff.

And she had lot of stuff to strut.

Rosie would start by turning off the lights, except for a single small bulb, or maybe a kerosene lamp, and when all the conditions were just right, she'd start the séance.

She'd place her small, empty hands in the middle of a large wooden table, which sometimes was even covered with dishes, then she'd close her eyes and turn her face upward at the ceiling, and she'd softly intone the séance words.

If there are any spirits in this room, let it be known by tapping this table leg three times, Rosie would speak, in a voice heavy with mystery and full of apprehension.

And if nothing happened she'd speak again.

If there are any spirits in this room ...

- stronger now, and more forceful. -

Let it be known by tapping this table leg three times. And the people watching would lean forward, and look around the room in anticipation.

If there are any spirits in this room ...

- ever stronger her voice would become, and she'd move her hands about in small circles on the smooth tabletop. -

Let it be known ...

- the table would slowly rise from the floor, and just as slowly settle back down. -

... by tapping the table leg three times.

- rise and fall, softly and slowly, rise and fall, the table would move, until it was quite apparent it was tapping its leg on the floor, all by itself. -

Harder the table tapped, and still the small hands moved slowly in tiny circles. Harder still the tapping came, in distinct groups of three taps each time.

This pattern kept up until Rosie knew that everyone in the room was sure that the spirits had answered her call. Then she'd stop her hand movements, the table would settle back down, and all the people would let out their breaths together, most not even aware that they had been holding it.

She'd open her eyes, look around and smile at the people who sat there with mouths agape, wondering just exactly what it was they'd seen tonight.

They'd all go away swearing that Rosie could call up the spirits, and the tales would grow as they were told over and over.

The strange thing was, most of them believed the tales, and not a single person among the ones who witnessed one of Rosie's séances could ever explain how she could do things like that, unless the spirits really did answer her call. Then there was the question of the dishes. Although the table was usually covered with dishes, they never rattled, not even one was ever broken, and that was another thing they couldn't explain. Of course, although Rosie was not a real small woman, she still wasn't big enough to lift a heavy table. Especially with only the palms of her hands resting on the tabletop.

Anyway, no one could ever explain how she did it, not even Rosie herself.

I never heard of Rosie actually trying to contact the dead, or anything like that. She seemed content to make tables move, and as far as I can tell she usually left it at that. Except for once.

If no one could understand how Rosie could make a table move, they surely couldn't understand how she made kernels of dried corn fall from the ceiling. But she did.

I might as well tell you this fact one more time, even though I've explained it more than once already.

Mama said that Rosie made corn fall from her bedroom ceiling. Nobody, and I mean nobody, would ever even hint that Mama would tell a lie. No way. If Mama said that corn fell, then you could take it to the bank that corn fell. And there were a lot of grown men in South Town who would be quick to fight a man if he heard him accuse Mama of lying.

So I can tell you this as gospel truth.

One night, in Springfield, Tennessee, at 401 21st. Avenue, dried kernels of corn fell from nowhere out of the ceiling. Mama said so.

It goes like this.

After a few years of the strangeness, Rosie became convinced that she was possessed by the Devil, and she became very scared of whoever or whatever was giving her the power to perform all these wild things. As was the usual custom, whenever someone was scared or needed to talk about something, they always ended up coming to Mama.

Rosie was no exception. But this time her story had a little twist to it.

Rosie, being married to Mama's brother Fred, claimed that it was his fault that the Devil had possessed her. That wasn't all. She told Mama, in private of course, that all of Mama's kids had the same power as she herself had, and they could make tables move and cats howl, and things like that. Unfortunately, Mama wasn't the only person to whom Rosie revealed this wondrous tidbit of information.

She also told Eva Mai and Norman.

Norman was Mama's oldest son, and Eva Mai was his wife, and once she found out what Rosie had said, she immediately said she'd leave if Norman even considered trying to séance anything at all.

Norman, being Norman, of course had to give it a try.

One night he tried a little séance and moved a great big chest of drawers around in the bedroom, using only the power Rosie said he had. That was enough for Eva Mai. Being true to her word, she left.

He promised never to do that again, and in a couple of weeks, she came back. I don't know if he ever tried it again, but I do know that I've heard this story all my life, and I've never been disposed to try and see if I have a little of the power myself. Well, I've wondered about it, who wouldn't, but I've never tried it. Not really. Not when I was serious about it. I was always afraid it would happen, and if it did, then what would I do?

But now, back to the corn.

It was right after Rosie claimed the Devil was inside her that the incident happened. Fred was gone that night, for one reason or another, and Rosie was afraid to stay at her house all alone, so she made her way up the street to our house.

Please Miss Lena, I got to have a place to sleep tonight. I just can't stand to stay down there by myself. I'm just too afraid. I can't sleep, and I thought if I could stay up here with you…

You can sleep in the bed with me, Rosie, Mama said. If the Devil comes, I expect the two of us can take care of him.

At this point, let me explain one other tiny detail.

The Devil would have had to have been a fool to come to 21st for any reason whatsoever, especially after dark, and let alone to try to get into bed with my Mama. That would have been the biggest mistake that horny headed, pointed tailed red rascal ever made. Either Mama would have beaten him to death with a claw hammer, or Daddy would driven him all the way back to Hell with his loud snoring.

Anyway ...

Rosie laid down on the double bed and closed her eyes. Mama pulled the string on the light that hung from a twisted cord from the ceiling, and laid down on the bed beside Rosie.

Thump, thump, thump, Mama heard something strike the bed covers.

She rose up and looked around, and saw nothing at all.

Thump, thump, thump, she heard again.

Mama got up and turned on the light, and as soon as she did, the noise stopped.

As before, at first she saw nothing at all out of the ordinary, and it wasn't until she walked back over and looked at the bed that she noticed several large kernels of dried corn lying on the top of the quilt.

Without a word, Mama scooped up the corn, turned off the light, and lay back down.

Thump, thump, thump, thump, the sound began again.

Rosie, Mama softly called, Rosie ... and got no answer.

Thump, thump, thump, thump, thump ...

So she got up again, turned the light back on, and it stopped again.

Rosie was covered from head to toe with one of Mama's old handmade quilts, afraid to look out from under the cover, and that's how she remained for the rest of the night. Mama says that every time she turned off the light, corn fell from the ceiling. There were no holes in the ceiling, and Rosie didn't have any corn in the bed with her, so she couldn't have been tossing it in the air.

But the next morning, Mama had scooped up a double handful of the hard yellow grains of dried corn, which she put in a little jar and sat it on the windowsill in the kitchen. The jar stayed there for a long time, and I don't know what ever happened to it. All I know is that one night, on 21st Avenue in Springfield, Tennessee, corn fell from the ceiling. Mama said it happened, so you can take it as the gospel.

Later on, Rosie divorced Fred, moved away from Springfield, and got religion. The power left her about the same time she left Fred, so maybe there was something to her wild claim about whose fault it all was. I don't know, I was much too young to remember any of this first hand. But this is the story the way Mama always told it to me, and you know how Mama was.

We had several other relatives that were strange and interesting people, and while I can't write about every one of them, there are a few stories that I just have to tell. Another of Mama's brothers was a handsome young man named Jim Walker, and there are so many stories about Jim that they would fill up a book by themselves. I've kind of hit the high spots, especially the ones I heard or lived first hand, and I must admit they make for some entertaining reading.

10

THAT RENOWNED SCOUNDREL, *UNCLE JIM WALKER*

Jim Walker was the youngest of Mama's brothers. In fact he was the baby of the family, and probably the chief mischief maker of the whole bunch. Mama always said that if anyone was going to get into anything, anything at all, they could always count on Jim to be ready. Truth is, Jim probably instigated most of the mischief they got into.

Jim was a good-looking man. All the women thought so, and I suspect Jim thought so too, though I'm not sure about that. I do know he had a large amount of confidence in himself. He thought he could do anything.

I'm not so sure he couldn't.

Jim was another Rinky Dink that went off to war and fought for the country, getting wounded and earning the Purple Heart. Once, years later, I asked him if he'd enjoyed being in the army, and fighting the enemy, and helping win the war.

Naw, boy, I didn't enjoy it. Most of the time we were scared out of our minds and we never knew if we were going to live or die. But I know one thing. A man has to fight for his country and he has to fight for what he believes in, and sometimes a man has to fight for what somebody else believes in. In the war, we did a little bit of both.

Did you believe in the war? Uncle Jim, I asked.

Well, I believed in what I was told, anyway. They told me if I didn't shoot the heck out of the enemy, either the enemy or the MP's would shoot the heck out of me. And I believed them. So I shot the hell out of every Jap and German I ran into. I shot 'em when we were in the front lines, and I shot 'em when I ran into one at a bar. I shot 'em between the eyes, and I shot 'em in the tail. So, yeah, boy. I believed in all that stuff.

Would you like to do it again?

Boy, ain't you got no sense at all? I ain't never seen nobody except a few crazies who'd want to fight that war over. You can bet your skinny little South Town butt there ain't no way I want to go through any of it again.

And then he laughed. And laughed, and all told I suspected that Jim wouldn't blink an eye about doing it again, if somebody told him he was needed again…

Jim sent Mama pictures home from across the sea, and she dearly loved to show everyone the latest picture of her handsome brother, standing so proudly in his uniform. And even one or two pictures of Jim holding on to one of his buddies so he could stand proudly. Maybe just so he could even stand. Jim was not a man to turn down a drink. He'd much rather turn one up.

When I was born Jim was already married to a dark haired girl named Rebecca Hulsey, whom everyone called Becky. Jim and Becky had four children, all boys. There was Spencer, of whom I'll write a little more later, and then there was James, Robert and Harold. I believe they were born in that order.

Although Jim and Becky lived in South Town when I was growing up, he moved his family, lock, stock, and barrel, to Detroit sometime in the mid to late fifties, and from then on he only visited in Springfield.

Actually, he didn't really move to Detroit. He moved to Romulus, Michigan, which is in Wayne County, and is on the southern edge of the city of Detroit.

He used to come home to visit Mama and the rest of the family about twice a year. On one visit he would bring Becky and the boys, and let them get to know their cousins and other kin, and let Becky see her family, most of whom still lived in Robertson county. On these visits, Jim would have a few drinks with Daddy and the others, but nothing serious, and mostly he just drove Becky and the boys around and let them visit as much as they wanted.

THE LAST OF THE SOUTH TOWN RINKY DINKS
THE EXTENDED VOLUME

The second time Jim came to town each year he came alone. During this second visit he made the rounds of the honky tonks and beer joints, drinking and raising cain, and bouncing from one gambling game to another. Perhaps there were a few women involved during these visits, perhaps not. Sometimes I drove Jim around several times when he was in town for his second trip, and although I saw him speak to a woman or two, I never saw anything that could be considered cheating on Becky.

There was a reason for that, as you might have guessed.

You see, Jim was a gambler. A really good gambler.

Oh, if anyone asked, he'd tell them that by trade he was a carpenter, and he was, and a good one at that. But his love, his joy, his passion in life, was always gambling. Cards or dice, made no difference. He'd roll the dice and deal the cards anywhere he could find a game. And I do mean anywhere.

Sometime along about 1972, after Jim had already been dead for several years, I was working as an assembly foreman in one of the plants in Springfield, and quite by accident I heard a story about Uncle Jim from a man who worked for me, and had known Jim back in the earlier days.

It was our afternoon coffee break, and several of us were standing around talking about life in general, and life in Springfield in particular, and somehow the conversation got turned around and we found ourselves talking about gambling. One story led to another and at some point in time I mentioned the fact that I used to have an uncle who was a mean man and one heck of a gambler. I went on to tell how he lived in Detroit and used to come to Springfield once or twice a year and play cards and shoot craps.

What was yo' Uncle's name, and when was it he was comin' into town to play? The man talking was an older black man who worked for me on the assembly line.

His name was Jim Walker, I said, and I guess he moved to Detroit sometime in the Fifties, so it had to have been in the late fifties or early to mid Sixties when he was coming back down here to gamble. Why?

Well, I thought that might have been who you was talkin' bout. I knowed Jim Walker back then. Good lookin' man, with dark wavy hair and laughed a lot? Wasn't scared of the Devil hisself?

Sounds like him, I said.

Well, the man I'm talkin' bout lived in Detroit all right, and said he had kin in Springfield. Want to hear a story bout him?

I'd love to hear a story about Jim, I said. Jim was just about my favorite Uncle. Where'd you know him?

Well, the first time I met him was down on 13th. Back before they cut Central Avenue through to Memorial Highway. You remember when 13th ended at South Main Street?

Yeah, I remember it all right, I said.

Then I guess you 'member when there used to be a whole lot of little clubs along 13th Avenue? Back when the black folk lived in that whole section?

Yeah, I remember that too. I've been down there once or twice with Daddy or Jim. There used to be a lot of gambling went on down there.

You know it did. Awful lot of it. And that's where I met your Uncle Jim.

Really, I said. You mean he was down on 13th gambling? Of course, I knew he used to go down there, but this was the first time I'd ever heard anyone talking about it. Jim usually didn't say much about his little episodes, seeing as how he figured that nobody could tell anything about him they didn't know.

Yeah, he used to gamble with the brothers, down on 13th. And they wasn't a heck of a lot of white men who came down there either.

What happened? I asked. The night you saw him down there.

Well, they was five or six of us sittin' on the floor, rollin' the bones, when Ol' Walker come strolling through the door, big as life, just lak he was down dere ever night. He was with a friend of ours, so nobody said nothin', him being white and all. He was already hittin' the bottle pretty hard, you know what I mean, and by the time it was his turn to roll, he was more than a little drunked up.

Well, that sounds just exactly like Jim so far, I replied.

Yeah, he laughed.

Anyway, he was about breakin' even when it come his time to roll the dice. He laid down a two-dollar bet on the floor and everybody covered it, and ol' Walker picked up the dice, blew on 'em as he shook 'em in his hand, then sent them bones skitterin' out in the middle of the floor. Rolled a seven, he did, first time out. Well, they was another friend of mine, kind of a bad boy, if you know what I mean, who didn't particularly want a white man playin' in the game, specially not if he was gonna roll a natural the first time he got his hands on the bones.

So anyway, this old bad boy, he reached out and picked up the money, looked at yo Uncle Jim, and said; You lose, white man. Down here, seven a natural born loser.

Well suh, bein' as we was all down on our knees in the dice shootin' position, you know what that is, Ol Walker just kinda leaned back on his heels, rockin' a bit, looked over at the man holdin' the money, and politely axed him. What'd you say?

Then the old bad boy, he leaned forward toward yo Uncle Jim and said, in his meanest voice; I said, down here, yo seven is a natural born loser, white man. So you just might as well get yo lily white butt back cross town, while you still can.

Ol Walker, he looked at the bad boy and kinda smiled for a minute. Are you sure that's the way you play down here, he asked him, still smilin' real big?

I'm sho, and that's a fact, the bad boy said.

When yo Uncle leaned forward again, the old bad boy and the rest of us noticed that he had a shiny little .25 automatic pistol in his right hand. He must have had it in his back pocket, I guess, all the time. Anyway, he leaned in toward the middle of the floor, laid that little pistol square in the middle of the bad boys forehead, and said;

Then I guess I'm just gonna have to shoot yo' ass, ain't I? Cause everywhere else in the world, a seven is a natural winner. And this little pistol says the same rules apply down here too.

The old bad boy's eyes got big, and he kinda sputtered, You mean, you mean, you'd kill me for two dollar, he spit out real quick?

Naw, feller, yo Uncle said. I wouldn't kill no man for two dollars. You need the money that bad, you can keep it. I'm gonna kill you because you're a cheatin' bastard who tried to steal my money. I don't care if it's two dollars, two thousand dollars, or two cents, ain't no way in the world Jim Walker's gonna sit here and let nobody cheat him. Course, now, if you was to decide you was wrong about the rules, and that y'all play the same way here as everybody else does, I might see fit to just take my money and keep on gambling. That is what I come down here for.

Yes suh, yes suh, that's the way it is, for sho. I don't know what made me mistake the rules that a way, the old bad boy said.

Yo Uncle Jim, he reached out and took the money out of the bad boy's hand, laid two dollars in the middle of the floor, picked up the dice, and started shakin 'em again. C'mon boys, he said, get yore money down, I feel mighty lucky tonight.

And he laughed like a wild man as the bones went hoppin' out across the floor again.

Is that a true story? I asked.

Bet yo butt it's a true story, he answered. I sho wouldn't make up a tale like that.

Well, that sounds like Jim, I gotta admit. He didn't have a lot of sense sometimes, and he always carried a little .25. And he was probably crazy enough to have used it.

Well, he made a believer out of a few of us that night, he said. I've played cards with him since then, and I shot craps with him, and never did have another incident. Whatever happened to the man, anyway.

He died, I said, back in the sixties. Wasn't but 46 or 47 years old. Died with a heart attack, like most of Mama's brothers, I told him.

Is that a fact. I hate that. I liked that man, I shore did.

I never met a man, or woman, who knew Jim Walker, that didn't like him. Unless of course, it was somebody who had crossed him at one time or another.

As we got back to work that day, I thought about the story, and I still think about it sometimes.

Now I don't know if that story is true or not, but the guy I worked with swears it is. I know it sounds a lot like Jim, for sure. Some of the older Rinky Dinks were about as rough and tough as they come. In fact, some of them were mean as a snake. Mama didn't have a brother who wouldn't hurt you in a fight, or just for the heck of it for that matter, if he was in a bad mood, or maybe drinking a little. I guess they just grew up that way, and never did grow out of it.

And Jim did die, like I said, some time in the late sixties. I could look it up and see what year it was, and just exactly how old he was when he died, but I'm writing as much of this from memory as I can, and cold hard facts get a lot colder and harder if I look them up and see them in black and white.

Jim was a reasonably successful man in the fifties and sixties, and owned his own home in Springfield, on Woodland across from where 21st joined Woodland. I used to love to visit Jim because he always had time to pay a little attention to me, regardless of how busy he was. I remember one time he gave me a beautiful knife.

Like I've already written, Jim served overseas in World War II, and like so many of the boys who fought over there, he brought home a few little souvenirs. The knife he gave me was one of those souvenirs. It was about eight inches long, and had a dark shiny handle. Inlaid in the handle was a diamond shaped piece of pearl, or mother of pearl, with a ruby red German swastika inlaid in the pearl. It was absolutely beautiful. The story Jim told, and I can't vouch for the truthfulness of it, was that he took the knife off the body of a dead German officer in one of the little towns they passed through. He said the knife reminded him of the war, and he wanted me to have it as a keepsake. But I lost it.

And it really wasn't my fault.

Spencer and I, Spencer was Jim's oldest son, used to spend a lot of time playing under Jim's house in the soft dirt. There was a large crawl space under almost all the houses back then, and the kids played in the shadowy coolness under the houses in the hot summertime. We had some play cars, and we used to get under the house and make little racetracks and towns and filling stations and things like that. Of course, we were always looking for a good sharp tool to use for digging. That's what I used the knife for most of the time. We'd sometimes cover up our toys and tools when we were tired of playing for the day, knowing we'd be back again the next day. Unfortunately, Jim's house burned one morning, and we were never able to find the German knife again. Many times after the house was rebuilt I thought about going back and asking the current owners to let me look, but I never did. I went back to the house and looked once, but the best I could tell they had laid a new concrete porch about where we used to play. Kinda makes me sad though, that I lost one of the best presents a boy could get.

After the house on Woodland Street burned, Jim bought a lot in a section of Springfield called Shannondale and built a new house there. He only lived there a short while though, before deciding to move his family north to Detroit.

But even after Jim left Springfield for the big city, he still led a colorful and crazy mixed up life.

We went to visit him once, in the summer of 1966. I know it was 1966 because I was already married and our first child was still a baby in diapers. I remember the diapers well, in this particular incident. We had to get off the interstate in the outskirts of Detroit to change a rather smelly diaper, and drove several miles trying to find another on ramp. It was very hot, and the old car didn't have air conditioning, and when we couldn't find a garbage can to dispose of the diaper, we were a pretty miserable bunch for a while.

Romulus, Michigan, is on the south side of Wayne County, a few miles from Detroit, and that's where we went to visit Jim and Becky and the kids.

Jim was a master carpenter, and it wasn't long after he moved to Romulus that he got a position as a building inspector for Wayne County. He moved up the social ladder in Romulus, finally culminating in his being the person nominated to meet President Johnson once when he visited Detroit. That visit happened to be at the same time as we were visiting Jim, and we watched as the Presidential procession rode by. They had blocked off the Interstate, and there were helicopters in the air, and to a young Rinky Dink from Springfield, Tennessee, it was a grand sight.

While visiting Jim, we went to a place called the Irish Hills for a picnic and to spend a few hours on the lake. I think this was the first time I had ever been to a cookout. We didn't have cookouts in Springfield at the time, at least not in South Town.

Jim had four cars, including a new Thunderbird, and he also had a brand new motorcycle, and had bought not only the house he lived in, he also owned two or three others on the same street.

I remember he also had an expensive banjo that he had picked up somewhere. Grandpa Walker was a fiddler, and all of Mama's brothers and sisters loved country music.

THE LAST OF THE SOUTH TOWN RINKY DINKS
THE EXTENDED VOLUME

While we were there, Jim said he had a Dodge station wagon that was in the shop having the transmission repaired, and he wanted me to drive him into Detroit to pick it up, and then follow him back home. Talk about a driving experience for a Rinky Dink that had never driven in a big city. We picked up the car and Jim drove like a wild man as he led the way back through the city toward Romulus, never stopping to see if I was behind him or not. I guess he must have known there was no way I'd let him lose me. After all, we had the same roots, the same background, and my inclination to be a little wild came from the same place as his did. We had much the same perception of normalcy, and Jim realized it, whether I did or not.

Romulus is a small township, and at that time, many of its roads were covered with cinders, and not blacktop asphalt as the ones I was used to back home in Springfield.

One afternoon, Jim decided that he wanted to drive into Detroit, and he wanted me to go with him. The only problem was that he'd had a few drinks, and I wasn't really sure about his ability to drive. But when we headed for the car, it only took about ten seconds for me to decide; Aw, what the heck, and climb into the car beside him. And off we went to the big city.

Jim had a tendency to drive fast anyway, and with a few drinks under his belt he had a tendency to drive even faster, so it wasn't long before we were clipping along the loose cinder covered road at about seventy miles an hour.

There weren't even seat belts in the car, and I was more than a little worried, to say the least.

Jim, I said, you might oughta slow down. You sure don't need a ticket.

I ain't gonna get a ticket, boy, hang on.

Seventy-five. Eighty.

Jim, maybe you'd better slow down a little, I was almost mumbling. The law'll give you a ticket for sure. I really was getting a little worried, and not really because I cared if he got a ticket. I was scared to be traveling that fast down that dang cinder road, to tell the truth.

Naw, boy, I ain't gonna get a ticket in Romulus.

Eighty-five. Ninety.

JIM. SLOW THIS THING DOWN BEFORE THE LAW STOPS US OR WE GET KILLED.

I ain't gonna get a ticket in Romulus boy, don't worry.

Jim was laughing like this was the best joke he'd ever pulled on anybody.

Dang, Jim.

Ha ha, Jim laughed. There ain't but one law in Romulus boy, and I'm it, he roared. Hell, I'm the only Constable in the whole township. Now hang on.

What the heck. I sat back, took a sip out of Jim's bottle of whiskey, relaxed, and enjoyed the rest of the drive into Detroit.

A year of so after that visit, Jim made one of his trips home to Springfield. For some reason he stopped somewhere in Kentucky and bought Mama a little red toy stuffed fuzzy bear. That was highly unusual. Jim very seldom brought anything with him. But this time, in what might have been a very real glimpse of the future, he told Mama he'd brought the little bear because he might never see her again. These were very prophetic words.

He had a little exciting news he wanted to share with Mama and the rest of his brothers and sisters on this visit as well. He'd found another house he was in the process of buying, and he was really excited about this one. It was a new brick house, and wasn't even completely finished, and had been tied up in probate court for a while. It seems the man who had started building it had died, and Jim was able to get the house at an extremely good price.

This is the house, he told Mama and Daddy that day, that I'll live in the rest of my life. Like I said, very prophetic words.

I was told later that before Jim had left Romulus, he'd driven around with Spencer one afternoon and had a long talk with him. He'd said that if anything ever happened to him, that Spencer would be the man of the house, and would have to help take care of the family, and had even gone so far as to drive past a cemetery and tell Spencer that that was where he wished to be buried.

And that was where he was buried, later that same year.

We went back to Romulus for the funeral, me and Helen, my wife, and Mama and Aunt Minnie and Goober, who by this time was already insisting that he be called Ray. We drove up in Clyde's car, and Minnie must have read every street sign between Springfield and Detroit.

While we were at the Jim's house, after the funeral, Becky told me this little story about Jim's last couple of days.

Jim had promised a friend of his that he'd help him put a roof on his house, and he'd spent most of the day before he died doing just that. Up on the roof in the hot sun might not have been what Jim should have been doing, but he was never one not to help out a friend when he needed help. Late that afternoon they had a big catfish supper, and Becky said Jim was in his glory, eating catfish, having a few drinks and just generally enjoying himself.

He awoke early the next morning with some chest pains, but didn't get Becky up right away, deciding instead to see if the pains would go away. Becky said it was around six-thirty or seven o'clock that he finally decided to go to the emergency room at the hospital. Even then, they sat in the car for about a half hour before Jim finally went in. He told Becky that the pains had gone away, but since they were at the hospital, he might as well get checked anyway.

They went into the emergency room and Becky said that Jim stopped a nurse and told her he was having serious chest pains and needed to see a doctor at once.

The nurse showed them into an examining room and told them to have a seat and wait a minute, and the doctor would be with them.

Becky said that Jim sat her down in a chair, walked across the room, took his wallet out of his pocket and walked back across to her.

He handed her his wallet, kneeled down in the floor beside her chair and rested his hand on her lap.

It's crying shame, honey, here I am dying with a heart attack, and they tell me to wait a minute.

Then he laid his head down in her lap, and died.

I really do remember the year. It's just at times I'd as soon not think about it. It was nineteen sixty-eight, and Jim Walker was 47 years old.

I don't think Mama or Minnie or Uncle Horace ever got over Jim's death. I know for a fact I never got over it. Jim was a heck of a man, and he was one of the original South Town Rinky Dinks. I'd say those of us that came later were walking in some pretty big footprints.

But if I know Uncle Jim, he'd be proud of the ones that carried on the tradition.

All of the strangely funny people that lived on 21st weren't directly related to me, but I grew up feeling like most of them were family. Take Daisy and Stanley Evans, for example.

11

DINNER (OR SUPPER) WITH
DAISY AND STANLEY

Daisy and Stanley were two very special people to many of the Rinky Dinks, and at times I think both of them, particularly Stanley, probably had quite a lot of influence over the way my mind finally learned to think (now there's a scary thought). Of course, no one ever influenced me the way Mama did, but in many ways, Stanley ran her a pretty close second.

Daisy's first marriage had been to a much older man in Coopertown, which is about 6 miles from Springfield. They had one child, a son named Charles, who was a good friend of mine back then, and was until the day he died.

For whatever reason, Daisy divorced her first husband and then married my Uncle Paul, one of my mother's younger brothers. A few years later Paul was killed in WWII, and after a period of time Daisy married again. This time, she married Stanley Evans, and that is a whole *nuther* story.

Stanley was a big, good-looking man, who dearly loved three things. He loved Daisy, he loved a good cold beer, and he loved kids. To tell the truth, I always thought Stanley loved me a little more than he did most anyone else, except for Daisy of course. There seemed to be a special place in his big heart for me, and to the day he died he was one of my favorite people.

When Stanley went into the service, maybe in nineteen forty three or forty four, he sent me a little blue tee shirt, a souvenir shirt, not a real one, that had the inscription, *Keep your shirt on Honey, will see you soon*. I still have it. I didn't see him a lot in his later years, but every time I did he was still the same ol' Stanley I grew up loving.

You see, Stanley read comic books. Funny books. The only grown person I ever knew that really read funny books. Not only that, when he was finished with them, he gave them to me. Stacks and stacks of them. He introduced me to Superman and Batman, to the Doll Man and to Green Lantern. I'm sure Stanley knew that my young mind would be opened by the books, and he also knew that imagination was the only way to get away from the reality that was South Town. Although I didn't understand everything he said, Stanley always tried to tell me that books were the key. Any kind of books. The funny books were the best way he knew to keep me interested in a world that existed outside my own, and to make sure that I knew the difference between real dreams and daydreams.

He once told me that real dreams are wonderful things. They give you something to work for, and offer a chance at being somebody.

You have to have dreams, Donald, he'd say. Don't ever believe anyone that tells you dreams are silly. Dreams turn a person into whatever he wants to be, and that's a good thing.

Yeah, well I want to be Superman, Stanley, is that too big a dream?

Naw, Donald, it's not too big, it's just that wanting to be Superman ain't a dream at all, it's a daydream. Now, don't get me wrong, daydreams ain't bad things either. Daydreams do for your soul what real dreams do for your mind. They lift it up and show it things it might not see anywhere else. So you see, daydreams are good, but Son, they just ain't real. You can daydream about being Superman, and that daydream will give you pleasure and make you feel good and all, but the fact is, you ain't never gonna be Superman. Not today, and not ever. That's what a daydream is all about.

But a real dream, that's something else. You can dream that someday you'll be a millionaire, or go to the moon, or be a movie star, and if you really work at it, that dream might come true. That's the difference between a dream and a daydream. Here, read another one of these funny books while I go see how Daisy is gettin' along.

Guess you can see why I thought so much of Stanley.

Daisy was a pretty woman, not very big, but she could make old Stanley walk the line. Looking back, I think she used to say things to me for no other reason than just to see what I'd say. Or do.

My favorite two tales about Daisy involve dinner time, or actually supper time. I was grown before I ever heard anyone call the evening meal "dinner." Everyone I ever knew called the noonday meal "dinner" and the evening meal "supper." Beats the heck out of me why that is, but it's true. Most of the time, I still call them that. Except when I'm around some of my Yankee friends. They wouldn't know what I was talking about. I have no idea when they'd show up if I invited one of them to have "supper" at my house. I know one thing for sure though. If I invited them over for "Sunday dinner" and they showed up around six or six-thirty that afternoon, they'd think I was a heck of a host when they found out we'd been through eating for three or four hours.

Anyway, the story goes that when I was three or four years old, I went to Daisy's house almost every afternoon to eat supper with her and Stanley. In fact, I was over there so much that it became quite a joke. One afternoon, after several days in a row of feeding me, Daisy told me that I couldn't eat with them that day because she'd broken my plate. I went home and told Mama what Daisy had said, and explained what I needed. Mama stood on the front porch and I expect she was laughing her head off as I purposefully headed back to Daisy's house with a small saucer. Daisy never mentioned breaking my plate again.

Like I said, Stanley loved a cold beer, or a hot drink of whiskey for that matter, and now and then he'd get into a little hot water with Daisy about drinking. Mama got another big laugh late one afternoon when I told her that I was for sure eating supper with Daisy tonight.

"Well, Honey," Mama said, "you ate dinner with Daisy today, didn't you? Are you sure you want to go back over there for supper?"

"Yeah, Mama," I replied, "I'm really sure I want to eat there tonight. Stanley's been out drinking today, and Daisy told me just as soon as he gets home, she's gonna cook his goose. I know I don't want to miss that kind of supper."

12

THE RINKY DINKS AND THE LION

Before I was born, when the Rinky Dinks consisted of my brothers, several of my uncles, and many of the most notorious citizens that ever called Springfield home, there was a story that was told about those kids. Mama used to tell me this story and laugh so hard tears came to her eyes.

I think she enjoyed it so much because so many of those kids were lost during World War II, and with this simple little story, their spirit lives on.

They said that once a man from "up North," I was never sure exactly where, came through Springfield researching a book he was writing.

He was a Sheriff "up North," I think, or maybe a reporter, and the book was about law enforcement all around the country.

His stories were printed in one of the big magazines, so the story goes, and he always sent copies to the towns he had visited, so the folks could see what he'd written about them.

One of his stops in the South was in Springfield, and of course, they had to bring him to 21st Avenue.

According to the story, he toured the street in a very thorough manner, albeit very quickly, and later wrote of the incident.

"In the small town of Springfield, Tennessee," he wrote in his article, "I was taken on a tour of South Town, a most remarkable place. While there, I was directed to walk down 21st Avenue, and had the opportunity to observe first hand the children of that street. To my knowledge, 21st Avenue may be the only street in the entire country where you could turn a wild lion loose, and the kids would either have him tamed or dead in an hour."

I never read the actual article, but many people swear it's the truth. If so, that's just another example of how other people viewed the South Town Rinky Dinks. I personally feel the northern writers observations were totally out of line, and are actually nothing more than speculation piled on top of misconception.

It's a fact, and everyone that ever lived in South Town knows it's the gospel truth, that there's never been a wild lion bred that could have lasted an entire hour on 21st.

13

FROM FRONT PORCH SWING TO NASHVILLE
THE RINKY DINK'S DISCOVER MUSIC

Jesse Davidson and his wife Miss Robbie lived next door to us, and they had two children, both girls. I think Jesse might have had an older child, but I don't remember if it was a boy or girl. Anyway, he/she wasn't living at home when we were growing up, so I didn't know him/her and therefore haven't written anything about him/her. The oldest girl at home was named Vonnie. Her name was really Mildred Yvonne, but everyone called her Vonnie.

The youngest girl was named Brenda, but the best I can recall, neither of them played with the rest of the kids all that much. Vonnie was too old to play with us, and Brenda just never wanted to. I don't know whose fault that was, and I don't much care, because I liked both of them then and later on as well. I do remember that Jesse and Miss Robbie had one of the only houses on the street that was fenced in.

It may not sound like much, but a fenced in yard was kind of a big deal on 21st. Actually, I was never sure why they had the fence, but I always suspected it was because they collected all kind of balls.

Baseballs, rubber balls, basketballs, footballs, big balls, little balls, shucks they collected any kind of ball that one of us kids happened to let fly over their fence. I guess they collected them. I know they sure didn't want to give them back to us. Some days when we couldn't find a ball to play with, one of us, usually me or one of the Wesleys, would slip over the fence in the back yard and crawl all over Miss Robbie's yard looking for one of the balls we had knocked it there. And most of the time we could find one.

Anyway, years after we'd all moved off 21st, Miss Robbie would occasionally come and visit with Mama.

In truth, Miss Robbie really was a very nice lady, a lot like the movies of the era always pictured a small town southern lady. I was delighted to find that she even remembered me and knew who I was the last time I ran into her, even though it had been years since I'd seen her.

Vonnie married a fellow named C.J. Brinley, who became a good friend of mine when we worked at Phillip's and Buttorff's together. I think he passed away a few years ago, and I hate to admit it but I'm just not sure if Vonnie is still alive or not. I hope she is, because she was a very nice person. Note: Vonnie passed a way a few years ago.

Brenda is still in Springfield, and I used to run into her every now and then. She's one of the most successful real estate brokers in the area, which also serves to remind folks that just because you were born and raised a South Town Rinky Dink, doesn't mean you can't make something of yourself. As far as I know, Brenda has never made any bones about being from South Town, and probably never will.

NOTE: We lost Brenda in February to Covid – 19.

By now you know that the Rinky Dinks managed to get by most of the time with very little other than imagination and the ability to entertain ourselves in simple ways. If we'd grown tired of playing for the time being, or if it happened to be raining, or maybe it was one of those cool summer nights we used to have so many of, at times like those we had to find something else to do.

We were good at that. Finding something else to do, that is.

We used to pass a lot of time in the summer evenings sitting in the swing on my front porch and singing.

I've always loved to sing. Did then and still do.

Back then, I used to learn every new song that I could, and I really loved to sit in the swing on the front porch and sing them. If you really wanted to, I guess you could say we were into swing music. (I can't believe I wrote that.)

I remember one of my favorite songs was called "You Saw Me Crying In The Chapel," and I used to sing it over and over.

The reason I began this chapter by telling about the Davidson's is because I'll swear Vonnie loved that one particular song even more than I did. Very few nights passed that she didn't sit out on her front porch and holler over to me.

Donald, sing that song for me.

Which one Vonnie?

You know which one, she'd holler back. Sing You Saw Me Crying In The Chapel. And sing it loud enough that I can hear it.

I had already had my public singing debut at Woodland Street grade school, singing "School Days" in a play. I was one half of a duet with a little girl named Shirley Harp (one of that other family of Harps, no relation) and I knew that the teachers thought I had a good singing voice. At least I think they did.

Of course, most of the time I only broke into song while sitting on my own front porch and most of the time I sang Hank Williams songs. Everybody loved old Hank. Men and women, boys and girls, Hank was everybody's favorite. I don't think it was because he sang all that well, but his songs were about the real things that people thought about. So most nights I'd get the swing going in a kind of nice, easy, back and forth motion and begin crooning away on something like "Lovesick Blues," or "Your Cheatin' Heart." Of course this was not only before everyone had a television, it was even before the evil "Rock N Roll" music became the rage of the age.

Rage of the Age.

Well, there's another phrase I can't even believe I wrote. If that doesn't date these stories, nothing will. Anyway.

One of the few times we ever went into Nashville was one Saturday night in the late summer of 1950 or 51. I think. I'm not sure, but I do recall it was hot, and we'd gone to the Grand Ole Opry to see Hank Williams.

I don't recall much about the show that night, or even much about old Hank. Sometimes I think I can close my eyes and see him on that stage, but I'm not really sure of that either. I was only around 10 years old, and to be honest, most all I can remember of the night was the ladies waving those big old cardboard church fans back and forth, back and forth.

But it is a great story to tell. I actually got to see Hank Williams perform on the Opry, even if I don't remember it all.

So, for a few years we used to sit out there on the front porch and sing and sing and I'd be lying if I said that even then I wasn't already thinking about making a career out of music in one form or another. I wrote my first songs during that period of my life, and while I haven't become a famous songwriter and I've never really been able to make a living writing songs, I still love to write 'em. Course, I've had quite a lot of my songs recorded, I just haven't been fortunate enough yet to have a song break into the magic top ten on the charts.

Charles Rippy had learned to play a few chords on an old guitar he had, and I guess we learned every song that Webb Pierce ever recorded. A few years later, Charles and I, along with three of four more of our friends later formed a band or two, or three, and played for a while in the skull orchard honky tonks along the Tennessee/Kentucky state line. In fact, we spent the better part of 25/30 years playing our music in and around Springfield, the Tennessee/Kentucky state line, and a few clubs in Nashville, Clarksville, Fort Campbell, Kentucky, and Hopkinsville, Kentucky. There was another pretty good Rinky Dink guitar picker named Larry Browning that played in one or two of the bands and we had some really great times, but those are stories for another book.

John Mayes had two brothers named Melvin and Deany who didn't live in South Town but visited Lawrence Thaxton's family every so often. They were both good singers, and we used to go up and down the street stopping at some of the houses for a little impromptu serenade.

One of the biggest Grand Ole Opry stars of the time was "Jumping Bill" Carlyle, and he had a hit record out called "Too Old To Cut The Mustard." Me and Melvin and Deany, and Lawrence when we could talk him into it, used to really like to sneak up under an open window at Lawrence's house and sing that crazy little song for Morris, Lawrence's dad. He'd come running out of the house like a cyclone, hollering at us, and making all kinds of funny faces, but he loved every minute of it. And so did we.

It was while singing on the front porch that I first learned that girls like a guy that sings to them. I guess I must have been a pretty good singer, because most every night that I was out there, some of the girls on the street usually managed to gather round. We were at the stage when we were beginning to be attracted to the opposite sex, but had absolutely no idea why.

It was only a year or so later that I learned that the front porch swing and school plays weren't the only places where I could sing.

I was not quite fifteen when I started singing regularly with a friend of mine from across town who also had learned to play the guitar. This friend will remain anonymous, because he is still a very good friend of mine, and may not recall this story exactly the same way as I do.

His father drank quite a lot, and was really proud of the way his son had learned to play the guitar and the way the two of us were sounding. The truth is, he was probably especially proud of us when he'd had a couple of drinks.

One day about one o'clock he came to our school and got my friend and I out of our classes. He'd found a place for us to sing, and had bragged about us so much that the people wanted to hear us sing for them live.

The place was in a little town about 15 miles from Springfield, and was at the home of an old black man who sold beer and homebrew. It wasn't a club or anything like that, just an old house where a few of the local county men, both black and white, gathered on hot summer afternoons to have a couple of cold beers and listen to a few songs on an old juke box.

It was a really hot day as we rode out in the country, and all the way there we kept wondering where we were going. Course, we were excited about going anywhere to sing, as well as being out of school. The old house wasn't much to look at, but when we got inside everybody seemed friendly enough so we sat down in a couple of old straight backed chairs and began to try to decide what to sing.

It wasn't really much of a decision. We didn't know very many songs other than the ones of Hank Williams and Webb Pierce, so my buddy tuned up a couple of strings and I took off with the opening lines of "Your Cheatin' Heart."

We were a smash.

We sat there for over two hours and sang every song we could think of, and they let us drink a couple of ice cold beers and gave us a hot barbecue sandwich or two. I decided then and there that all I'd ever do was sing. This was the life. We were out of school, singing for grown people, and they were giving us cold beer and hot barbecue, how much better could it get?

How much indeed?

I've played in a lot of bands since those days, in front of big crowds and small ones, in honky tonks and in churches, and I've come a long way from that front porch swing and that old black man's front room, but every time I've ever picked up a guitar and sang a few songs for the folks, I've asked myself that same question.

How much better can it get?

To this day I still get the same answer.

It don't get better than this.

14

WHAT EXACTLY IS A GRAPEFRUIT?

Another typical story of the times is one concerning grapefruit, a fruit not many people in South Town were really familiar with during the years following the depression. This story comes from Billy Gragg, one of the South Town Rinky Dinks who grew up there a few years ahead of me.

There were a lot of folks around the area who didn't make a lot of money, and at times needed a little help making ends meet, and feeding their families. Back then, when they went and asked the government for a little help, people said they were on relief. I guess that's what they now call welfare, and I know folks who had money back then looked down on folks who were on relief, just as they look down now at folks who are on welfare. To tell you the truth, it doesn't now and never has made much difference to me if someone got a little help or not. I figure folks have to do what they have to do to take care of their families. Anything short of stealing, that is. Of course to this day, if a man is really and truly hungry, or his kids are doing without food, I don't necessarily think that borrowing an occasional chicken or a few ears of corn could be called stealing. And I know for sure that most of the people on relief, or welfare, or whatever you call it didn't want a handout from anyone. Most had rather have worked, but back then, just as now, sometimes that's not possible.

Anyway, there was a relief office uptown in Springfield where folks could get a little help, and now and then they gave away baskets of fruit. I guess they thought people needed as much vitamin C as possible.

The story goes that at one point in time the relief office received a truckload of grapefruit, and promptly began distributing them, mostly to the kids in South Town.

Billy Gragg, his brother and another kid were coming from town when they happened to pass the office and saw the grapefruit inside. Hurrying home they got their small coaster wagon and almost ran the mile or so back uptown. They loaded the wagon up with the large yellow fruit and headed back toward South Town.

As they slowly pulled the wagon down the street they were stopped several times by folks wanting to know what they had. They tried to explain the strange fruit, but they really didn't know much about them either.

Now you have to remember that the folks in South Town were always more than ready to share whatever they had, especially food, with the other folks that lived there, and it was perfectly natural that whenever the boys passed someone who wanted a grapefruit, they'd give them one.

They were doing pretty good until they came to the house of a man named Cox. Now, I'm not sure if it was Clarence or not, but I'm going to say it was for the purpose of this story. I think I'm right, but it doesn't really matter, this could have been almost anyone in South Town. Anyway, Mrs. Cox saw the boys with their wagonload of grapefruit and walked out to the street to take a look.

What do you boys have? Mrs. Cox asked.

These here are grapefruit, Mrs. Cox, one of the boys answered.

Don't reckon as how I've ever seen any of them afore, boys, she replied.

No Ma'am, but everybody says they taste real good. Would you like to try to fix up a few for Clarence? We'll be glad to let you have some.

Why, that'd be nice of you boys. I'll bet Clarence would really like to have a mess of them grapefruit fixed up.

The two boys happily unloaded several of the grapefruit on Mrs. Cox's porch and continued on home with the rest.

The story could be ended here, and would be useful in pointing out how un-selfish even the kids in South Town were, but there is a little different ending that also might give some insight to the times, and the place, and the habits of the people.

Seems a few days later the same two boys went back to the relief office, loaded up their wagon with grapefruit again, and once again headed toward South Town.

Once again Mrs. Cox came out in the street to meet them.

Well, boys, she said, I see you've got some more of them grapefruit.

Yes Ma'am, we picked them up a while ago. Would you like to have a few more of them to fix for Clarence?

The boys swear Mrs. Cox looked at them, sadly shook her head, and replied.

Lordy naw, boys, I 'preciate it, but I don't want no more o' them things. When you give me that last batch I swear I must have worked fer two or three hours just a'peelin' em. Then I tried boilin' em, fryin' em, and even roasted a couple, and I swear I ain't been able to cook 'em no way a'tall that Clarence could eat a single bite of one of them.

I lost my brother Norman in 1948, when I was seven years old. He was the third child that Mama and Daddy had lost, leaving only me. I was a little too young at the time to realize what growing up without a big brother could mean, but at just exactly the right time, someone came along.

15

ALONG CAME BUD

At the first of this book I mentioned that I've been lucky enough to have had a few men I looked up to and admired in my life. These days the catch phrase is "role model" or "mentor." Well, I don't know if they were mentors or role models or not, but they were certainly heroes of mine. Let me go over them one more time.

My Daddy was one of them, and so were several of my uncles. There was Jim and Horace Walker and Clyde Cannon and the one and only Ernest Mayes, and don't forget Stanley Evans. And as I've mentioned elsewhere, John Mayes was a big influence on me. But if there was one man who had the most influence on me, outside of Daddy, of course, that man would have to be Jewell Bryant Bollinger. The man everyone called Bud.

Bud was the older brother I didn't have, at a time when I needed one the most. He was the one who let me drive his cars, and took the time to talk to me about life, and helped me to realize there was more to the world than the narrow, half paved streets of South Town.

If I grew up seeing things just a little off center, it was Bud, and of course Mama, who influenced me the most. Mama saw things differently from anyone else I've ever met, including Bud, and of course, I guess I do too.

But there'll be more about Mama later. This chapter is about one of the greatest rascals of South Town, a man everybody knew, and almost everybody liked. I suspect that even the ones who said they didn't like Bud probably really did. Fact is, Bud was one of those guys you couldn't keep from liking.

Bud came from a well-known and well respected family in Robertson County. His parents were farmers; good, honest, hard working people, the kind of folks everyone used to call the "Salt of the Earth." I knew Bud's Mama and Daddy, and his brothers and sisters, and every one of them was cut from the same cloth. A lot of people in town thought Bud was the "Black Sheep" of the family, and maybe he was, but it never made a lot of difference to me.

I knew his sister Lola May better than I did any of the others, and I liked her from the minute I first laid eyes on her. Dark hair and dark flashing eyes, Lola was a good looking woman, and although she never married, Lola would have made a good wife to any man. They just don't make any finer ladies than Lola May Bollinger. I might mention that Bud's brother Clayton and his sister Betty have made very successful lives for themselves, and continue to be upstanding citizens and pillars of their respective communities.

But now let me get on with my story about Bud.

Bud Bollinger came into the lives of the Rinky Dinks sometime in the early fifties. He came roaring down 21st in a souped up 1946 Ford, and changed the way most of we kids saw the world.

With steel taps on the bottoms of his shoes, an un-filtered Camel cigarette hanging out of the corner of his mouth, and a devil may care grin permanently carved into his lips, he was exactly what every boy of the fifties wanted to be.

The old "Happy Days" television writers could have used Bud as the pattern for Fonzie, except maybe that in real life Bud might have been a little bit cooler than the TV character.

Bud drove fast, he raised cain whenever he felt like it, and he was a handsome devil who loved the ladies. Not only that, Bud was a really good ball player. He was a catcher. Bud had the first catcher's mitt and face mask any of us had ever seen, and he could hit a ball a country mile. And that was enough for the Rinky Dinks.

Bud had been in the service and hadn't been out for a very long time when I first saw him play ball at Woodland Street School. Bud was catching, and I think his team must have been behind a run or two. Anyway, there were two strikes on the batter, and Bud called time out. He stood up, reached into his pocket and pulled out a cigarette. Without a word, he lit the cigarette, took a couple of quick drags, and then assumed his catching position. He laid the butt down on home plate, looked at the batter and said;

This one's for the Navy.

The batter struck out, the inning was over, and Bud's team won the game their next time at bat.

I liked that. So did most of the Rinky Dinks.

I think Mama and Daddy and Eva Mai had known Bud for a few years, but none of us kids knew him, or knew anything about him. He'd been married two or three times, I think, had been in the Navy, and had a motorcycle, as well as the souped up 46 Ford.

Kids back then didn't say things were cool, that came along a little later, but you can bet your bottom dollar that's what we all thought. Back in those days when someone was, well, cool, everyone called them slick. And Bud was slick, you can bet on that.

I remember the first time I saw Bud.

Eva Mai Birdwell was married to my brother, Norman Harp, and they had a baby, a little girl named Mary Evelyn who got sick. I think this was in 1946 or maybe 47. The baby was diagnosed with tuberculosis, and died that same year.

When they ran tests on other family members, they found that Norman also had an advanced case of the dreaded disease, and it was already too late to do anything about it. I remember him lying in Mama's bed in the living room, and everybody sitting up with him at night, and sometimes I think I remember the night he died. But I don't really know if I do or not. I remember Charles Fryer came over and gave me a quarter, and I remember the doctor coming to the house and then the long black ambulance took Norman away.

Eva Mai kept on living with us after Norman's death, and at some point in time she started "seeing" Mama's brother, Horace Walker. I don't know if Eva was ever serious about Horace, but I think he was serious about her. Actually, I didn't pay a lot of attention to things like that back then. I know they went to the Moonlight Drive-In Theater a few times, because they took Goober and me along. We were still small enough to stretch out in the back seat of the car for the ride home after the movie. And although the old drive-in movie site is only a couple of miles outside town it seemed like a very long drive to us back then.

Occasionally in the summer, some of the folks on the street would get together for a few cold drinks and a little dancing. Some of the men could play guitars and fiddles, and everyone loved the few minutes when the music could take them away from the battle they faced everyday just trying to get by.

It was at one of these little get togethers that I first saw Bud.

We were down the street, I don't remember at whose house, but it was full hot summertime, the guitars were ringing and most of the men were feeling no pain. Folks were dancing and singing, and a lot of us kids were running in and out, listening and singing along.

Suddenly the screen door flew open and in walked a guy I'd never seen before.

For a moment, the entire room stopped and everyone looked at the man standing just inside the door. He grinned and looked around the room and after a few seconds, I heard somebody say,

C'mon in Bud, grab yerself a beer and sing us a few songs.

And he did.

But first he did a little dance.

Bud wore steel taps on his shoes, several on each shoe in fact, and when he started dancing, those taps started talking, and I could almost swear I saw sparks flying off them after a few minutes.

Bud tapped around in the floor and told a few jokes, and after a few minutes he sat down in a chair beside the man who was playing the guitar and began singing. And not just any old songs, either. Bud started singing gospel songs.

Gimmie that old time religion...Gimmie that old time religion...

Come, come, come, come, Come to the Church in the Wildwood...

He had a deep bass voice, and sang great harmony, and it wasn't long before everybody there was lost in the most beautiful gospel refrain of all;

Amazing Grace, how sweet the sound...

It was about then that I noticed Bud was looking at Eva Mai. And she was looking back.

Bud and Eva started dating, and then they got married. I'm not sure what year that was, but it was just in time for Bud to take over the big brother chore of seeing that I came into my teenage years on the right foot.

Or maybe it was the left foot.

I know there are some folks that wouldn't call it the right foot, but if I know Bud, he'd have shown those folks his right foot, especially if they had anything at all to say about the way he lived his life. Or about me. Bud would fight a grizzly bear with a willow switch over any one of us kids, and me and Goober in particular.

Bud and Eva moved into the corner house across the street from us after they got married, but Goober didn't move with them. The only home he'd ever really known was at Mama's, and there was no way he was going to move.

Bud was a better than average automobile mechanic, so he built a garage by the side of his house and made his living repairing cars. He was also a heavy equipment operator and mechanic, and one heck of a good welder.

If it's beginning to sound as if there was nothing Bud couldn't do, well, that was pretty close to the truth.

I don't remember there being a lot Bud couldn't do.

Why, you might ask, didn't this multi-talented man become a big success and make a lot of money and leave South Town?

Well, I don't think Bud was all that interested in money, to begin with, and probably didn't want to leave South Town anyway. One of his biggest drawbacks was that he liked to take a drink. Actually, he liked to take a lot of drinks. I now realize that Bud was an alcoholic, although that wasn't a popular name back then. He'd rather work when he wanted to, fish and play ball when he wanted to, and take a drink when he wanted to than to be considered a successful businessman.

But Bud had one other fault that kept him from becoming the wealthy, successful businessman he might have been.

Although Bud made his living working on things, he knew the folks in South Town didn't have much money. But just because you didn't have any money didn't mean he wouldn't work for you. Bud would repair your car, weld up whatever you had that was broken, come over and work on your house or do whatever you needed, whether you had the money to pay him or not. It was that big heart of his that kept him from making as much money as he could have made somewhere else, working for other people.

Over the years, Bud did just about as much free work as he did paying jobs. He could never turn anybody down. I said that's a fault, and I know most people think it is. Especially a lot of successful people who wouldn't repair a hole in their mother's roof if it was raining cats and dogs unless she paid them for it. But it really wasn't a fault. It was a gift. Bud was a rough man, loud and ready to fight. He drank and he raised cain, and he never had much money, or at least he never kept much money. But Bud had a heart bigger than three or four ordinary people.

To this day, I don't have much use for a man who has to be paid for everything he does.

When I first started hearing the term, "Good old boy," it was used a little bit different than it is now.

Someone would say something like...

You know Bud Bollinger, don't you? Saw him last night up town. He was drunker'n a skunk.

Yeah, but he's a good old boy. He'll give you the shirt off'n his back. Do anything in the world for a man if you ask him to.

That's a fact.

Yeah it is. And won't take a penny for helpin' you, neither.

I know it. Ain't worth a dang, is he?

Naw, but he's a good old boy.

And that's the way it was.

Bud was a good old boy, and he would give you the shirt off his back. That's the reason he didn't have a lot of money, or a big fine car, or a nice house, or, for that matter, a whole lot of shirts. He did too much, for too many, for too little. And the thing is, while Bud did a lot of work for his friends and neighbors who needed help and couldn't afford it, a lot of the time the folks he was doing for were better off than he was.

And many of those were the same folks who looked down on Bud. Of course, they were the same folks who looked down on almost everybody in South Town.

Another of Bud's strange little quirks was that he liked to lie a lot.

Maybe I could sugar coat it a little and say that he liked to tell tall tales, but that just ain't the way it was. Nope, Bud just plain old liked to lie. I'm sure he liked it, because I know for a fact that he did a spectacularly good job of it. Old Bud was a twelfth degree black belt in stretching the truth. He stretched the truth to proportions that the truth seldom sees. Bud would walk ten miles through a hailstorm to tell you a lie, when he could have just as easily told you the truth without leaving the shelter of his own front porch.

For years I thought Bud told the stories because he just wanted to see how much he could make folks believe. And I still think that's how it started. But later on I think he started to believe the stories himself.

But that's not too strange, is it? A good liar can make a lot of people believe a lot of things. People will believe things they know aren't true, if the right person tells them they are. And Bud was that kind of person.

He could make folks believe things.

All kinds of things.

Once, Bud and his brother Clayton and a couple of other friends, Leonard Sawyers and another guy named Black, built a stock car to race.

There was a dirt track in Old Hickory, and one in Bowling Green, and a big track in Nashville where they raced the cars on weekends. This was before the days of NASCAR®, and the organized racing teams. Most of the cars were built in small garages and driven by the guy that built it. They were loud, fast, and dangerous, and of course Bud loved every minute of it.

I'm not out to upset the other partners in the race car, but the way I remember it, the partners supplied most of the money and Bud did most of the work on the car. Bud was also the main driver when they took the car to the track.

Some folks said that a lot of the time Bud would warm up before a race with a pint of Jack Daniel's or Jim Beam. That may be true, and if it is, it may be the reason that he usually finished pretty far back in the pack. The best I ever remember the car ever finishing a race was second, and I think that was only once.

After Bud got the car ready to race, he took it up in the field and tried it out by racing around and around in the grass. He was trying to see how fast the car would go, and how hard it was to roll.

I'll tell you, that was a sight to see.

Ten or fifteen little Rinky Dink kids scattered around the field, and Bud ripping and roaring all over the place. He'd rev the engine, pop the clutch, spin the wheels and fly around the field, then stomp the brakes and cut the steering wheel hard and see if the car would roll. It never did.

Off the top of your head, do you think any of us boys standing there watching wanted to be driving that car? You say that's a stupid question. Of course it is. OK then, do you think any of us boys standing there watching didn't want to be driving it? Oh, that's the same question? Shucks.

I don't want to get into the racing stories, except for one. The last time Bud raced the car, I think it was the last time, was in Bowling Green, Kentucky. It was one of the biggest races we'd been in, and just before Bud climbed in the car, he downed a half pint of whiskey. (At least, that's what they said.)

He was running his best race of the season, running in second position against the toughest competition he'd faced, when the whole thing kind of went south.

Bud came roaring down the back stretch, around the third and fourth turns, and just as he came out of the fourth turn and headed down the home stretch, the car veered to the right, hit the beam that the fence was built on, and flipped over and over down the track, right in front of the grand stand bleachers. We only had two laps to go, and there was a good chance Bud could have actually won the race, if he hadn't flipped it. He climbed out of the car without a scratch, walked back to the pit, and I guess that's when they decided not to rebuild the car.

Later, Bud used to tell folks how he and I raced cars in Florida.

Of course we didn't race cars anywhere, but Bud could make folks believe we did. I was only about fourteen or fifteen at the time, but that never seemed to bother Bud.

There was a little honky tonk a few miles outside of town, called the White Way Inn, that Bud used to visit quite often. They used to call it the White Way Inn and the Black Way Out, and if memory serves me well,

Lola May worked there for a while. Anyway, I went out there with him every chance I got, which was also quite often, although I didn't tell anybody about it.

As I've already mentioned, Bud had a souped up 46 Ford that would really run. The car had a floor shift in it and there was a hook on the dashboard that he used to lock the car in second gear so he could keep both hands on the wheel.

We were sitting at the White Way one night, Bud drinking beer, me drinking an R.C. when some good old boy got to talking about how fast his car would go. Well, that wasn't the kind of talk Bud could let slip past.

The good old boy said;

My car'll do ninety miles an hour, and I'll bet five dollars it will. The old boy said.

Son, that ain't nothin', Bud said. My old Ford'll do ninety miles an hour in *second gear*. And I'll bet ten dollars on that. And, by God, Donald will drive it.

Bull, the good old boy said, and tossed a ten-dollar bill on the bar.

Hop in, Bud said, and threw his own ten down.

The only instructions he gave me were two really simple things.

Now, when you get up to about fifty miles an hour, Donald, hook this sucker in second and shove it to the floorboard.

There's a dangerous curve on the road between the White Way and Springfield, and I went into it at about eighty-five. I think I was doing ninety when I came out of it, but I was the only one looking. Bud and the other guy were hunkered down in their seats and had their eyes shut tight.

When we got back to the honky tonk and the other guy shakily got out, Bud picked up the twenty dollars, walked back out to the car, looked at me and said,

What the hell wuz you trying to do boy, kill us all?

You said, hook the sucker in second gear an...

Yeah, yeah, I know what I said. How fast did you get anyway?

I was a little past ninety when I took it out of second. I started backing off at a little past a hundred.

Is zat the truth, he asked?

Yep, I replied.

The truth is, I never looked at the speedometer after I hooked it in second. I don't have any idea how fast we were going.

But I told Bud I knew. And he believed me. That's what counted. Bud always believed me. Or at least he always said he did.

Bud did a lot of things for me. He put me on the first motorcycle I ever rode. I wrecked it in Mama's rose bush, but I didn't get hurt, except for a few thorn scratches. The next day, Bud put me on the dang thing again. Learned a lesson, don't you know.

Once when I was fifteen, I wanted to go to a party, but I didn't have a way to get there. Bud pitched me the keys to his car and said,

Don't wreck this sucker.

That's all. No don't do this, don't do that. No be carefuls. No put in gas. No nothing.

Just one sentence.

Don't wreck this sucker.

And I didn't. Not that night, and not ever. I had a little fender bender a few years later in the same car, but I was parked and some old guy ran over me. That's the truth.

But the first night he let me take the car out alone, I went to the party, did whatever kids back then did at parties, then came home. Didn't wreck the car. Made a heck of an impression on all of the kids at the party though. Course, Bud knew that all along.

The old car was a 1949 Pontiac, and we had a lot of fun with it.

Once, Bud was operating a bulldozer in a field a mile or so outside town, and me and Eva Mai took his lunch to him. It had been raining really hard that morning, but the sun was out by lunch and when we got to the field, Bud was way over on the other side, a long way from the highway. Eva decided we'd drive across the field to where he was working, and we got almost all the way there when the car suddenly ran into a spot that was nothing but mud. The car got stuck, and no amount of wheel spinning would get it out. Then the engine died and wouldn't start, and so there we sat.

Bud finally saw us and came chugging over to the car on the bull dozer. After he'd eaten, he decided the best way to get the car to the road was to push it with the dozer. Needless to say, the blade on the front end of a bulldozer doesn't match the rear bumper of a 1949 Pontiac, and by the time we were back to the highway, the bumper was pretty much history. Didn't bother Bud at all. He brought a bumper home from a junkyard a couple of days later, put it on the car, and never said another word about it.

(Note: There's a little more to this story than the part I've told, but some things are best left unsaid.)

Bud and Eva had three kids, and to this day I feel like their big brother. I should, they stayed at our house as much as they did at home. There was David Jewell, who everybody called Scooter Bill, which was later shortened to just Bill. Bud's sister, Lola May, began calling him "Scooter Bill" because he learned to kind of scoot along on the floor instead of crawling, and the nick name stuck for many years. The other two children were named Jimmy Wayne and Deborah Faye.

Debbie was the prettiest little girl I think I ever saw, at least until I had my own two beautiful little girls. Anyway, Debbie grew up to be a pretty woman. Bill and Debbie still live in and around Springfield and Greenbrier, and I see them every now and then. Probably not as much as any of us would like.

We lost Jimmy on a cold rainy night exactly a month to the day after his fifteenth birthday. He was in a car with Bill and two of their friends and they were on a dark county road just outside of Springfield. The driver hit a bridge over the railroad tracks and the car flipped over and fell top first twenty or thirty feet to the tracks.

Bill and one of the other kids lived, Jimmy and the kid who was driving didn't. I've never been able to talk about the accident, and I sure can't write about it. There is a cold hard rock where part of my heart used to be. That's the part of me that died that rainy night, and will never live again.

I've got so many stories about Bill that I can't possibly put them in one chapter, so I'll save them for later.

I've left out as many stories as I've told, for a lot of reasons. There was a dark side to Bud that sometimes overshadowed most of his good qualities, but the important thing to me is that Bud never once let me down. From small things to big things, he did his best to live up to how he knew I looked at him. And that was as a hero, a man who stood head and shoulders above the rest. And I still see him in that way.

Bud did a lot of things later in life, and I didn't see him as often as I would have liked. We all get busy and let the really important things slide, and I guess that's my only excuse. He and Eva Mai got divorced, and although Bud lived in Springfield for the rest of his life, we just didn't see each other as much as we had in years past.

Bud fought a good fight against the Big "C" for several years, and we finally lost him a couple of years ago. I figure God needed somebody to do his welding, and keep his equipment operating, and so He finally called Bud home.

I know for a fact that there isn't a better bass singer in Heaven's chorus, or a better shade tree mechanic on the Streets of Gold.

And if God ever gets up to bat, takes two strikes at the ball, and then hears someone say;

This one's for the Navy...

I know who'll be squatting down behind the plate. There'll be an unfiltered Camel cigarette lying there, slowly burning... and God will strike out.

And if God ever has to stretch the truth a little, I know who he'll ask for advice on how to do it.

Bud, I sure do miss you.

16

THE LONG ARM OF THE LAW

You might think that kids that grew up as poor as the Rinky Dinks would have had quite a lot of trouble with the law, and the truth is we did have a few brushes with authority, but not nearly as many as could be expected.

There were a couple of kids from South Town that spent some time in reform school, and later spent time behind bars. Some spent the time at the county jail, and some at the state penitentiary, but for the most part, the rest of us managed to avoid jail, and as a whole we kept our noses pretty clean.

There were several reasons for that, I suppose. Our parents tried to teach us wrong from right, and didn't hesitate to lay into our backsides with a willow switch or a leather razor strap if we strayed too far from the path. And of course all the preachers told the same story, that sin against man was the same thing as sin against God, and either would result in us burning forever in Hell, Hell, Hell. Needless to say, we were all scared to go to jail. We didn't want to be locked up, and most of us thought we knew what happened once you were behind bars. And we sure didn't want that.

But one of the main reasons we spent so little time in trouble with the law was the law itself.

The law was different back then. If a policeman spotted a kid doing something wrong, he was much more likely to take him or her home and let the parents administer the punishment. Sometimes, when the mood struck the officer just right, he might come up with a little creative punishment of his own, without benefit of judge and jury.

Don't hold me to the kids I've named in this story, because I'm not really sure which of us it happened to. But, the story happened, and it happened pretty much as it's written.

I think it was me and Lawrence and Wesley Birdwell, and maybe Wayne and Thomas Lee and maybe even one or two of the others who were out playing that day, when one of us came up with a brilliant idea to have a little fun.

We found an old cardboard box and being creative kids we decided to make a little fort beside the road. The box was really large, the cardboard was strong enough for building, and we built the fort in front of an empty house, so no one would call us down about it. Then we sat there for a long time trying to decide what to use the fort for.

I honestly don't know whose idea it was to make the mudballs.

It had rained during the night, and the ground was wet and there was a little water in the ditch in front of the mission, so we somehow got around to mixing up a little black dirt with the water, and pretty soon we had a good supply of walnut sized, squishy, wet, dirty mudballs.

I might as well point out right now that the only thing mudballs are good for is to throw at something. The question is what.

We sat behind the cardboard walls of our fortress and came up with a plan. We would wait until a car came down the street, and then as it passed we'd jump up and plaster it with mudballs. Then we'd hide in the fort, and if the driver stopped the car, we'd retreat back to the empty house and crawl under it and hide until they went away.

Good plan, right? Yeah, right.

It didn't work at all. In fact, the bottom dropped out of our well laid plan with the very first car that came down the street.

Wesley saw a car turn onto 21st up by Mrs. Gragg's store, and shouted at the rest of us to get ready as it headed slowly down the street. We hunkered down inside the fort, fingering the mudballs, hardly able to restrain our laughter. Whoever was driving the car was surely gonna be surprised when they rolled past us.

THE LAST OF THE SOUTH TOWN RINKY DINKS
THE EXTENDED VOLUME

We snickered and giggled as the car approached. With both hands full of mudballs, and mischief in our hearts, (as the preacher would say) we sat and waited, and then, without even a signal, all of us leaped to our feet as the car passed and hurled our missiles as hard and as accurate as we could.

This was one of the times when our many hours of throwing a ball back and forth backfired on us. We were just too good. Every single mudball hit the target. Every one. Our high, shrill laughter was just forming however, when we realized the horrible truth. The slow moving car was a police car, making one of its infrequent passes down 21st Avenue, and we were caught red handed.

Make that black handed.

I don't remember if the car was white or black and I don't remember who the officer was. All I remember is staring at the four or five huge splatters of mud on the car, and the policeman was already getting out of the car and headed toward the now fragile walls of the cardboard fortress. He was a huge man, fifteen or twenty feet tall, and as wide as a small truck. And mean. He didn't have a sign of a smile on his face. Thank God he also didn't have a gun in his hand.

We hastily crouched back behind our thin shelter, trying to kick the rest of the mudballs into the higher grass, and hoping beyond hope that he hadn't seen us.

Not a chance.

Suddenly the front cardboard wall went flying out into the street. I'm not sure if I had my eyes closed and my fingers in my ears or not, but it wouldn't have mattered. I'd have seen and heard him anyway.

What yew boys doin'? His voice boomed down the suddenly silent street.

None of us answered.

I asked yew boys a question, he said. What chew doin'?

Nothin'. We ain't doin' nothin'. It was my voice, I'm sure of that, but it didn't sound like me. We're just havin' a little fun, the same squeaky little voice said.

Yore Daddy at home, Donald, the policeman asked?

Naw sir, he ain't, he's workin' for Mister Rawls today. The squeak came again.

Well, all yew boys get on back up to Donald's house, and I'll be there in a minute.

We hang-dogged our heads and shuffled our way up the street to my house, where Mama was already on the front porch.

By now Mama knew we had thrown the mudballs at the police car, but I suspect she also knew what the policeman had in mind.

Remember I told you at the start of this book that we had a water faucet in our front yard? Cold running water, right there by the porch.

Yew got a bucket I kin use? Miss Lena, the policeman asked when he got out of his car.

Yes sir, I have, Mama said, and started into the house to get it.

Could yew brang me a few old rags too, if yew got any?

Mama came back out on the porch and handed the bucket and a handful of rags to the policeman. Then without a word she sat down in the swing to watch.

Course you know by now that he made us wash all the mud off his car, and while he was at it, he just went ahead and let us clean the entire car. It looked a lot better when he left 21st. that day than it did when he came to 21st. Mama never said a word, and other than the small scolding and having to clean the car, the incident was never brought up again.

But I'd say the Rinky Dinks learned a lesson that day. It doesn't matter if you're safe and secure inside your fortress, if you start throwing mudballs, sooner or later the mud is gonna hit the fan, and you're gonna get spattered just as much as everyone else. In this case it was sooner. Actually we were lucky it was a cop that was the first one that stopped. I hate to think what could have happened if it had been one of our Dad's cars. We would have still spent an hour cleaning the car, but we'd probably have spent a day not being able to sit down.

There was another incident with the law that me and a few of my generation of Rinky Dinks got into, and a couple that some of the earlier Rinky Dinks instigated that I think you'll enjoy.

I've also mentioned the small branch that cut its way down through the fields between 21st. and Woodland Street School. It started somewhere back in the woods on the other side of Woodland Street, and crossed through Rinky Dink territory all the way till it disappeared in the woods somewhere the other side of Highway 431.

It was just a small branch, not big enough to swim in, and it had no fish other than a few tiny minnows, but we spent a lot of time there, laying on the bank and daydreaming, and sometimes eating the plump, juicy plums that grew on one or two small trees on the bank.

Again, one of us got the bright idea that we could dam up the branch and make a great swimming hole.

We went all over South Town gathering bricks and rocks, and took them to the branch and started our project.

It took us all of the first day and most of another to complete the dam, using the rocks, bricks and a heaping helping of the dirt from the creek branch.

We sat there all that afternoon after we'd finished the dam and watched the water rise.

The next morning the branch was overflowing its banks and water was making its way into the yards of some of the houses on Woodland Street. By lunch the water was all the way to the back of one of the houses and a policeman was knock, knock, knocking on my front door.

The law, and a few parents, spent most of the rest of the day standing on the banks of the lake watching a handful of bedraggled, muddy, soaking wet Rinky Dinks tear down the dam.

It took us all afternoon to finish clearing away the mud and rocks, and it wasn't long until the water was back down to normal.

Again, the only punishment we got was undoing the damage we'd done. If kids today did anything like that, they'd probably spend a few hours in juvenile court, and somebody would sue somebody, and people who once were friends wouldn't be speaking to each other.

I think the way it was handled then made much more sense than the way it would be handled today.

Everyone remained friends, nobody got sued, we didn't spent any time in court, and we never dammed up the branch again.

Several of the times the law visited 21st. was quite a lot more serious than these two times, however.

Sometimes they visited 21st. Avenue's resident bootlegger, taking away tubs filled with bottles of whiskey, and sometimes they came to return the whiskey, minus a few bottles they kept for evidence. At least, that's what everyone always said.

I also remember there were a few shooting's in South Town, and once two or three people were killed on 21st. when a man shot his wife and her friend and I think another man.

Then there was the time when a lot of the men on the street got together and decided to hang a man who had stolen one of the men's wives. The men heard he was coming one afternoon to get some clothes and other things, and they got a long rope and found a good stout limb to throw it over.

The man came to the house about when they expected him to, but somehow he got wind of the plot and ran off down along the branch toward South Main Street as fast as he could run. Sometimes I think I remember seeing him flying across the fields, but I don't know. Maybe I've just been told the story so much it seems like I remember it.

But one thing I'm sure of. I guess it's a good thing this happened at a time when we didn't have the little branch dammed up. He never would have escaped through the water.

Once, my brother Carlos and one or two of my uncles, I think it was Jim and Fred Walker, and I think maybe a friend of theirs decided to steal some shoes and re-sell them. They broke into a shoe store on the East side of Main Street and made off with an undetermined number of pairs of shoes. I guess the robbery was pretty successful up to this point.

The trouble started the next morning when they took the shoes to a shoe store on the West Side of Main Street to try and sell them. Problem was, I think maybe the same family owned both stores.

Needless to say, they got caught. Also needless to say, they spent some time in the Robertson County Jail. 500 Willow Street was the address of the jail, and I believe I still have a letter my brother Carlos, (Kink) wrote to Mama.

Now this robbery was already going along at a pretty crazy pace, but take it from me, it gets even crazier.

With Carlos and Jim and I think maybe Fred in jail, another of my uncles, Horace Walker, decided to stage a massive jail break. And he came up with a doozy of a plan.

One Saturday morning, Horace went uptown to the Midway and bought one bottle of beer. He drank most of it, and smeared the rest on his clothes. The idea was to make everyone think he was drunk.

He stalked up and down Main Street, raising cain in general and being as loud and obnoxious as he could for about thirty minutes before the law finally came and arrested him.

They put Horace in the drunk tank at the jail where he continued to make as much noise as he could.

That morning, someone had somehow managed to smuggle a file into the jail to Carlos and Jim, and while Horace was making as much noise as possible, they were filing their way through the bars.

The best laid plans of mice and men, as someone once said, so often go astray. And this was not the best laid plan in theworld. Actually, it wasn't even in that category. The end result was that they didn't break out, Horace spent a few more days there than he had intended, and I think they arrested Jim's wife Becky for smuggling in the file.

A few days after the incident, Mama went down to the jail for a visit.

Who do you want to see, Mrs. Harp? The Sheriff asked.

Mama just looked at him for a few minutes, before giving the obvious answer to the plainly stupid question.

My whole family, if you don't mind, she dryly replied.

By the way, during World War II, a Springfield man enlisted in the Army, and gave his permanent address as 500 Willow Street, which, of course, was the address of the jail. I think in the history of the Army, this was the only time a jail has been listed as the permanent address of an enlistee.

We had one or two other experiences that might have resulted in the law becoming involved, but somehow or other didn't. And we did a few things that might have been considered dangerous, if we'd only had enough sense to recognize danger when it smacked up right square dab in the face. A good example is the time we…

Next chapter please.

17

TELEVISION COMES TO TOWN

    I don't remember what year it was that Geraldine Osborne got a television set, but sometimes she'd let us come to her house and watch Superman. George Reeves was Superman in the TV series, and I know for sure that the show inspired the Rinky Dinks to do things that we never would have thought of otherwise.

    Geraldine was Clyde Cannon's younger sister. Clyde was married to Mama's sister Minnie, making him my Uncle, and Geraldine and I always called ourselves cousins. Anyway, Gerl was married to a man named Richard Osborne, and Richard made a pretty good living as an auto mechanic. They had three children, Wanda, Rita, and Ritchie, but I don't know if any of them had been born when this little incident happened.

    Richard and Geraldine lived in a small house that was technically on Blair Street, but was just a few steps around the corner from 21st, and was well within our daily roaming area.

    Richard had bought Geraldine a small television set, and like I said, sometimes we would get to go over and watch it. Of course, we still preferred funny books most of the time, but the new fangled TV was kind of interesting every now and then.

    I used to sit and watch Superman fly all over the place, and it always brought out the creative urges in me. At one time or another, I tried my best to fly with every kind of homemade invention I could dream up.

    I've already written about making wings and kites and trying to fly off the coal house and down the long hill in the South Town woods, and the truth is that if a little flying was all that Superman inspired us to do, things would have been much better all around. But once, wanting to watch Superman caused me and Wesley to pull a really stupid stunt.

It was Sunday, and Superman came on early in the afternoon, and there were several of us playing in our back yard. There was me and Wesley, and Goober and Thomas Lee, and probably Wayne and Roger.

And all of us wanted to go to Gerl's and watch the show. However, we knew she would only let two or three of us in the house. That's all the room there was, and anymore than that would have been a little too much for her to handle.

So me and Wesley hatched up one of our little plans.

We rummaged around in the coal house and came up with a good sized length of rope, and without a second thought, we tied up Goober and Thomas and left them in a small tent we had draped over the fence behind the toilet. We put gags in their mouth, and made sure the ropes weren't tight enough to hurt them, them we merrily marched off to Gerldines to watch old Superman fly around and save Lois. A little later we could have used Superman's help to save us.

The show was about half over when the front door flew open and Mama walked in. Mama didn't get mad very often, but when she did, everyone in the entire world knew enough to stay out of her way.

This was one of those times.

And it was me she was mad at.

I'd rather Daddy had whipped my behind five times than for Mama to do it once. Not that I got very many whippings, because I didn't. Neither Mama nor Daddy thought you had to whip a child for every little thing that the child did wrong. And neither do I. But they did believe that punishment was called for in some instances, and this was one of them. And I think the same way. I have very rarely spanked any of my own children, preferring to talk to them instead, but still I think there are times when a spanking teaches a lesson in a way nothing else does.

I don't think Mama used a switch that day, although she might have, but it doesn't matter. My butt was the target, and she gave me a smack, right on target, for almost every step all the way back to our house.

Now for any of you who might read your own way of thinking into this form of punishment let me say up front that I know there are people out there who think spanking your child is child abuse. Well, I say it's not. I say a judicious spanking, properly applied to an unruly child's rear end, is one of the most effective ways a parent can show love for that child. It is effective in establishing that you must accept responsibility for your actions, and it re-enforces in your mind that doing harm to others may actually result in some amount of harm to yourself. A spanking hurts, but I have never believed that the results are life long, nor traumatizing. A spanking is a few swats on the butt, nothing more nor less, and is used to teach a child a lesson. I also believe that some lessons are better taught with a spanking that with all the words in the world.

Although we didn't think about it at the time, we could have caused a serious accident by tying the kids up. They could have smothered, they could have tried to escape and hurt themselves on the ropes, or a dozen other things could have happened.

But you can bet we thought about it from then on. I've never held a piece of rope that I wasn't reminded of the incident. And I've never tied anyone else up. Say what you may about spanking your child, and what a spanking teaches, but one thing I know for a fact is that it taught me a lesson I've never forgotten.

It also made me realize that the one Superman power I wished for, other than being able to fly of course, was super tough skin.

As it turned out, I guess I got that last wish. And it's a good thing. You need super tough skin if you're gonna spend any time at all in the music business.

18

WAYNE LEARNS TO RIDE A BIKE THE HARD WAY

Wayne Wilson didn't have a bike, not at this particular time anyway, and he still hadn't learned to ride, so one day we decided to take care of that situation once and for all.

We figured getting Wayne on one of our bikes and giving him a little shove down Carter Street would be the fastest and easiest way to teach him to ride. And it worked.

Well, it kinda worked.

I seem to recall that when we told Wayne about our plan, he grinned.

Wayne did that a lot.

I've already told you that Wayne's older brother Wesley probably had more common sense than most of us, and he might have had some good advice about learning to ride a bike, but I don't think Wesley was there at this particular time.

Anyway, let's see if I can set up the story for you.

Carter Street was a narrow little street, covered mostly with white limestone gravel, that ran beside my house and up to the back side of Woodland Street School, where it dead ended at a couple of iron posts that were set in the ground and held a chain between them. There was a slight downward slope to Carter Street from my house to the little branch at the bottom of the grade, and then a steeper hill ran from the branch up to the school. You've already read about the branch being dammed up by the kids, but now let me tell you about the bridge, and how the branch looked on either side of the road.

I think I remember when there was no bridge at all over the branch, but I'm not really sure. I know that at some point in time they laid a big concrete culvert in the bed of the branch and built a plank bridge. After that they rolled in the big gravel trucks and spread the dusty white limestone gravel all along the road and over the planks and the culvert. And that's the way I mostly remember it.

Heading from my house down the hill and to the bridge, here's the lay of the land.

There's a coal house in my back yard sitting on the left side of the street, and sometimes we had a little garden behind it. And occasionally we even kept a pig there.

Next there's just a big field, with an old fencerow at the back of our yard. By the road, close to the fencerow, there's a hedge apple tree. I don't know what the real name of the tree was, but it had monster thorns, and grew good sized yellowish green fruit. But it's not a fruit you can eat. The fruit is hard and bumpy, and we never found anything at all they were good for, except to throw at something. Tin cans mostly.

A little farther down the road, still on the left, is a large sugar maple tree. We spent many days sprawled in the shade of that old tree, talking about life, and wondering what we were all going to grow up to be. None of us really had a clue back then, and some of us still don't.

There was a fencerow, mostly overgrown with weeds, that ran from the side of the tree almost all the way to the branch.

On the other side of Carter Street, starting at the corner of 21st., were more of the same kind of little run down houses.

Bud and Eve Mai lived in the house on the corner, which had also been where Daisy and Stanley had lived. Bud had built his garage at the side of his house, and that's where he worked on cars, and did welding for people.

Next to Eva and Bud lived an older lady named Mrs. Straughter. She always kept several chickens in the back yard, and now and then, as chickens are apt to do, they'd get out of the fence and go pecking and strutting all over the place. At those times, Mrs. Straughter would put a few tiny pieces of gravel in a brown paper bag and tie it to the end of a broomstick. She'd come out in the street and shake the bag, making a rattling noise, trying to call in the chickens. I don't remember if it worked or not, but it probably did. I do remember that she looked like she was three or four hundred years old, and always wore long black dresses and a hat that covered most of her face. Most of the kids thought she was a witch, especially when she came out with her broomstick and gravel-in-a-bag to call her chickens.

Mrs. Straughter had a grown brother, or maybe it was her son, who was locked away in the asylum. Sometimes he would come home for a visit, and you can bet that when that old boy was hanging around the maple tree, most of the kids kept their distance.

I think Mrs. Straugther was Lily May Smith's mother, and Lily May lived in the house with her, but I'm 100% on this one. Lily May was married to Charlie Smith, and I think they had five children. The three girls were named Edna, Patsy, and Suzy, and they had a brother named Charlie, but who everybody called Buddy. There was also another child who was born with one of the crippling diseases and had to be cared for all of the time.

Next to Mrs. Straughter, and the last house before you reach the branch lived an extremely nice lady named Mrs. Warren. Mrs. Warren had a grown son named Buddy, but I really don't remember a lot about him. Mrs. Warren's house was one of the newer houses in South Town, and one of the few that had a block foundation. Most of the other houses, especially those on 21st. were perched precariously on single concrete blocks or rock pillars. There were a few pillars in strategic places under the houses, which served as the only foundation the houses had, and also kept the house sitting two or three feet off the ground, depending on the slope where the house was built.

This made for some awfully cold winters as the wind could blow under the house, but we never had any pipes that froze up, not even in the coldest years. If you'll think back to the very first of this book, you'll know why. We didn't have any indoor plumbing. But it made a good place for the dogs to get in out of the weather, and I couldn't count the litters of puppies that were born under our house.

I remember once the police had to come and shoot a mad dog that had crawled up under Eva Mai's house, and then somebody had to go under the house and drag out the dog's body. (A mad dog is a dog that has rabies, and is acting funny and foaming at the mouth, for those of you who don't already know that) I don't know who finally wound up actually crawling under the house, but to this day I sometimes still hear the sound of the shotgun.

The houses being off the ground also gave us a cool place to play in the summer, and we spent many afternoon digging in the dirt under one or the other of our houses.

Across the branch from Mrs. Warrens and part way up the hill was the house of Frank and Virginia James. (No, not that Frank James, although he did have a brother named Jesse.) Frank's nickname was Bubby, and Virginia was one of the kindest ladies anywhere in South Town.

On up at the other end of Carter Street, right before you reach the back of Woodland Street school, is where Jerry Mantlo lived. Jerry was a year older than me, and one grade higher in school, and we were very good friends. Jerry had a sister named Faye who was one of the prettiest girls in South Town, but she kept to herself most of the time. At least, we seldom saw her on 21st.

Jerry's house was at the side of the ball field at the school, and either the school or Mister Mantlo had put up a tall, chain link fence to keep balls from hitting the house. The house sat directly on the borderline of right field, and a lot of balls hit the roof of the house, even with the fence being there. Now and then one would go over the fence at just the right angle and break out a window, but that didn't happen very often.

Across from the Mantlo's house there were three or four newer houses that had been built several years after most of the houses on the street, and I seem to remember that a disk jockey for radio station WDBL lived in one of them.

Now that you have a feel for Carter Street, let me get back to the fact that Wayne Wilson didn't know how to ride a bike, and we were getting ready to teach him.

We started at the corner, by the light pole, right in the middle of Carter Street, in the hard white limestone gravel.

Get on the bike, Wayne, somebody said.

I don't know bout this, Wayne answered.

Get on the bike, it ain't nothin' to it.

I don't know bout this, Wayne said, but had already put one leg across the bike and was thinking about sitting on the seat.

OK, now just push off nice and easy, and you'll coast all the way down the hill.

Uh, don't turn loose yet. I ain't ready.

Nothing on earth shakes and wobbles as much as a bike when you first get on and don't know how to ride. There is no way in the world to hold the front wheel steady, and your feet have a natural tendency to search for the ground on both sides of the bikes frame, even as you cautiously start trying to get it rolling forward.

Wayne's feet found the ground several times in the first forty or fifty feet, but miraculously he managed to stay aboard the slow moving bicycle.

It took us three or four minutes to reach Mrs. Straughter's house, even though it was close enough that I could have thrown a rock and hit it.

Wayne was doing pretty good by this time, and had begun to build up a little bit of confidence.

I think I can do it, he yelled.

I know you can, I yelled back. Pedal it.

He did.

The street sloped downward a little more as it passed Mrs. Straughters, and was its steepest just before it reached Mrs. Warrens.

The branch was at the bottom of the hill, on the other side of Mrs. Warren's, and the water was a little deeper on the left side of the bridge than it was on the right, which turned out to be a good thing in this case.

Wayne was really catching on to this bike riding by now, and the three or four that were teaching him to ride were running along beside and behind him, shouting encouragement.

Pump it Wayne, we yelled, pump it.

And he did.

Pump harder, pump harder...

And he did.

Hit the brakes. hit the brakes, hit the bra...

And he didn't.

The branch had closed in on the speeding bike much faster than we thought it would, and although the bridge was wide enough for two cars to pass, the idea was that you had to hit the bridge first.

Wayne also didn't do that.

We had never once thought about telling Wayne that the way you put on the brakes on a coaster bicycle was to push the pedals backward, and keep applying pressure until the thing skidded to a stop.

Wayne didn't know how to stop.

We watched in horror, or in fascination, as Wayne continued to pump the bike as it headed away from the bridge and directly toward the branch.

Over the bank the bicycle flew, Wayne hanging on for dear life and still desperately pumping in an effort to get the thing to slow down. Wayne and bicycle hit the water hard, but it was on the right side of the bridge in the shallowest part of the stream. Which, as I said, turned out to be a good thing.

When we saw the bike and rider tumble out of sight and into the branch, it seemed as if it took us hours to get there.

And when we did...

The bike was up-ended in the water, and so was Wayne. The bike was a bit the worse for wear, and so was Wayne.

Not only that, but Wayne was half submerged in the now swirling, muddy water, barely holding his face above the surface. I think that might have been carrying it a little to the extreme, because the branch was only eight or ten inches deep, and there wasn't any danger of Wayne drowning. Not much anyway.

We did the only thing we could do, in an emergency like this.

We jumped in and saved the bike.

It wasn't hurt too bad, just a bent front wheel and the chain had slipped off. Nothing we couldn't fix. We could always get Ernie to straighten out the wheel.

Wayne sputtered and spit a few times, then hauled himself to his feet.

How'd I do, how'd I do? Did I ride that bike or not?

Dang right, you rode it. Ready to try again?

Well, if you'll show me how to put on the brakes first.

We did, he climbed back up one of the other bikes and rode it back up the hill, then flew down the hill again. This time he came to a sliding stop on the bridge.

I looked at Wayne...

It's about dang time, I said.

Wayne grinned...

I have a great picture I took of Wayne and Linda about 1992 or so, back stage at the Grand Ole Opry. They're standing with Opry star Charlie Louvin, a member of the Country Music Hall of Fame. Don't know why Wayne has his eyes shut; the bright lights maybe, or is he just being cool. He could do that, ya know. Or maybe that's just a later version of that little grin I told you about.

He did that a lot...

The two iron posts with the chain stretched between them that sat at the top of the hill on Carter Street were to keep anybody from driving their car onto school property, and as far as I know they always did their job. The school, of course, was Woodland Street Elementary, and it deserves a chapter by itself.

160

19

WOODLAND STREET SCHOOL
READIN', RITIN', and RITHMITIC'

Just in case the preceding pages have left you thinking that the Rinky Dinks were a little backward, or maybe even just a tad bit stupid, let me set the record straight. We weren't backward and we weren't stupid, it's just that we simply weren't all that interested in what was going on anywhere other than South Town.

Our little corner of reality was a pocket-sized universe, and we were quite happy there. Our parents had survived the depression and World War II, and to tell the truth I think they had just as soon we weren't all that interested in things that went on elsewhere.

They believed, at least Mama did, that anytime the world had a serious problem, a lot of America's poor people lost their lives because of it. And maybe, just maybe, if we ignored it long enough, the world would forget about my generation of kids and none of us would have to ever have to fight a war we had nothing to do with.

Of course, we weren't completely shut off from the rest of the world, even if we would have liked to have been.

Oh, we had a window to the world all right. That window was called Woodland Street School.

Woodland Street School. The old red brick building sat in the curve of the road where Woodland Street turned into 22nd. Avenue. It was about a block from my house on 21st. and all of the kids walked to school every day. We never rode a school bus until we started high school, which was on the other side of town.

Woodland Street School wasn't a big school building, and it wasn't very fancy either. The best I can remember there were classrooms for grades one through six, an auditorium and a cafeteria, and a connecting hall. Later they added on a small gymnasium, but even then it was still a small school.

I even think I remember most of my teachers.

In the first grade I had Mrs. Thomas; Mrs. Traughber was my second and third grade teacher; Mrs. Estes taught me in the fourth; Mrs. Grace was the fifth grade teacher; and Mr. John Strange was the Principal of Woodland Street School, as well as the sixth grade teacher.

Miss Grace's last name was Youngblood, and a couple of years after I left Woodland Street School, Miss Grace and Mister Strange got married, but both continued teaching at the school, as far as I know they both stayed there for the rest of their careers. Also, for quite a few years, Mister Strange was also the Mayor of the small community of Adams, Tennessee, some fifteen miles northwest of Springfield.

By the time I was in the fifth with Ms Grace as my teacher, I'd begun to write a few things, mostly poems, and I recall that once she read one of them and took a few minutes to talk to me about writing, and to encourage me to write as much as I could, about any topic I liked. She was the very first teacher that saw in me some writing potential, and of course I took her advice about writing as much as possible.

I was in the first class that Mrs. Estes ever taught in Springfield. She came to Woodland Street School to teach fourth grade, and most of us instantly fell in love with her.

She was a warm, witty person, and loved what she did. She was also the first person in the school system to introduce yours truly to a paddle.

I got my first politically correct lesson in the fourth grade, thanks to Mrs. Estes. Of course, at that time nobody had ever heard that particular phrase. She reinforced the lesson with a couple of licks from a thin wooden paddle with a few small holes in it.

The story goes like this.

About a half block from the school, down on Woodland Street, was where Ray Harris lived. Ray and I were close friends almost from the day we met, which was probably in the first grade. Every now and then I used to walk up Woodland Street on my way to school, and when I did I'd always stop at Ray's house so we could walk together. And sometimes in the afternoon, I'd go by Ray's house on the way home from school and we would throw a ball around for a while.

On the day in question, I stopped by Rays on the way home to play catch, and we ended up by climbing a small tree that grew by the sidewalk in his front yard.

For years, all the kids in South Town had been told that the few small trees and the dirt mound in Ray's front yard was in reality an old Indian burial ground. We used to sit for hours and imagine what kind of Indians might be buried there, and if maybe there were any bows and arrows or knives buried there too.

That's what we were doing this particular day. Sitting in the lowest branches of the small tree, talking about the Indians and wondering if maybe we might even be descended from them.

We had no idea that we were doing anything wrong, or that anyone would ever think anything about us climbing the tree. After all, most of the kids had climbed the tree at one time or another, and none of us thought anything about it.

But Mrs. Estes did.

The next day when we went to school, Mrs. Estes politely explained to us that playing in the old burial ground, and especially climbing the tree, was actually desecrating the sacred ground, and that we would have to be punished for it.

We didn't really understand it, but back then you didn't question the motives of your teacher, or whether she was right or wrong. She was right, always. And we knew that for a fact.

Which one of you wants to be paddled first, Mrs. Estes said.

I'll guess I'll go first, Mrs. Estes, I said, and headed for the cloakroom.

Punishment was almost always carried out in the cloakroom where no one else could see, unless of course they were making an example out of you, in which case you'd get a couple of swats on the rear end in front of the whole class.

Anyway, I stood waiting in the cloakroom for Mrs. Estes to come in and paddle me, still not completely sure what was going on.

I remember that she was almost in tears herself as she walked into the cloakroom with her paddle. It was also the first time she had ever paddled anyone.

I don't recall how many licks I got, but it probably was only one or two.

I do recall the lesson I learned that day.

After she had completed the punishment on both of us, she took us back into the classroom and explained in detail to the whole class why she had taken the action she had taken. I learned a lesson about respect for others, even when they are long dead, that I have never forgotten.

The paddling didn't hurt me, I got over the embarrassment by the end of the school day, and the best I can tell I don't have any lasting scars on my psyche.

I can tell you with all honesty that I never climbed that tree again, nor have I ever in any way been disrespectful to the dead, of any race.

I later learned that there is a good chance that I do indeed have more than a drop of Indian blood coursing through my veins, and I also learned that the burial ground was probably more ancient than just a hundred years or so.

I often wondered what happened to the small mound and the few trees that stood on that spot. They didn't tear down the houses on Woodland Street when they built the projects, so I imagine the burial ground is still there.

I wonder if the kids who live there now know about the old Indians who once roamed the woods of South Town?

Probably not.

I'll bet a dollar to a doughnut that not a single child has been paddled over climbing those trees again.

To all of us kids the ball field at Woodland Street School seemed as big as any major league park in the country. Not that any of us had ever seen a major league park, we hadn't, but we'd heard about them on the radio, and I guess we just couldn't imagine any field being any bigger than ours. It lay on the west side of the school, bordered by 22nd Avenue, and ran all the way to Cherry Street.

Across Cherry Street stood the Pet Milk plant, and if any of us managed to hit a ball all the way across the street and into the parking lot of the milk plant, we were just as happy as we would have been if we'd hit one out of any major league park in the country. (Assuming we ever got to see a real park, that is.)

Some of us did hit a few balls that far, but it didn't happen very often.

I don't remember what year it was that we started playing more ball at the school park than we did up in our field, but I guess I was thirteen or fourteen years old at least.

It was along about then that someone had the very bright idea of opening the playground, with good adult supervision, during the summer, and making it available for the kids of South Town to use for ball games and other activities.

Ray Harris' mother, Mrs. Mary Alley, was hired to supervise the playground, and she did a fabulous job of not only keeping our interest up, but also of keeping us in line. And that wasn't very easy. On either count.

Mrs. Alley was one of the most positive forces that ever entered the lives of the little wild-assed bunch of Rinky Dinks that gathered around her every day. She taught us a lot of important things, like sportsmanship, and being a good loser, and things that helped mold the kids into adults. And like I said, it was no easy job.

But she seemed to thrive on it.

She taught us how to mold little plaster figures, and how to plat lanyards and bracelets and necklaces, and she taught us that it didn't matter where you came from, it was what was in your heart that counts. And Mary Alley was one of the first persons outside of our parents, and our teachers at Woodland Street, that told the kids in South Town that we could be anything we wanted to be. Hard work, education, and honesty could be the magic carpets that we could ride to anywhere we could dream of.

Mary Alley loved the kids of South Town, and we all knew it. And we loved her. She invested years of her life in trying to improve the lives of all of the kids she loved. And it wasn't for the money she made. It couldn't have been. To start with, she probably didn't earn all that much anyway, but I always had the feeling that she would have worked just as hard if they hadn't paid her anything at all.

Mary was our buddy, and even now when we meet on the street, the old feeling is still there. The memories run deep, and the summers we spent at Woodland Street School with Mrs. Alley are among the fondest memories of all.

Mary was married to a man named Hap Alley. While I've written quite a lot about Mary, I haven't mentioned Hap. Well, Hap was at the school most nights, played a lot of ball with various teams, but was most at home pitching horseshoes.

I'm not sure, but there may have been a dollar or two change hands over a few of the horseshoe games. Mary didn't hold with gambling, but there's always the outside chance that she just didn't know.

I do seem to remember that Hap and my nephew Ray teamed up to beat the socks off almost everyone they ever pitched against.

Over the years the horseshoe games at Woodland Street School were almost as popular as the ball games. Notice I said almost?

I started my singing career, which I've already written about, in a school play at Woodland Street, singing "School Days" as one half of a duet, and I still have the eight by ten pictures of two of the little plays I was in.

Some of the kids didn't really live in South Town, but as long as they lived south of the railroad tracks, they still attended Woodland Street.

There were more kids that went to school there than I can recall, and I don't want to get into trying to name them all anyway.

I've already mentioned most of the kids I played with regularly on 21st. but there are a few more that I'd like to include.

There was Bobby Dean Pentecost, who was one of my very best friends all the way through school, and there was Jerry and Jimbo Pearson, two brothers who were as good as any two athletes that ever lived in Springfield. Both were star football and basketball players in high school, both went on to be college stars, and both became Coaches. Not only that, but both coached at Springfield High School later in their careers. As far as I know, at the time of this writing, Jerry was still a coach somewhere in Tennessee. Jimbo had a massive heart attack and died very young, and the world lost a man who made a difference in everyone whose life he touched.

I went to school for twelve years with a kid named Jerome Ellis, who later became an outstanding teacher in Springfield, and was later the Robertson County Superintendent of Schools for quite a few years. He was an excellent one, I might add. I won't mention Jerome's middle name, as he used to be quite sensitive about it, but I will remind him that I know what his middle name is, and another book isn't out of the question.

All of them were raised as South Town Rinky Dinks. Not bad for poor town kids, huh?

There were others like Leon Leftrick, Joe Brown and Pat and Terry Hutcherson who were also great athletes and good friends.

Our coach for many years on the first teams at Woodland Street was a man named James McEwing, whose nickname was "Hicky."

Some of the early teams that Hicky coached ran up a win/loss record that any team would love to have, and not many ever attain. Hickey was very much a local legend, and worked with the softball programs in Springfield until his health finally failed.

The first organized team I played on at Woodland Street had Jerome Ellis, Ray and Charles Harris, Larry and John L. Evilcizer, Jerry Pearson, Wesley Wilson, Pat Hutcherson, and of course me. We didn't substitute very much then, because we all wanted to play all of the time. We first started playing other neighborhoods in Springfield, and gradually progressed to playing teams from the surrounding towns. Some of the later teams had some really good ball players too.

There was Goober, excuse me, I mean Ray Harp, who was probably one of the best, if not the best center fielder that ever played at Woodland Street or in Springfield, and there was Jacky Harris, who might have been the best hitter, and was a great first baseman as well. There were also players like the Wilkerson kids, Kenneth Carroll, Joel Pentecost, and Wayne Wilson. I think Bobby Lee Jones may have played too, but I can't quite recall it. All of them were good ball players, and all of them could have played on any team in the area. Woodland Street was lucky to have had such a crop of good kids, and the kids were lucky to have had Woodland Street School.

And here's a fact that you can check on, one of the few that I'm absolutely certain of. We won a lot more games than we lost. We hit the ball hard, long, and often, missed very few ground balls, and almost always made good throws. Remember those "hours at a time" of play I kept talking about? Well, this is when it started paying off.

Once when I was in the sixth grade, Mister Strange came out on the playground and told a bunch of us that they were going to have a field day down at the high school, and did any of us want to go. We didn't have any idea what a field day was, but we were all in favor of taking part.

He explained that there were to be contests in running, high jumping, broad jumping, distance baseball throwing, and several track events.

Of course we wanted to go. We could run and jump with the best of them, all of us could throw a baseball like a rocket, and while we didn't know what a track event was, we were pretty sure that we could catch on, especially if it had anything to do with running, jumping or throwing. I really wanted to win at least one ribbon at the field day. I'd never been to the high school before, and I wanted to make a good showing my first time there.

We practiced our butts off on running, jumping and throwing a baseball for a few days, as if those things weren't second nature to us anyway, and I remember what Mama told me the morning of the meet.

Now Donald, she said, don't think anything of it if you go on down there to the high school and don't win any ribbons. The boys at Main Street School have been practicing all year for this event. Just do the best you can, and I'll be proud of you.

Yes, Mama, I said.

Out loud, that is.

Inside, my answer was a little different.

I knew that if any of those North Town kids beat me, they were going to have to put on one heck of a performance.

South Town Rinky Dinks were hard to beat at running, jumping, and throwing a baseball.

As it turned out, most of them didn't beat me.

When I got home that afternoon, I slumped into the house and quietly sat in a chair in the front room.

Now Honey, Mama said, I told you not to feel too bad if you didn't win.

I don't feel bad, Mama, I said, and pulled five ribbons out of my pocket. I had two blue first place ribbons, two red second place ribbons, and one yellow third place ribbon. I'm not sure, but that might have been the most individual ribbons won by any kid that day.

I was kinda proud of that. Jerome Ellis did throw the baseball a little father than I did, and he got the blue ribbon and I got the red ribbon, but I finished first in the high jump and one of the relay races.

Jerome and I had thrown against each other every day in practice, and sometimes he threw farther and sometimes I did. That day he did. I was glad he won. At least, I was glad he won if I couldn't.

But sports isn't all we studied at school.

We also discovered girls.

All in a friendly way of course.

There was Mona Rae Freeman. She was the little blonde haired girl that every boy at Woodland Street School fell in love with. Then there was Patty Moats, another little blonde haired girl that everybody fell in love with.

Whew, boys, here I have to mention Barbara Nell Dorris.

Bobby Nell.

If all of the boys fell in love with Mona Rae and Patty when we were small, most of us had our first fantasies about Bobby Nell. We were teenagers then, and our society was not nearly as open about things as the kids of today are, but we felt the same things, you can bet on that.

When Bobby Nell walked down 21st in her short shorts, it's a fact that the temperature in South Town rose eight or ten degrees. She was probably the first girl I ever thought of as being beautiful, and I still remember her that way.

There are a lot of kids that I haven't named, and it's not because I wouldn't like to. But I have to stop somewhere. If anyone reads this and wants to tell me a few stories they'd like to have written, I'd be more than willing to listen and give it another try a little later.

All told, I have a lot of truly fond memories about Woodland Street School and all of the kids there. I think the values we learned, and the ideas that we first heard about have stood us in good stead. Woodland Street School, like all of the small community schools of that era, is well behind us. But what they left us will never be out of our minds, for we still live by most of those same principles, and have for most of our lives.

John Strange, Mrs. Grace, Mrs. Estes and the other teachers, and good people like Mrs. Alley left their mark on South Town, and all of the Rinky Dinks are better off because of it.

> School days, school days, dear old golden rule days,
>
> Readin' and ritin' and rithmitic,
>
> Taught to the tune of a hickory stick.
>
> School days, school days…

DADDY

BIRTLE ODELL HARP
AUGUST 9, 1901 - FEBRUARY 14, 1978

This poem is dedicated to Daddy, Birtle Odell Harp. I was the last of his children, and the only one to live to reach thirty years of age. Daddy never talked about his family, neither his parents nor the three children that came before me. I believe it was because he felt the loss with too much intensity, and he couldn't bring himself to express the depth of emotion he felt. I feel the same way when I think of him and Mama. In the latter days of his life, I finally brought myself to tell him I loved him, and was surprised that he told me he loved me too. I still do love him, and I still miss him with every day that passes. And I'd like see him come home from a day of fishing and tell him one more time; "That's a heck of a catfish, old man."

E. DON HARPE

DADDY

Daddy had a penny, that once belonged to Shirley Ann
And when he thought no one was looking, he'd hold it in his hand
And he'd think about the baby girl that he and Mama lost
Then he'd slowly a drink a beer or two, and a silent tear would fall.

Daddy had a buckeye, that Kink carved with a nail
When he was seventeen and had to spend some time in jail,
Then Kink went off to fight a war, and didn't come back home
So Daddy'd rub the buckeye, take a drink, and sit alone.

Daddy had a pocket knife, that had once been Norman's pride
He put it in his pocket, the night that Norman died
Sometimes he'd sit out on the porch for hours at a time
Stare at the ground, and take a drink, and sharpen on the knife.

I never found the courage to ask about his private Hell
And he never one time volunteered to tell me how he felt
He seldom talked about his kids, but I guess somehow I knew
That the pain's a little duller when you have a drink or two.

Daddy was laid to rest in February of seventy-eight
In his Sunday go to meeting suit, a small smile on his face
The smile was there because he knew, in death just as in life
In his pocket was the penny, the buckeye and the knife.

20

THE RINKY DINKS TAKE A HOLIDAY
BUT NOT A DAY OFF

Holidays were special for the Rinky Dinks in more ways than one. A holiday always meant a lot of food, usually some kind of ball game, and some of the holidays involved fireworks. Granted, they weren't the huge, spectacular fireworks displays we are accustomed to now, but all of us liked them just the same. The Fourth of July was always celebrated with firecrackers, and Christmas meant sparklers and Roman candles. Daddy used to buy a few small pinwheels that he would stick up on a fence post in the back of the yard and light. We loved to see the sparks as the little wheels spun, and I can still close my eyes and bring those moments back.

But there other occasions when fireworks weren't all that made noise.

Most of the men on the street would take their shotguns into the back yard and shoot several rounds along about sunset on fireworks days.

I remember Daddy trying to get me to shoot his 12 gauge double barrel shotgun one fourth of July. I wasn't very old, and I wasn't very big, and I didn't much want to fire the big gun, because I knew how hard it kicked. It hurt your shoulder every time you shot it, and I wasn't really wanting to do it, but Daddy insisted. He shouldn't have. Mama heard me saying I didn't want to shoot it and came out in the back yard to see what was going on.

Birtle, what are you trying to get Donald to do?

I just want him to shoot the shotgun, that's all.

But he don't want to shoot the gun.

Well, it won't hurt him none.

Maybe not, that's not the point. Ain't you always taught him not to shoot the gun unless he was shootin' at some kind of meat?

Yeah, but this is the Fourth of July, and I just wanted to let him shoot it once or twice, and I don't know why he don't want to.

Well, if you want him to shoot it so bad, why don't you take off running down across the field, and I'll see if I can talk him it taking a shot or two at you with it.

Now, Lena, I wanted him to shoot it up in the air.

Well, then climb up on the coalhouse, and he can shoot at you up there.

That was the end of that discussion.

A few years later, once I got a little weight on my skinny little frame, I fired the shotgun every now and then. And it did kick. Not bad enough to hurt for a long time, but enough that you knew you had been shooting it.

I'm not sure which holiday the Rinky Dinks enjoyed the most. Chances are, like most kids, Christmas was the big one. But I remember other holidays in South Town, and I'd like to start with some of them.

The Fourth of July was always important for us. The world was in a much different frame of mind in those days. World War II was barely over, and patriotism was dear to most people's hearts, so the fourth was celebrated with a lot of enthusiasm.

The Fourth meant picnics, Old Glory waving high and proud, people singing, and hot barbecue, baseball games and maybe a visit to the creek for few hours of relaxing and swimming.

Springfield has a sister town named Greenbrier in the Southern end of the county that traditionally has a Fourth of July picnic. I remember many times when we all piled in our old car and headed the six miles down Highway 41 to join in the festivities. They had fresh cooked pit barbecue, potato salad, and even a few rides for the kids. Seems they always had a few horses around for the town kids to try out. The Fourth was probably the biggest holiday for Greenbrier of the entire year, and I know for a fact I don't remember anyone who didn't think the Greenbrier picnic was the place to be on the Fourth of July.

Then there was Thanksgiving.

THE LAST OF THE SOUTH TOWN RINKY DINKS
THE EXTENDED VOLUME

Food. Food, food, food, food and more food. Thanksgiving in the South is the best time for feasting on all of the great dishes Southern women are so famous for. I don't want to say anything about the cooking in any other part of the country, but boys, let me tell you that if you ever slid your feet underneath the table to a real down home, Southern Thanksgiving dinner, you'd be willing to throw rocks at all of the other cooks you've ever known. And yes, I know you think your Mom was the best cook in the world, but believe me when I tell you that you ain't never tasted nothin' like the food I grew up eating. My Mama's green beans, cooked in the big old iron skillet till they were almost black, would make you dump the funny looking, stir-fried, bright green stringy things you used to think were great in the nearest trash can, and re-cycle the aluminum cooking pan they were cooked in.

The best Italian cooking in the world ain't in the same league with turkey and dressing slow cooked all day until it absolutely melts in your mouth.

Next to Christmas, I guess my very favorite holiday had to be Halloween.

Halloween to the Rinky Dinks was not, I repeat, not a one night affair. Oh no. We started three or four nights ahead of time, and made the most of every minute of darkness.

After all, this was the only time of year when we got to get out a bunch of old clothes. paint our faces with lipstick and powder, or maybe just throw an old white sheet around ourselves, and go out "spookin'."

Like I said, we didn't just go out on Halloween night. We went out spookin' two or three nights in a row, but it was all just innocent fun, and we never did any thing to harm anyone while we were at it. The closest we ever came to bothering somebody was turning over an outhouse or two, or soaping up someone's windows.

Sometimes they had a Halloween party at Woodland Street School, and when we went there we always got a small bag filled with candy.

Back then Trick or Treat back then meant exactly what it sounds like.

You either gave us a treat, or we gave you a trick.

Once again, it was never anything more serious than soaping a few windows, or turning over a few toilets.

Halloween has now turned into a "Politically Incorrect" holiday, with many people opposing it as being an anti-christian holiday, or claiming that it promotes children to develop a "hostage" attitude. In my opinion, most of the opposition is simply due to some people being too cheap to buy a few dollars worth of candy to hand out to children other than their own. And not wanting to take the time to fool with anything other than their own business.

I guess there are a few people that oppose Halloween on a religious basis for real, and they have their right to their belief. In my opinion it has been blown completely out of proportion, and I personally think that if some of these folks would just lighten up, let the kids celebrate Halloween the way we used to, and not put ideas into their heads, everything would be fine.

Now let me try to describe Christmas for the Rinky Dinks.

It sure wasn't like Christmas is now.

For one thing, we didn't get hundreds of dollars worth of toys. Shucks, sometimes we didn't even get tens of dollars worth of toys.

But, we got all the toys our parents could afford to have Santa Clause bring.

Actually, most of my Christmases were pretty good. We always had big bowls of fruit and nuts sitting around on the table, and Mama started several days or weeks early baking the Christmas cakes. Still, the fact is that we didn't always get a bunch of toys. I remember one Christmas when all I got was a little plastic spotted cow, and once when I got a baby doll. A black baby doll. That year, Daddy hadn't made much money in December, and by the time he got what little pay he had coming and Mama got to go to the ten cent store, that was all that was left. Or at least, all that was left that she had enough money to buy. But it didn't make a of a lot difference, the best I can recall. I played with the cow, and I played with the doll, and I thought both were wonderful presents, and both were great Christmas'.

South Town had a way of turning kids into realists at an early age. We had no other choice.

Most Christmas' however, were a little better than that. Most of the time I got a shiny new set of cap pistols, and maybe some silver spurs and sometimes even one of those little hard, pressed felt cowboy hats with the string lanyard that hung underneath your chin. They always had a big wooden ring, or else they had a plastic ring that looked like a boot or a sixgun or some other western thing.

In fact, almost all of the boys on the street got a set of guns just about every Christmas. Anyone who happened to be on 21st. Avenue on Christmas Day would have seen a whole bunch of little cowboys make-believe galloping up and down the street, shooting their brand new pistols at anything that moved.

Since I preached so hard about Halloween, let me say a few things about toy guns. We all grew up playing with cap pistols, and most of us learned to handle real weapons at an early age, and I don't think any of us have ever shot anyone, or was considered dangerous or subversive because we owned a gun. I know what would have happened if we had taken a gun to school. Mister Strange would have blistered our butt with his nine hole birch wood paddle, then he'd have personally escorted us home where our Dad would have promptly used a belt or a razor strap in the same place that was still stinging from Mister Strange's whipping. There would have been no doubt in our minds what would happen to us if we were so stupid as to take the gun back to school. None of us were that stupid.

They wouldn't have had to call the police to handle the situation. Between school authorities and parents that had control over their children, the matter would have been resolved once and for all.

While I'm at it, I might as well tell you that I think that if parents taught their children that they have to be accountable for their actions, and that not only the parents, but the school teachers and the police have every right to punish them when they got out of line, we would see a turn around in juvenile crime.

Someone has to have control over children, and it absolutely has to start with the parents.

But I guess that's enough of that. Besides, I know I don't have all of the answers to this problem, and I know that some of you think I don't have any of them, but I do know enough to admit that a problem exists, and to know that a solution must be found very, very quickly. I also know that solution must involve responsibility, accountability, and discipline.

I guess it was because we got so very few toys at any other part of the year, that most Christmas' our parents didn't make us wait until Christmas day for Santa to come. About seven thirty or eight o'clock on Christmas Eve, Mama would send me down to see if Santa had been to Wesley's house yet. Of course he hadn't, but by the time I got back home, dragging Wesley with me, Santa had already been down my chimney and made his escape into the sky. It didn't take me very many years to figure out what was going on. I couldn't have over fourteen or fifteen before I knew the real secret of Christmas. Yes sir, by then I had it all figured out. When Mama sent me outside, it was a signal to Santa that the coast was clear, and he could safely start his visit to 21st. Avenue. Even Santa had to be careful around the Rinky Dinks.

Yep, we celebrated all of our holidays differently then. Like everything else, the holidays were simpler, filled more with love than anything else, and enjoyed just as much as they are now. Maybe even a little more.

We always had Christmas plays at Woodland Street School, and I was usually in them. Most of the time I played a wise man or a shepherd, and got to dress up in a faded old bathrobe and carry a home made stick with a big crook on the end of it.

And even though we might not have had as much as some folks to celebrate over, we did know the true meaning of Christmas, and believe it or not, the Rinky Dinks were also familiar with the inside of a Church.

Speaking of holidays, the first time I ever went on a Florida vacation is next up. When you put a Rinky Dink on a beach, it's just another sand box. Or is it?

21

THE WORLD OUTSIDE OF SOUTH TOWN

IS A BEACH.

I began my senior year of high school in the fall of 1958, and to say that it started with a bang would be a vast understatement.

That fall was one of the most enlightening periods in my young life, a period in which I first learned that sometimes parents have a reason for telling kids what to do and what not to do. In this case, what not to do was what I should have taken a little more seriously.

It was really quite an experience, no one was hurt in any way, and the old saying is that a lesson learned the hard way is a lesson learned well.

I know for a fact that this particular old saying is the truth, for that was the fall that Bobby Dean Pentecost and myself learned one of the cold hard facts of life, and the lesson has never been forgotten.

Bobby Dean's parents, James and Annie Pentecost, had some very close friends who had moved from Springfield to Daytona Beach, Florida a couple of years before, and who had been trying to get Bobby Dean's Dad to bring the family down to visit. Well, the fall of 1958 was when James finally decided the time was right to load up the old 56 Chevvy and head for the beach.

Bobby Dean asked me to come with them, and being the really cool guy that I was, it took me almost thirty seconds to make up my mind. Of course I jumped at the chance. Jumped? Sure I did. I leaped up and down and ran around in circles. I had never been much of anywhere before, and the thought of actually seeing the ocean was the most exciting thing that had ever happened to me. Other than some of my everyday experiences, that is.

Now, it's important to understand that even though Bobby Dean and I didn't have much of an idea where Florida was, we didn't really even care very much. We were ready to go. We had looked up Florida on a map page in a geography book, so we knew it was South of us, we knew it was hot, and we suspected there were several million girls there in small bathing suits. So it didn't really matter that we didn't know exactly how to get there. Anyway, we figured James knew where we were going, so we just settled back to enjoy the tip, and left the driving to him.

As it turned out, James didn't know for sure where Daytona Beach was either. He just headed South and stepped on the gas, stopping several times along the way to ask if we were going in the right direction.

The only time Bobby Dean and I had second thoughts about where we were and where we were going was when we stopped at a little filling station somewhere in Georgia and James asked the gas attendant if this was the same road that Butler's Beer Joint was on. Butler's was a small beer joint/cafe that sat at the intersection of Highway 31W and Highway 41 in Goodlettesville, Tennessee, just outside Nashville, and Butler's was a long way from wherever we were in Georgia. Of course the gas station attendant didn't have a clue what James was talking about, and didn't give really care, but being a friendly sort he managed to sell us some gas, a "block" of Juicy Fruit chewing gum, a couple of RC Colas, and then pointed us in the general direction of Daytona Beach, Florida.

Remember this was 1958. There were very few interstates and very few divided four lane highways anywhere in the country then, much less in the South. So we just kept driving South and East until the highway ended at the edge of the biggest patch of water we'd ever seen. We figured this must be the ocean, and for once we figured right. After we found the Atlantic Ocean, it was simple enough to find Daytona Beach, and not even a lot of trouble finding the house we were looking for.

We checked in with the folks we were visiting, (for some reason I can't recall their names) and while James and Annie settled in to catch up on old times, me and Bobby Dean jumped into our bathing trunks and headed the half mile or so to the beach. We wanted to go swimming in the ocean just as quickly as we could, and to us time spent talking was time wasted.

When we got to the beach, we stood there for several minutes staring as hard as we could at the horizon, looking at the place where sky met water, trying to see if we could somehow spot land on the other side. We weren't exactly sure what country was directly across from Florida, but it didn't take us long to agree that we couldn't see a thing. Except a few fishing boats of course, and we figured they probably were from somewhere close by, as they appeared to be so small. (I never said we were the smartest kids that ever visited Florida. Do you recall reading that anywhere in this book? No, of course you don't.)

The first day we bought a couple of small rubber inflatable rafts, and spent all afternoon paddling as far out as we dared, then riding the surf back to the beach. Later that day we found an enormous sea turtle that had washed ashore, and made pictures of each other sitting on its back. To this day the hours Bobby Dean and I spent on the beach of Daytona stands out in my mind as one of the most enjoyable times of my life. It was the first time I had ever seen the ocean, the first time I had ever been swimming in salt water, or ridden a wave to the shore, or seen such a big turtle, and the memory is as crystal clear now as though it had happened yesterday. I know that Bobby Dean felt the same way, for we talked of that afternoon many times later in life. Neither of us ever forgot what it was like when two kids that had never been anywhere first saw a little of the outside world.

The next day we shared another experience that was a first for both of us.

After another day spent at the beach, when we came home we found that our friends had ordered pizza pie for supper. Of course, we didn't have any idea what a pizza pie was, but we knew we liked apple pie and chocolate pie, and we figured that we could take a bite or two of any kind of pie, even one made from a pizza. (Whatever that was.)

Imagine our surprise when the pizza pie arrived and we saw that it was a great big bread thing, covered with cheese, and had little pieces of meat and tomato on it, as well as some suspicious looking things we didn't recognize. If I remember it correctly, some of those suspicious looking things turned out to be mushrooms and anchovies.

Neither me nor Bobby Dean had ever seen either of these food items before, but undaunted, we helped ourselves to a slice of the pizza pie, and tried our best to eat it.

We had no luck whatsoever.

For some reason, this delicacy just wasn't suitable to tongues that were used to eating beans and taters. We faked it for a few minutes, talking about how delicious the pizza pie was, then walked outside to finish eating our slices. Once out the door, we quickly threw away the half eaten pizza pie, washed our mouths out with the rest of our RC Colas, and declared then and there that we'd never try that stuff again. Of course, later on, several years later actually, I once again tried pizza and found that I really liked it. I suppose Bobby Dean did the same thing, but the memory of that first taste has never been completely washed from my mouth, and I've never picked up a slice of pizza without remembering Daytona Beach, Florida, 1958, with Bobby Dean and his folks.

During 1958 they were building a super speedway at Daytona Beach, and James wanted to see what it looked like. We took a drive out there one day and spent the afternoon being shown around the not quite completed speedway by a man who claimed to know a lot about what they were doing. He told us how the track would look and how many people could watch a race, and how much the top guard railing cost, and a lot of things that seemed strange to us. Of course, being from South Town and not wanting anyone to think we were dumb, we let on like we believed him, but we really knew he was just trying to impress us with his own self importance.

Later, when the speedway was officially opened, we saw the man's picture in the paper. Seems his name was Bill something or the other, and he was the President, or the owner, or something like that of the whole track. Not only did he know what he was talking about, he was such a nice man that he spent a couple of hours with some folks from Springfield, Tennessee, telling us all about his pride and joy. Thinking back, I wish we had gotten an autograph and a picture, but we didn't. We didn't even take a picture of the track that today of course is one of the most famous racetracks in the world, Daytona International Speedway.

It was the next to the last night we were to spend in Daytona Beach that Bobby Dean and I had an experience that was to teach us, at least I know it taught me, a lesson I have never forgotten.

We knew that afternoon would be the last one we would spend at the beach, and we wanted to make the most of it, so I suppose that's why it was after dark when we finally decided to start back to our friend's home. We had walked to and from the beach each day we had been there with no incidents whatsoever, and even though it was after dark, we didn't really think anything could happen. But you can never tell what might happen, especially if you disregard all of the things your parents have tried to teach you. Which we did.

THE LAST OF THE SOUTH TOWN RINKY DINKS
THE EXTENDED VOLUME

Bobby Dean had been playing a game on the boardwalk and had won a small metal horse. It was six or seven inches tall, and reasonably heavy, and Bobby Dean carried it in his hand as we walked back to the house. Having grown up in less than desirable circumstances, many of the kids I knew carried a pocketknife, and I was one of them. Actually, I had a rather large knife, having purchased a huge Stiletto switchblade from an Army Surplus store in Nashville earlier that summer. I had the knife in the waistband of my blue jeans, seeing as it was too large to fit into my pocket, and as we walked I kept my hand in close proximity to the handle of the knife. I didn't think anything would happen, but I didn't want to take any chances just the same.

We were walking alongside the road, and had covered about half the distance to the house, when all at once a large white car pulled to a stop just in front of us and a very kindly, older gentleman rolled down the window and spoke.

Hi there, boys, the man said, his voice very friendly. How far do you have to go?

Well, Mister, Bobby Dean said, we don't have very far at all. We just live about a half mile up the road.

It's an awfully hot night, boys, would you like a ride?

I don't think it ever passed through either of our minds that all of our lives we had been told to never, never, get in a car with a strange man.

Bobby Dean looked at me. I looked back and him and touched the knife at my belt. I shrugged my shoulders. He shrugged his. It really was an awfully hot night, and we were more than a little tired. Maybe a ride would be all right. After all, it was only for about a half mile. And Bobby Dean and I were confident in our ability to handle a given situation. I had my knife, didn't I, and didn't Bobby Dean have the metal horse. Nothing to worry about.

So, doing exactly what we had been told over and over not to do, we climbed into the car with a strange man. As it turned out, this really was a strange man.

In fact he was the exact same kind of man our parents had warned us about. He was a homosexual, very much in the closet, and one of the kind of men who didn't mind traveling a few hundred miles to a town where he thought his luck might be a little better. Of course, if he had tried picking up boys in any town where he was well known, it would only have been a matter of time before the police, or one of the kids fathers had caught up with him, and he wouldn't have liked that one little bit.

It didn't take Bobby Dean and I very long that night to understand that we had made a mistake. A bad mistake. Actually, when he asked us if we drank beer and if we liked girls, we knew then and there it was time for us to get out of the car, and for him to get somewhere far away, and the quicker the better.

It was like a little light came on in our heads, almost at the same time. Bobby Dean turned and stared at me in the shallow light from the dashboard and I stared back. He gently pushed the metal horse against my leg, and I elbowed him softly, letting him know that I had my hand on the knife in my waistband.

Mister, I guess you'd better be pulling this car over, right now, one of us managed to say. We'll be walking the rest of the way home.

Now boys, don't be afraid. I didn't mean any harm. I'll let you out right now.

And he did.

As the taillights disappeared into the heavy salt air, I somehow had the sense to note the license plate, and was surprised to see that the car wasn't even from Florida, but was from a state several hundred miles to the North.

Bobby Dean and I slowly began walking home, feeling more like kids than we had felt in a long time. We felt young, a little bit afraid, and we felt very stupid. You might say that we felt more than a little like what we really were. Two green country kids from South Town in Springfield, Tennessee that didn't know very much at all about the world, and the real things that happened out there.

We decided not to tell anyone anything at all about this incident. After all, nothing had happened, we were safe, and the stranger was gone. In later years, I sometimes wondered if perhaps we should have reported it to someone. Although we weren't hurt, the man may have actually been dangerous to some other kid at some other point in time.

I do know that it was because of that night in Daytona Beach that I formed an opinion about a so-called life style that remains with me to this day. I believe there is something inherently wrong about an old man who will drive hundreds of miles and cruise darkened roads trying to pick up a young boy for sexual purposes. There is nothing gay at all about a person who acts in this manner, nothing happy and carefree about a habit or a life style that causes a man to prey upon unsuspecting children. It was this personal experience with a homosexual that leads me to believe that this life style is wrong.

There is one other thing I can tell you for sure about this experience. Neither myself nor Bobby Dean was ever completely sure exactly what the stranger wanted to do to us, or what he wanted us to do to him. We do know, however, that if he had made one move toward actually touching either of us, he would have heard the snick of a switchblade knife, and probably would have felt the hooves of the metal horse somewhere in the vicinity of between his eyes.

In South Town some of the men said that there was only one cure for a man who liked little boys, and that was to cut off a few things. I don't know if that would have happened, but as young and inexperienced as we were, anything is possible. Now wouldn't that have been a heck of a way to end our first visit to the Sunshine State?

And wouldn't it have been a heck of a way for the stranger to end his Florida vacation. He goes down a stud, comes back home a gelding.

There is one other thing I can tell you for sure. I know that if we had told our Dad's what had happened, it wouldn't have been safe for the stranger to drive the streets of Daytona Beach, and if they had found out where he was from, his home town would have have lost what they thought to be an upstanding citizen. And once the law found out the truth about the man's habits, there probably wouldn't have been much done about the justice the fathers had taken into their own hands.

However, I am very glad to say that other than that one painful memory, the rest of the Florida vacation was, as I've already said, one of the best periods in my life. Bobby Dean's Mom and Dad were among the best people that ever lived in Springfield, in any part of Springfield, and Bobby Dean and I shared a friendship that comes along only once in a great while.

South Town Rinky Dinks? Sure we were.

Friends all of our life? Absolutely.

Bobby Dean married a pretty young girl named Carolyn Fay Leftrick, they raised a fine family in Springfield, and up until a short time ago I always thought there would come a time when Bobby Dean and I would get together to talk about the old days. The days at Woodland Street School, and at Springfield High School, and especially the 1958 trip to Daytona Beach, Florida.

But it didn't happen.

In February of 1997, Bobby Dean Pentecost lost the battle to heart disease, a battle he had fought long and valiantly. Springfield lost a native son, a Rinky Dink who was a far better person than most. I lost a good friend. A lifelong friend. A friend who will be missed, but who will live forever in my heart.

22

THE RINKY DINKS GET RELIGION

The wild-eyed old Preacher had a Bible in his right hand and a large white handkerchief in his left, and he was in his element. The cloth cover on the Bible was black, and was as worn and faded and sweat stained as the old mans face. The handkerchief was almost as white as the Preacher's long flowing hair, and like the Bible had plainly seen better days. The handkerchief fluttered about in his hand like a wounded butterfly as the Holy-Roly minister stalked the small wooden stage like a wild lion, pounding on the Bible as he preached the Word of God. He alternated between using the handkerchief to wipe the sweat from his forehead, and as a pointing device to emphasize some particularly important point about the many pitfalls that led folks straight down the highway to Hell.

He was preaching Hell-fire and brimstone, and the amens, although they rang loud and often, were swallowed up by the heat and humidity of the August evening. The heavy, humid air pushed down against the large canvas tent that stood on the corner of 20th Avenue and Blair Street, and there were hand held fans aplenty in the audience, gently waving to and fro to the rhythm of the Preacher's sermon. Nearly everyone in South Town was at the tent revival meeting, and on this night the Revival had the religious fervor of people on the mountaintop.

God offered these people something that nothing or no one else did. A ray of hope. In the years following the Great Depression there was precious little hope for the poor people of the rural South, and the preacher knew that. So he called on God to come down and visit upon these people a miracle, to give them a sign that the hard times were almost over. But even though they believed the Preacher's words, deep down they knew that more than likely the hard times would never be over. At least not for most of them.

And so they gathered at the tent meeting and prayed for a miracle, not for themselves, but for their children. They prayed their kids would have a better way of life, a life that wasn't confined to the dead end streets of South Town.

There was an old brown Sears guitar lying across a feeble straight backed wooden chair which sat behind the preacher and a little to his left. Only minutes before, a young man had been on the stage with the preacher, picking the guitar while the preacher and two women sang all of the old favorite gospel songs.

Weary voices which somehow became a little stronger as they sang, rang out to the chorus of "I'll Fly Away" and "Amazing Grace." It didn't take much imagination to picture the morning dew on the roses when they sang "I Come To The Garden Alone," and tears filled the eyes of most of the congregation as the Preacher and the two women sang the beautiful favorite, "The Old Rugged Cross."

In the back of the tent, scattered about on the grass like fresh cut weeds, sat a handful of suntanned children. Most of them were dressed in overalls and plaid shirts, and almost without exception the boys had their right pants leg rolled up halfway to the knee. That was to keep it out of the way of their bicycles chain. The bicycles were resting on the kickstands in the field behind the tent, or lying helter skelter about on the ground where they'd left them.

The Rinky Dinks had come to see the preacher.

Not for religion, probably, but for the show. And what a show it was.

I cut my religious teeth on tent meetings like this one, and spent many Sundays at the Baptist Mission on the corner of Cherry Street and 21st Avenue. I've already touched on the Mission, but there is a little more I'd like to write about going to church.

I started attending the Nazarene Church on Main Street when I was eleven or twelve, and up until the time I graduated from high school the church played a very significant part in my life. Most of my activities were centered around whatever the Church had planned for the young people to do. We usually had fifteen or twenty or even more kids in our youth group at the church, and we spent a lot of time together. We had class parties, Lamp Lighter meetings, and we were encouraged to try our best not to miss any church services at all. We went to church on Sunday morning, Sunday night, Wednesday night, and usually had some kind of church meeting on either Friday or Saturday.

THE LAST OF THE SOUTH TOWN RINKY DINKS
THE EXTENDED VOLUME

We had a bunch of South Town Rinky Dinks in the Nazarene Church, but the church itself was on the other side of the railroad tracks, just outside Rinky Dink territory.

Counted among the Rinky Dinks that attended the Nazarene Church, besides me of course, were all of the Evilcizer kids, Larry, John L., Sue Anne, Betty Lynn, and Gary. Their parents, Tom Bill and Mattie, also went to the church, and the Evilcizer's spent a large amount of time, money, and patience working for the church, and every service you would find them picking up folks and giving them a ride to and from church. I rode with Larry a lot of the time, especially when it was too cold to walk. The Evilcizer's were good folks who loved the Church and loved the Lord, and let it show in their lives.

Then there was Wesley, Faye, and Wayne Birdwell, Melvin Tanner, Faye Mantlo, Marjorie Norris, and the Benton sisters, Elsie, Helen, and Lillian. Josie Coleman was the Benton's cousin, but she didn't live in South Town. Josie lived out in the country, on M. Etta Lahr's Road, and came to church as regularly as the rest of us did. Most members of the Kiger family attended the Church, and I hope they forgive me if I can't remember all of their names. I can remember Betty Sue better than the rest, because we kind of dated off and on for a few years.

One of my very best friends in the Church was a kid named James Bilyeu, pronounced "Blue" if you don't mind, and for several years if you saw one of us, you could bet that the other wasn't very far away.

James and I had many strange, crazy adventures together, including the cold snowy night I stood up with him and his blushing young bride as Brother Slifer administered their wedding vows. Mary Jo giggled her way halfway through the ceremony because she couldn't get James' ring to fit on his finger, while James and I just stood there with big silly grins on our faces. I'll have to save most of the stories about James and me for the second book about the Rinky Dinks, assuming, of course, that there is a second book.

Of course, like the rest of the Rinky Dinks, I knew all of James' family. The Bilyeu's were as much a part of South Town back then as any family that had ever lived there. Like a lot of the folks out there, James' parents were straight-laced and a little old fashioned. They were always considered very religious, and in fact, I think his father preached some every now and then. To tell the truth, the way James could talk I always thought he might eventually become a preacher too. But he didn't. After we grew older, he managed our band for a while, and almost got us killed one night up in Kentucky, but again, that's another story.

The Bilyeu family were all good people, and I'm proud to say that they were all my friends. Like most of the rest of us, the Bilyeu kids turned out to be hard working, honest people, and Springfield should be glad that they chose to remain there. They would be a welcome addition to any town, and Springfield is lucky to have them.

James' older sister Ruth married a fellow named W.B. Adams, and he and I later worked together at the Mansfield Tire and Rubber Company. W.B., or Billy, as most people called him, was a supervisor at the plant, and one that I learned quite a few tricks of the trade from. I guess the best way to describe Billy is to say that he was one of those rare individuals who had true style, in the old fashioned sense of the word. He was well liked, and thought the way to get the most work out of people was to treat them fair, talk to them as if they had enough sense to understand what he wanted done, and then let them do it. And it worked. It worked for Billy, it worked for me, and it still works, as a matter of fact, for those few people with enough sense to recognize a real skill of supervising people.

Anyway, if there is another book, I'll have to try and remember all of the old stories about James and me. And about kids like Kenneth Carroll, and Ralph Leftrick, and Pete Kirkland, and all of the rest of the guys I went to high school with. I guess we were pretty typical teenagers, for the fifties, that is, but you've got to remember that a few of us were Rinky Dinks, and that little fact does tend to spice things up somewhat.

But enough side tracking. Let's get on back to Church now.

There were some kids in the class who lived in North Town, but not very many. Patty Summers lived on Willow Street in North Town and she's about the only one I can actually remember that wasn't from South of the railroad tracks.

That could be because Patty was the one person I thought most about during those years.

You see, Patty Mary was the first girl I ever truly loved, and we dated off and on through high school, settling most of our arguments with a duel we called marshmellows at ten paces, or MATP. We had our up's and down's, and there a lot of good memories associated with Patty and those few short high school years. But in the end, it wasn't me who won the heart of the fair young lady. After graduation, Patty married Larry

Evilcizer, and as far as I know, they've had a good marriage. Both of them have remained good friends of mine, and I can't think of two people who deserve a better life. I can't recall one single time that Larry ever did anything that could be considered wrong, or hurtful to anyone else. Unless of course it was in a karate tournament. It's possible that Larry was the best karate expert that ever came out of this area, and there's even a chance he could have been among the best in the country. But even during the early days of our rivalry, when both of us were head over heels in love with Patty Mary, we remained friends. And we still are.

Patty and Faye Birdwell were best friends back then, and the last time I spoke to Faye she said they still are. They had another friend named Christine Vaden, who was in our class at school, and I saw her a lot after we graduated from high school. She worked in the office at Phillipps and Buttorff for quite a while with us, and I can't imagine a nicer person that Christine. She later married a good old boy named Joe Brown, and to the best of my knowledge they are still married and are still in Springfield.

There were a lot of great kids that went to church at the Nazarine, and while I won't try to name them all, I will do my best to recall some of them.

Brother Slifer's daughter Marita was at church every time the doors opened, and if I remember it right she may have been "dating" John L. Evilcizer. Randle (?) and Maggie Coleman were great people who were very faithful in the church attendance, and they had three very pretty daughters. If I remember their names correctly, they were Carolyn, Gail, and Sheryl. Carolyn was a year behind me in high school, I think, and Gaile was a couple of years younger. Randle and Maggie were really good people and we used to have class meetings at their house now and then. Actually, I think there may have been another daughter, but I can't remember for sure.

I've already mentioned the Bentons, Evilcizers, and the Bilyeus, and that's about all I can recall off the top of my head. I know I've left out more than I've named, but again, it was a long time ago, and some things I just don't recall.

Another thing about that Sunday school class is that there were always more girls than there were boys, which you would think would really make us guys happy. But when you remember how tough the rules at that Church were, you can see that just because there were more boys than girls didn't really make a lot of difference.

Let me explain it a little more, just for fun.

If you know anything about the doctrine of the Nazarene Church of the fifties, you know that they didn't like for anyone to do anything that they thought was not praising the Lord. That included skating, bowling, movies, mixed swimming, (they called it mixed bathing) and any other activity that let us have fun, or at least that's the way it seemed to most of the teens in the Church. For some reason, these rules, and whoever made up the rules, were especially against dancing. I was never quite sure why, but dancing seemed to generate more than its share of evil feelings for the elders of the Church. I didn't understand that then, and maybe I still don't understand it. Anyway, all of the rules that I couldn't understand were the reasons I got away from the Nazarene Church pretty soon after high school. I understand they've changed now, and all I can say is that it's about time. I know several people who felt the same way I did, and I don't think I was the only who left the Church for the same reasons.

The teenagers weren't the only targets of the Churches strict rules.

The women in the church weren't supposed to wear any makeup, nor any jewelry, with the exception of a wedding band, and they couldn't wear long pants. I never have figured that one out.

Smoking was a no-no by anyone, man, woman, or child, although some of them did it anyway. And of course, no drinking or cursing would be condoned by any member of the Church. Like I said, they regarded anything that didn't give praise to the Lord as being sinful. And we were reminded of that almost every Sunday.

It was during this particular period in my life that I met another person who was to become one of my life long friends. He was from South Town, born on Mantlo Street, and as much a Rinky Dink as any of us, and he turned out to be one of the most valued friends I've ever known. His name was Samuel Traughber, and he didn't attend the Nazarene Church. Actually, to the best of my knowledge he was only inside that Church once, and that was one Friday night in September of 1965 when he stood beside Helen and myself at the front of the Church, as the best man at our wedding.

I've included him in this chapter because Sam taught me a valuable lesson about religion, although he probably doesn't even realize it.

THE LAST OF THE SOUTH TOWN RINKY DINKS
THE EXTENDED VOLUME

Sam was a devout Catholic, and as such he didn't think he should visit my Church for one of our services, but that didn't stop me from visiting with him at his Church once or twice. And to my surprise, I didn't find Catholic's to be that much different from the rest of us. And I think that is the valuable lesson I learned. For some reason, after seeing the strangeness of the Catholic services, it dawned on me that even though people worship God in many different ways, we all worship the same God, and the result of that is while the ceremony's are different, the worship is mostly the same, regardless of the name of the Church we attend.

Sometimes I call him Samuel P. Curly Q Traughber, and sometimes I call him Sammy, but mostly I just call him Sam. But make no mistake about it, he is one of the people I'm most proud to call friend. And in another context, I might say that I've never called him that he didn't answer.

I met Sam in 1955 or 56, and up until I moved away from Springfield I still saw him quite often.

Sam is a few years older than I am, and by the time I met him he was already doing things I'd never heard of. Strange and wonderful things that I couldn't wait to try.

Interested? I thought so. But it may not be what you're thinking.

Actually, the things probably weren't so strange and wonderful to anyone that didn't live in South Town, but they were as strange to me as if they had been invented on the moon.

For instance, Sam knew how to water ski. Water ski. I'd never heard of water skiing, let alone met someone who knew how. And he knew how to roller skate and ice skate. And I could hardly wait to learn.

Sometime in the fall of 1956 or 1957, I'm really not sure which year it was, Sam introduced me to the sport I grew to love as much or more than any other sport I ever played. Several of us loaded into his old Ford one evening and we took off for Eighth Avenue in Nashville, to a small, eight-lane bowling alley, and from that night on I was hooked.

Bowling became my sport of choice, and for years I bowled two or three or four nights a week. Helen and I bowled in doubles leagues, and I traveled all over this part of the country bowling in amateur tournaments.

And I loved every minute of it. I quit league bowling in the early eighties, after Nikki and Derek were born, but for years I got more than my share of enjoyment out of rolling that sixteen-pound ball. And I have Sam to thank for that.

There was another particular game I learned during that time, this one not from Sam, but from one of the members of the church. It was another game that I really enjoyed, and was one that James Bilyeu and I spent many a day perfecting. That game was ping pong.

The Benton girl's older sister had married a missionary, and they had spent quite a lot of time in Japan before moving back to Springfield. They moved into a house across the street from Woodland Street School and during the first summer that they lived there they taught some of the kids that played around the school how to play Japanese style ping pong. And some of us got pretty good at it. We could back away from the table and play the slam style of ping pong and beat almost everybody in town that still played the other way.

But I didn't beat everyone I played. Not quite.

During my Junior and Senior years in high school, James and I began to spend quite a lot of time going over to Trevecca College in Nashville.

Trevecca is a Nazarene school, and I was pretty sure that was where I wanted to go to college. Especially since we had met several people, read that girls, who went to school there, and they really wanted us to join them the next year.

During the times when I wasn't going with Patty, I usually dated a young lady from Trevecca named Lois Kolar, and Lois and her family were really pushing for me to come to Trevecca.

James and I tried to go over there once every few weeks, and it was during one of these visits that I learned a lesson about ping pong I've never forgotten. The fact that it was also a lesson about life makes it even more valuable.

James and I were visiting Lois one weekend, and we happened to go over to the student's recreation room to see what was going on.

There were a couple of ping-pong tables set up in the room for the students, and of course we started a game almost as soon as we got there.

THE LAST OF THE SOUTH TOWN RINKY DINKS
THE EXTENDED VOLUME

James and I were pretty evenly matched, and the game seesawed back and forth for awhile, until all at once Lois caught my eye.

She introduced us to a pretty young girl who had been standing watching us play, and the girl said that she also loved to play ping pong, and would one of us like to play a game with her.

Sometimes always being the one who steps up is a burden that can turn out to be more than a Rinky Dink could carry, especially on shoulders as thin as mine were at the time.

But I don't remember that ever stopping me from jumping right in.

I'll play you, I said, and handed her a paddle.

I promised myself that I'd take it easy on her, her being a girl and all, and me being such a wham bam super duper ping pong player.

I stood up close to the table and very softly hit the hard white plastic ball in her direction.

With its peculiar little hollow sound the ball bounced over the net and she returned it rather easily.

I hit the ball back to her, being careful not to hit it very hard.

She hit it back with a little more zing, causing me to lose the point.

I shot her a questioning look, a slightly raised eyebrow, and served the ball again, this time a little harder.

She drove it back at me like a bullet, the ball fairly screaming as it passed by me like a rocket on its way to the moon.

I shot her another look, served the ball with as much force as I could muster up, and when the ball passed me again, even harder than the last time, I knew I was in trouble.

She beat me three games cold, with me scoring almost no points, in spite of the fact that I played her as hard as I knew how, using every trick I had learned, and slamming the ball on almost every shot.

After the game I learned she had lived much of her life in Japan, and had learned that style of ping pong several years before I had. And was much better at it. In fact, she was a champion tournament player, and had beaten almost everyone she had ever played.

I didn't feel quite so bad about losing to her once I found out all of this, and I learned never to take any situation at face value.

Actually, the most valuable lesson I learned concerned the equality of the sexes.

And that lesson is that there ain't no equality of the sexes, boys. The girls will beat you almost every time, hands down, at almost everything that requires timing, speed, and a killer instinct.

Now I'm not intending for you to think that I regret my years spent in the Nazarene Church. I don't regret them at all. In fact I value them highly. I learned a lot about religion, a lot about the Lord, and in so doing I learned lessons that have stood me in good stead throughout the years. And I really loved the people at the Nazarene Church. There wasn't a better congregation in Springfield. I still see some of them, and you'd be surprised at how many still attend that same Church.

And even now, some forty years later, when I close my eyes and say a little prayer to God, I can see Brother Kenneth Slifer standing at the front of the Church, his eyes closed, fervently leading us in prayer in what was absolutely the most somber voice I have ever heard. I always thought, and I still do, that if Brother Slifer couldn't get through to God, I seriously doubt if anyone in the world could.

But the image that stands out in my mind the clearest is still that old tent revival meeting, with the Preacher's eyes blazing and his white handkerchief fluttering in the air, and deep down in my memory I can hear the distant refrains falling softly on the evening air...

On a hill far away, stood an old Rugged Cross,
> the emblem of suffering and shame...

23

THE WALKER CLAN

Billy Walker was a large rawboned man whose weight tended to run to muscle instead of fat. He had a ready laugh and a ready temper, and used them both as he saw fit. Actually, this pretty much describes most of the Walker men, such as Odell and Horace. Willard, Billy's' dad, was a good-sized man, but as I recall not quite as large as Billy.

Billy joined the Army at an early age, and then volunteered for the paratroops shortly after that. From what I recall, Billy was a jump instructor for quite a while, and was stationed at Fort Campbell, Kentucky, the home of the 101st Airborne Division.

I'm pretty sure Billy was in the Army during the Korean War, and may have served a hitch or so in Vietnam. I know he went where he was sent, showing the same sense of duty that many other of the Walker men have shown over the years.

For a lot of years I've heard the story about Billy having a few beers at the Midway Café one hot Saturday afternoon, getting into a fight with a black man in a parking lot in Springfield, and then trying to outrun the law back to Clarksville. I can't vouch for the truthfulness of it, however, it sounds like something that could have happened. After all, he wouldn't be the first of the Walker boys to take a drink and then take a swing at somebody, nor the first to try and out run the law.

If I remember correctly, Billy moved back to Springfield after he retired from the Army, but after a couple of years he relocated to Germany, where he still lives, assuming he's still alive, that is. Sad to say, I don't even know.

Billy is married to a pretty German lady named Frieda and at some point in time he decided he'd rather live over there than here. Of course, this also isn't a first for a Walker kid. Well, moving to Germany may be a first, but many of Mama's brothers and sisters moved away from

Springfield to seek their fortunes elsewhere. Jim spent the last few years of his life in a small town outside Detroit, which I've already written about, and Lucille only came back to Springfield when she was close to death, but still managed to die in Detroit.

Fred spent some time in Detroit, and Annie Bell never moved from Portland, Tennessee where her husband Henry Petty was from.

We visited Annie Bell and Henry in Portland once or twice a summer, and I remember the huge cherry tree that was in her yard. I remember it as being big, but maybe that is because I was so small at the time. I also remember Annie Bell picking fresh strawberries from her garden and whipping fresh cream to put on them. Fresh strawberry shortcake became one of my favorite desserts, and has remained so all of my life.

Henry was a long tall lean drink of water, and about as good a man as ever lived. In all of my life, I don't recall ever hearing one bad word spoken about Henry, and that's saying something for the men in our family.

I used to really like Helen Petty. She was funny and friendly and loved Mama almost as much as I did. Billie Francis Petty, another of Annie Bell's daughters, was a pretty girl and I think she was already married when I was still 8 or 10 years old. She married a man named Billy Hunnicutt and I think they lived in Gallatin, Tennessee, or maybe Hendersonville, Tennessee. Billy Hunnicutt was an engineer but I don't know where he worked. They had a child or two but the only one I remember is a son named who was also named Billy. I later became an industrial engineer in the appliance industry, and I think I was a little inspired by Billy Hunnicutt, even though I didn't really know him all that well.

Some, such as Paul, Jim and Horace joined the military, and some stayed home, but my point is that they were all strong minded men and women who made their own decisions about where and how they wanted to spend their lives.

The fact is that some, such as Paul, went into the military and didn't come back. He was a sailor on board the USS Birmingham when it came under attack by a Japanese Kamikaze plane and from a report I recently found on the internet, the deck of the ship ran red with blood from the wounded and dying. Paul was killed that day, and I've often watched

Mama walk by and touch his picture and I've wondered what thoughts were running through her mind.

Horace was burned very badly while serving, and Jim may have been wounded as well. Fred was turned down when he volunteered, and the story is that after he moved to Michigan he tried again and was turned down for the second time.

Andrew Walker, their father and my grandfather had passed away in 1941, and even though the children were close to each other, they were individuals and spent their time as they each desired.

Andrew and Mattie had, I believe, sixteen children, but I'm sure I can't name them all. I'm pretty sure this isn't the correct order, but here goes the names that I recall or have been able to find..

Mama, Lena Viola, was the eldest, and after her came Horace, Odell, Willard, Almon, Hubert, Annie Bell, Minnie, Fred, Clara, Lucille, Paul and James.

This is thirteen of them, and these are the only names I've been able to find. I'm only sure on the order of two of them. Mama was the eldest and James, or Jim, was the youngest.

But let me get back to where they lived and what they did.

Horace remained in Springfield, living in the same old wood sided house Andy and Mattie had lived in, and took care of Mattie till she passed away, sometime in the late forties or early fifties.

Minnie was married to Clyde Cannon, and they also remained in Springfield till the end of their lives.

Minnie and Clyde never had children, but Clyde's younger sister Geraldine had a child who was born with MS, and who never grew from the baby stage. This child was named Mackie, and Minnie and Clyde kept him all the days of his life, and loved him as if he were their own. I've often wondered what it would take for a woman to do this. Take on the responsibility of the care of such a child, one that was not hers, and to love that child unconditionally for as long as he was alive. If this doesn't buy this woman some special place in Heaven, then maybe we should all rethink our desires on going there. I spend quite a lot of time with Minnie, more in fact than I did with any of my aunts or uncles, and I never once heard her complain about the choice she had made. To me, this makes her one of God's chosen, and if there is life after death, Minnie and Clyde are in a better place, and Mackie is a strong healthy child, and they are together still.

Willard married a pretty girl named Allie May Brown, and they had what I also thought was a very strong relationship. Both worked at the famous Springfield Woolen Mills, at least until the time when Willard's bad health reached a point where he had to quit work.

While most of the Walker clan were big strong people, for some reason almost all of them tended to develop heart problems. Several of them died in their forties with heart attacks, and I think this heart problem was the reason Willard had to quit work. Not long before the time that Willard quit work, Hubert, another of the brothers, had died while laying blocks, and Lucille had developed the same problems.

Some years before, while shooting some dynamites caps, Willard had lost the ends of a finger or two, or maybe a thumb, I don't recall exactly which, and I was never sure if he was working with dynamite or simply playing with the caps. For years I've thought he was just shooting them off for the fun of it, because that sounds like something one of them would have done. Anyway, he lost parts of some fingers, but I seem to remember him laughing about it a few times when he was at our house.

Remember, Odell had lost a leg while hopping a freight train, and it stands to reason that the brothers did a lot of things just for the heck of it, or because it struck their fancy at the moment.

The Springfield Woolen Mills where Willard and Allie May worked sometimes paid their Christmas payroll to their employees in silver dollars, and I remember once Willard came by the house and gave me and Goober one each for Christmas. I kept mine for years, but have no idea what eventually happened to it.

Allie May is a book all by herself, and I'd like to share a few little tales about one of the most fascinating ladies that ever came out of Robertson County, Tennessee.

She worked at the Woolen Mills until it closed, and then she went to work for another company, I think in another town, and she drove back and forth to work every day of her life.

In fact, she liked to drive so much that in the last couple of years of her life I grew very worried about her being on the streets in a car. She was still very active even up into her eighties, driving herself wherever she wanted to go, and refusing help from anyone at all. Anyway, I was worried enough that I watched the papers for stories about accidents and stuff like that, and to tell the truth I was probably worried enough that I might have parked my car if I knew for sure she was out and about that day.

Allie May was one of the most active senior citizens Springfield ever produced. She took part in the Senior Olympics every year, traveling all around and entering the contests. She had started power walking and for years I don't think there was a person of any age in Springfield that could have out paced her. She walked miles and miles every day, and it paid off in gold medals in competition time after time.

She was in her eighties when she started taking classes in clog dancing, and as my wife and I were in the same class, I can say with firsthand knowledge that none of the younger people were a match for her in endurance. Well, Helen may have been, but I know I sure wasn't.

Once during a clogging class she slipped and fell and I was afraid she had broken her arm. As it turned out, she actually did fracture it. I helped her up from the floor and then went and called her daughter Juanita and told her about the accident. Juanita immediately came to see how her mother was, but Allie May showed her displeasure with me quickly.

I can take care of myself, Donald Harp, she said. You didn't have to call anyone to come see about me.

Of course, I knew she was right, but I also knew Juanita would want to know, and so I made the call.

Allie May had the distinction of being one of the oldest, if not the oldest, person in Springfield to ever go back to high school and her diploma. She had told me at one of the clogging classes that this had been a goal of hers for years, and she was in her seventies or her eighties when she completed this dream.

I never met a person who did not have great admiration for Allie May. She was a strong woman before it was trendy to be so, she had a mind of her own and used it and never asked for any special treatment in anything in life. She was determined, I guess the word would be, to do whatever she wanted to, and she never let an obstacle stand in her way.

I had already moved away from Springfield when Allie May passed away, and didn't know she was gone until after the funeral. She was truly such a remarkable woman, I can say that knowing that not only will I miss knowing she's around, but Springfield, Tennessee lost one of the most unique and wonderful ladies that has ever called that town home. Springfield was lucky to have Allie May choose to live there, and whether or not anyone in town realizes it, there may never be anyone who will be able to take her place.

I believe Willard and Allie May only had four children, as that is all that I can remember. If I have missed one, or even more, and if any of them ever read this wildly strange account, then I apologize. I have said over and over than I am only writing what I can personally remember, and that my memory is not all that clear on some points, and all that I can remember is four children.

They were Dot, Doodle, Juanita and Billy, and these are not in any order that I am sure of. I'm not sure which of them is the elder, and I might not tell if I knew.

Dot was a tall, dark good-looking woman, given to the Walker dry sense of humor, and if I recall correctly she moved from Springfield sometimes in the Sixties or early Seventies. I'm not sure where she moved to, and I only saw her a few times after that. Most of the time it was when she came to a funeral of one or the other of the brother and sisters, and I believe the last time I saw her was when Mama died. I don't know much about her after that and I wasn't around her all that much growing up. She was always nice to me, and seemed to be a very likable girl. I'd like to have known her better, but it seems as if we were all too busy finding out what we were going to do with out own lives to get too involved with anyone else.

Then there was Doodle. Well, here name was Lula, but everyone always called her Doodle. I think the name was appropriate, because the fact is that Doodle was crazy. Not in a bad way of course, in a very good way. Doodle was always one of the funniest people I have ever known, and could make a sack of rocks laugh. Her humor was a lot like Mama's, and sometimes tended to be a little on the risqué side, shall we say. She always had a smile, and even in the midst of some personal turmoil, she managed to keep her spirits up and to hold on to her sense of who she was and what she wanted. Some of my best memories of all come from the times when we had to opportunity to visit. Doodle would stop by to see Mama every chance she got, and she always impressed me with her outlook on life in general and the way she lived her own life in particular.

Doodle married a man named Clarence Bates and they had two children that I can remember. I think the oldest was named Jerry and maybe the youngest was named Ronnie, but I'm not real sure about that. I don't remember much about Clarence but it seems as if he and Doodle were divorced. I don't know what happened to him, and it's been years since I've seen her. Again, the last time was probably at Mama's funeral.

Juanita was a very good-looking girl, but when we were younger I wasn't around her as much as I was Doodle, so I didn't know her as well. She also had that sense of humor, and was also a strong willed woman. She knew what she wanted and went after it to the best of her ability. Which, by the way, was quite a lot.

She became office manager of one of the areas most prominent trucking companies, and was a very successful business lady for years in Springfield.

Juanita had another thing going for her that made me take notice, however. She was married to a handsome young man named Russell Draughon, who had a devil may care smile and a twinkle in his eye, and every time you saw him you just knew he'd been up to some strange new undertaking.

I might as well say that what caught my interest was the fact that Russell was a guitar picker and a singer. I've always been into picking and grinning, and was already playing in a lot of local bands, so the fact that Russell could hold his own with a flat top or singing an old Hank Williams tune was impressive to me.

Russell worked up town at an appliance store, and he used to make guitar cords up for me. He'd make then a little longer than the commercial kind you could buy, and he'd take a little extra time making sure all the ends were soldered on perfectly, and I used to just like to hang around Russell and talk. He was an interesting and intelligent guy, and as I was a few years younger, he could make me feel a little bit special just by taking the time to talk to me.

I always liked Russell, and I wish I'd had the opportunity to spend a bit more time with him. I'd liked to have gotten him on stage with my band at the Food Bar or the Blue Angel Club and seen how the ladies liked him. I'll bet they would have lined up to hear just one more song. If you read this, Juanita, tell the truth now, you know that's so.

Course, I've already written about Billy, but to tell the truth I never got to know him really well either. He was already in the Army before I was big enough to take an interest in anything other than ball games or bike riding, and even though he sometimes came to visit when he was in town, I never got real close to him. Being in the military, he was gone more than he was home. I think he served in more than one combat zone, as several Walker men did, and I will guarantee you he did so honorably and well.

I do remember that he had that same old big ass Walker laugh, and the same tendency to knock a man's block off if he took a notion to. There were other strange character traits that most of Mama's brothers had, and I think Billy may have picked up those as well. Not that they were bad things, they certainly weren't, but sometimes they could be pretty hard to understand.

Even Mama would tell you that sometimes her brothers could be a pain in the ass, and even as a kid I could see that in some of them. I liked them all, maybe because I had some of the same blood, and could be a pain in the ass myself, but there was always something about them that was just a little bit over the top. I never tried to figure it out and still haven't. I just understood that they grew up in an environment that was tough on most people, and they learned to cope in anyway they could. They worked hard, they raised families, they fought for the country, and many of them died young.

Mama always said they were trying to cram as much living into as short a time as possible, because they never knew when the next heart attack might have their name on it. Seems I got in on that bit of the action as well, having a massive heart attack at 43 and quadruple bypass surgery at 53.

I don't know if that was the reason, but it's probably true. Mama had the best insight into things such as that as anyone I've ever known. What I do know is this. Mama and her brother's and sister's were a group of men and women who were strong and proud, who loved life and each other and who loved their families. Sumner County and Robertson County, Portland and Springfield, Tennessee, heck, the whole world is a better place because these people lived there. They weren't millionaires and they weren't saints, they were just ordinary everyday folk who made the best of a hand that may not have been the best one ever dealt by God. But they played it out, and they won.

MINNIE AND CLYDE
(NO RELATION TO BONNIE AND CLYDE)

Sometimes, as I was writing these stories, I found myself remembering bits and pieces of things that were so deeply buried in my memory that I had to break them out one tiny little chunk at a time. Some of my memories of Minnie were like that. I could plainly recall big things, like the trip to Detroit we took when Jim died. Minnie must have read every road sign in 500 miles. I never knew she had eyes that good. She could see signs for half a mile up the road, or at least it seemed that way to me, and by the time we had reached the middle of Kentucky, I was ready for her to take a nap.

Of course, she didn't do that. She wanted to see everything there was to see, and not only that, she wanted to tell us everything she saw. Twice.

But we dearly loved Minnie.

She was the aunt that was always there, always available, always ready to do whatever she could to make some little hurt disappear, or to try and put a smile on your face when all you wanted to do was cry.

Minnie was married to a man named Clyde Cannon, and for as many years as I knew Clyde, I don't recall him saying a bad word about anyone. Now, I don't recall him saying a lot of good words about anyone either, but I think he said more good than bad.

Clyde was an avid fisherman, and, like Daddy, was a catcher of fish. I've said that not all fishermen truly know how to catch a fish, but Clyde was one of those who did.

He and Daddy and a few others managed to go fishing once or twice a week, and seldom came home empty handed.

Clyde was also a pool player. And a pretty good one at that. He played bank pool, and spent a lot of time at Charlie's Pool Room uptown in Springfield. He had a bunch of guys, most of them around his age, that he played with on a regular basis, and I'm pretty sure a few dollars changed hands during the games.

Clyde was the first person I knew who had his own cue stick. He had found one that he liked and had managed to get Mr. Charlie to sell it to him, and he kept it in a rack in a little room at the back of the pool hall.

Several of the men Clyde played pool with did the same thing, and they were very particular about who they let touch their cues. Each stick had its own feel, and they didn't want anyone to do anything that might change the way the stick handled. Of course, I don't know that you can do anything to change the way a pool stick handles, but they thought so, and who was I to disagree?

I've spent many an afternoon playing pool in Charlie's Pool Room, and actually played a lot of games with Clyde. Even though their game was closed, and not just anyone would be asked to play, sometimes when someone didn't show up Clyde would ask if I wanted to take a cue.

The others didn't really object, and at first I suppose they saw me as an easy mark. A kid who they could beat for a few bucks or so, and at first that's pretty much what they did.

It was a different story in a few years after I had learned the game. To me, pool was just another ball game, and I've never met a ball game I didn't like. I've also never met one that I couldn't learn to play well enough to hold my own.

Their game soon became a place where I might pick up a few bucks, instead of just contributing to their winnings. I didn't always win, but I did sometimes, and I didn't embarrass myself or them by playing badly or by conducting myself in a way they didn't approve of.

Now these old guys could shoot. Don't ever think that just because a man has a little gray hair or a bit of a belly, that it means they can't do anything. Most of these men had been playing pool ever since the end of World War II, and they had grown to be very good at it. I saw shots back then that would make any of the famous pool hustlers or the tournament players you see nowadays on television take a second look.

As an occupation, Clyde was a painter, a house painter, and was good at that also. He had a pickup truck that had an air compressor in the bed, and he had paint guns and all of the equipment to do an excellent and highly professional job.

He worked in and around Springfield, and also went over into Kentucky quite often on jobs, and it was at an old farmhouse in Pembroke, or Pembrook, Kentucky that he once took an old RCA wind up Victrola as part of his payment. An old lady lived there, but was getting ready to move and wanted to get rid of a few things. Clyde painted her house for her to make it sell for a better price, and she gave him the Victrola and a big bunch of the great big records that were made back in the 20's and 30's.

Clyde brought the Victrola home but just couldn't find any place to put, so Minnie suggested that they give it to me for my birthday, which was just a few days off. They knew I loved music, and they thought the gift would be something I would really like.

I soon found out that there was nothing wrong with the old player, and I even learned a few of the songs on some of the records.

I learned an old Irish song called "Roaming In The Gloaming" and still remember most of the words.

There were also some comedy records, which now seems a bit unusual for that time. I recall one of the titles was; "Uncle Josh and Aunt Nancy Putting Up The Kitchen Stove." I have no idea why I still remember that, but as I said, writing this has brought back a lot of things I thought long forgotten.

The workings of the Victrola wore out some years ago, and I kept the cabinet as long as I could. Two of the legs got broken off in a storage building I once had some furniture stored in, and over the years the finish had taken quite a beating. I finally gave it away about 10 years ago, and I don't know what happened to it after that. I wish I could have kept it in the condition it was once in, but it just didn't work out.

Once, when I was about 19 or 20, I needed to buy a car. My old Ford had given up the ghost and if I was going to work I needed transportation.

Clyde found a 1957 Dodge at a car dealership uptown, I won't say which one, for a reason you will soon learn, and he finally dickered them down to $70 as the full price for the car.

I was working at Phillips and Buttorff in Nashville, building stoves, earning $1.60 an hour, and I brought home about $50 a week.

With my full paycheck in hand that Saturday morning, I walked the mile or so from my house to the car lot, where I was to meet a salesman and sign the papers to buy the car.

As has been most everything in my life, this didn't turn out exactly that easy. My paycheck was in the neighborhood of $50, and they wanted $70 for the car. I didn't have the other $20, and didn't have anywhere to get it.

So we compromised. I gave them my $50, they called Clyde and he came up and co-signed the note for the remaining $20. That may be the lowest amount any car dealership has ever requested a co-signor for.

I was a little bit upset at being asked for a co-signor for $20, so I decided to pay them off at the rate of $2 a week. They hadn't set up any payments for the debt, and as they had been such jerks about the whole situation I made sure it took as long as possible for me to get them paid off.

Clyde laughed about it every time he told the story, but in the long run it was the car dealership that lost out. Clyde had bought a car and a pick up truck from them, as well as several other vehicles over the years, but he never went back. He took his business elsewhere. I don't know if he ever told them why he did that or not, but if anyone from the dealership had ever asked, I'm sure they got an earful.

I remember once when several of the kids had managed to come up with the quarter it took to get into the swimming pool, and I couldn't get one anywhere. Eve Mai had given Ray a quarter but didn't have one for me. Mama didn't have any money to spare, Daddy was working, and I was really upset.

I went and sat on Minnie's porch swing for over an hour, not saying a word, just swinging and trying to understand why this had happened.

I had tears in my eyes from the hurt, and never knew Minnie was on the telephone, talking to Mama.

THE LAST OF THE SOUTH TOWN RINKY DINKS
THE EXTENDED VOLUME

Without a word, she softly slid into the swing beside me and kissed me on the top of my head. She took my hand and pressed a shiny half dollar into it, and smiled when she saw the look I gave her.

I have never told anyone this story, but I have never forgotten it either.

Over the years I have tried to do as many small favors as I could, because I learned that what may seem small to one person can be life shaking for another.

Clyde had a younger sister named Geraldine, whom I have already written about, but there is another story that I have not yet told.

Geraldine had a baby, a boy named Mackie, and he had one of the crippling diseases. One of the ones that never let him grow, or develop, or learn to crawl or walk or talk. Minnie and Clyde kept Mackie all of his life, caring for him as lovingly as if he were their own. They never had children, and the love they had for this small child was as big as the mountains. They never once complained, or asked for help, and I'm sure they never one time considered placing Mackie in any kind of hospital or home.

Minnie and Clyde owned a small four-room house on 18th Avenue. They were one of the few families on the street that owned their own home.

The house was only four rooms, but somehow it was big enough to hold more people other than just Minnie, Clyde and Mackie.

Clyde's father, a man everyone called "Old Man Cannon" lived with them for the last years of his life, and so did Uncle Jessie Wright. Uncle Jessie was Grannie Walker's brother, and I never learned the story of why he lived with Minnie and Clyde.

There is no way to describe the heart of a woman who will do this. No way to tell how many points she must have built up in heaven for being the person she was on earth.

Mackie passed away and then so did Old man Cannon and Uncle Jessie, and then a few years later we lost Clyde. But that didn't stop Minnie from trying to do as much for family members as she could.

Off and on several of Horace's boys spent a lot of time at Minnie's and when our son Jason was born in 1970, Minnie was the only baby sitter he ever knew. She kept him while Helen and I worked, and after she died I found that she had pictures of him on almost every page of her photo album

She passed away in the early eighties, and we laid her to rest beside Clyde one beautiful morning in a little graveyard out in the country. Along with a lot of other people, I sat in the cemetery and cried like a baby as they lowered her casket.

I can't help but think that Minnie was an extraordinary woman. I don't remember Minnie ever having a public job, but she lived her life serving others. While she didn't go to church every Sunday, I don't see a God that would deny her a mansion in heaven. She'll need it, because she will have so many family members that will want to spend eternity with her and Clyde.

INTERLUDE

I've written pretty much all that I set out to write about in this book. I've told what I think and hope is a lot of interesting and innocent stories of the South Town Rinky Dinks, and even though I left out quite a bit, I probably told about as much as most of you care to read.

I wrote about how I remembered the town of Springfield, which I'm sure will take many of you on a stroll down memory lane. Of course, Memory Lane for me will always be 21st Avenue.

I'm also sure that some folks won't be satisfied with my modest thoughts on our fair city, but that can't be helped.

I must admit I had been thinking of writing these stories for several years, even before Mama died. In fact, Mama was the first person that suggested that I write them, and I wish to God I had written them when she first asked me to. I could have had so much more first hand information to use, and the stories could have been a lot more factual. I know that Mama would have enjoyed them so much. Actually, I have a feeling that maybe she knows I'm writing them now, and is reading along on every page.

But I didn't write them then. It was years later that I finally made up my mind to chronicle the adventures, or misadventures, of myself and my relatives and friends.

The actual writing came about in this fashion.

A few years ago, in December of 1993, one of our dearest friends decided, for some reason known only to herself, that life had become too difficult to face, and once she decided that, she took it upon herself to end her life. In so doing, we lost one of our favorite people.

The Rinky Dinks gathered at her funeral and through tear dimmed eyes we once again talked over the old times. Once again someone, I believe it was Fay Birdwell, suggested that the story of the Rinky Dinks should be written. This time, for some reason, I listened.

So it is that this book is not only dedicated to the persons I've already named, it is also especially dedicated to the memory of Jane White Thaxton. Jane was married to Lawrence Thaxton for over thirty years, and was his one true love. We loved her and we miss her.

I do have one more chapter, and that's the one about Mama. It's also about Daddy, and some of the other family members, and it is the most personal chapter in the book. The other stories have been mostly for the enjoyment of my readers, but I must confess that I wrote this last chapter for myself. There are memories that I want set to paper, and I know in my heart that my memories of Mama belong here, in the pages of the book that tells the stories of the kids and family she loved more than she loved life itself.

Being as I know what I have written, I will tell you that the last chapter deals more with emotions than stories, and some of the memories have proven to be very unsettling for me. I suspect that many of the emotions I was feeling as I wrote the lines may show through. The tears I shed as the images flooded my mind won't show on the paper, but if you read this chapter, all it will take is a little imagination for you to see the stains.

And so, you might want to end your reading of this book at this point. If so, I hope you've enjoyed the stories of the kids everyone called the South Town Rinky Dinks.

If you choose to read the last chapter, then be my guest as I introduce you to the lady that over the years of a lot of raggedy little South Town Rinky Dinks called Mama.

That one word says it all.

THE LAST OF THE SOUTH TOWN RINKY DINKS
THE EXTENDED VOLUME

GOD AND MAMA

LENA VIOLA WALKER HARP
FEBRUARY 19, 1899 - JUNE 12, 1985

Dedicated to Lena Viola Harp, the woman a lot of rag tag South Town Rinky Dink kids called Mama. I am sure that Mama is living in one of the finest shotgun mansions in Heaven. She is dressed in pure white un-starched robes, with a golden halo gleaming above her head and great wings upon her back. And if God truly has the ultimate wisdom He is supposed to have, I'm sure that He consults with her each time He gets in over his head, not only when he is attempting to deal with one of Heaven's Children, but on any matter that requires an uncommon amount of common sense, enough love to share with everyone, and the ability to make other people feel important and needed.

GOD AND MAMA

God saw Mama coming and He met her at the gate
He took her hand and said "Come on in, another minute would have been too late.
For tomorrow with the rising sun, Judgment day begins,
And tonight I'm closing Heaven down, you're the last one who'll get in."

"You're closing Heaven down," she said, "I just don't understand.
There can't be everlasting life, without a promised land?"
But God just looked at Mama and slowly shook His head
"I'm sorry, but I've made up my mind," were the only words He said.

Then Mama looked at God and said "Tell me, would You please,
Are all my friends and loved ones here, who meant so much to me?"
God smiled and slowly stepped aside and said "Just take a look."
And sure enough she saw them all, as He had promised in His book.

For a moment or so she stood there, and she smiled and waved and at them
Then she turned and started leaving, her expression sad and grim.
God gently touched her shoulder, and said "Is something wrong?"
And Mama wept, "I can't stay here, I don't think I belong.

For although my loved ones beckon, wanting me to cross the line
There are still too many precious friends that I've just left behind.
And I promised them there'd come a day when I'd be with them again
So if you're closing Heaven down tonight, I don't guess I'll come in."

When God saw Mama leaving, he touched her once again
And said "Don't turn away my child. Come, I'll lead you in.
And there'll be room for everyone, for you have made me see
As long as there is one like you, Heaven will always be."

25

MAMA

(ONE WORD SAYS IT ALL)

Mama, this is from me and Helen and Goober, and from those of our children that had a chance to get to know you. We love you, and there isn't a day that passes that we don't think about you.

There's an old Southern saying that fits Mama to a "T."

Used to be, when country people wanted to give a woman the highest compliment they could give them, they almost invariably said the same thing;

She's a Good Woman.

That's what they always said.

They always said that about Mama, and they were right.

Mama was a good woman.

Mama wasn't a big woman, at least not in physical size, but she was a giant in all of the ways that really counted. She had to be, in order to put up with all the hardships she put with, live without all of the little things she never asked for, and never expected to get, and most of all, she had to be a giant of a woman to have put up with a lot of the things Daddy did.

Now it's important that you don't get me wrong on this one. Daddy wasn't a mean man, not to Mama or to any of the kids, and to the best of my knowledge he never cheated on her, not in the fifty-nine years they were married. And I never once, not in my entire life, saw Daddy raise a hand to strike Mama.

He just wasn't that kind.

But Daddy was a stubborn man, opinionated and out-spoken, and a man that wanted his own way most of the time.

Daddy went fishing a lot, but seldom took us with him. He hunted, but we never went along. He went to Florida every five or so years to visit his brother Esco, but we never made the trip with him. He worked hard, and always kept food on the table, the bills paid, and clothes on our back, but the rest of his money he spent on whatever he wanted to. Which was usually fishing or beer.

And I guess that was all right with Mama, at least she never seemed to mind. She stayed at home and raised her kids, and seldom if ever complained about her lot in life.

That by itself is a testimony to the kind of woman she was. Maybe not by today's strange set of politically correct rules, but by the standards of her day she was a good wife and mother in every sense of the word.

I guess the best way to tell this story is to start by saying that Daddy was a carpenter, a good one, and he busted his butt for $1.50 or $2.00 an hour for years building and remodeling houses in and around Springfield. Daddy very seldom complained about how much money he made, but after I grew up I learned that he could have made a heck of a lot more money working somewhere other than Springfield. For some reason, it never occurred to me to ask him why he didn't pack up Mama and his family and leave the little one horse town. Years later I finally came to understand why. It's because Springfield was home. That's where most of the family lived, and where most of the rest were buried. Mama and Daddy couldn't leave Springfield, they had spent too many years there, and there were too many drops of their blood soaked into the South Town dirt for them to ever let go.

Besides, Mama let me in on a secret.

Once I asked her the question about leaving Springfield, and the answer she gave me is not what I expected. It took me a long time to accept it, but I guess I accept it now, and I'd like to pass it along.

Mama, why didn't you and Daddy just pack up and leave this old dried up little town? You'd have been a lot better off if you had.

I was about twenty when I asked this question.

Mama would have been about sixty-two at this time, and her answer was typical of the way she always managed to get me thinking.

Would we? How do you figure, she replied.

Well, for one thing, Daddy could have made a lot more money in a city than he did here.

Maybe so. Probably so. So what?

So what. So what? You could have bought a lot more stuff that you wanted.

Maybe so. So what?

Mama, what are you talking about?

Honey, we didn't like the big city when we lived in Detroit back during the war, and we never did want to live in Nashville, so that only left Springfield.

Naw, Mama, it didn't. You could have moved to some other country town. It didn't have to be a big city. Any place would have been better than Springfield.

Mama looked at me for a long couple of minutes.

Honey, I don't know if I can explain it or not, but let me try. You see, there aren't any other country towns. All of them are Springfield. They've all got the same little shotgun houses, the same Main Street, the same movie house, and the same ball games. You can only do what you can do, no matter where you are. You can move a hundred miles away, or a thousand, and except for the weather, things are always going to be pretty much the same. You see, you can change towns, but it's a lot harder to change yourself. If we'd have moved fifty times, every little town would have had a bunch of kids that looked just like the ones in the town we just left behind. The schools would have taught reading and writing and arithmetic, and your Daddy would have still been a carpenter, building houses for other people.

So why move? It doesn't matter what a town's name is, they're all the same. That's because people are the same.

They laugh when they're happy, cry when they're sad, cuss bad luck, and give thanks to God for good luck.

So in my opinion, honey, it doesn't matter where people live. All country towns are Springfield, regardless of what name is written on the maps.

So, there's no sense moving around all over the map, when all little towns are the same. Besides, this is where everyone is buried. We can't just move off and leave them alone, now can we?

That's it. That was her secret. She understood that there is something about all of us that will cause us to live our lives much the same, regardless of what town we live in. We are creatures of habit, not very much given to change, and those habits and un-changing traits will determine what we do. And what we do is all that we will do, in whatever town we call home.

So the only thing that can really make you choose one town over another is where the people you love live, and where the rest of the people you love are buried, and that's why we never moved to some other little town.

Looking back, I think that's probably why I stayed there for most of my life too.

Mama and Daddy were married in 1919, and lived in Portland, Tennessee for a short while before moving to Springfield. When they did move here, it was in a horse drawn wagon, and it took them all day to make the trip. They packed up everything they owned and came to Springfield to make a better life for themselves. And I guess they did.

Like I said, Daddy was a carpenter, and a good one, and Mama stayed at home and raised the family. Over the years, she also helped raise a lot of other kids who lived in South Town.

She never once, that I can ever remember, failed to offer anyone whatever help she could give. She never turned anyone away from her door, and she always managed to find enough food to set just one more plate, every time someone came to our house hungry.

I don't recall her ever saying anything bad about anyone. Not that she liked everyone she knew, it's just that she didn't believe in saying bad things about people.

She gave advice when people needed advice, listened when they just needed to talk, and she always knew the difference.

She was a strong woman, she had to be, and once I asked her the secret of her strength.

I'm not really strong, she said, it's just that most of the time when something really bad happens there's only two ways you can handle it.

You can live through it, or you can kill yourself. I've always chosen to live through it.

I thought that made a lot of sense.

And Mama had to live through an awful lot.

She was the oldest in a family of sixteen children, and outlived all of them but one. That means she saw fifteen brothers and sisters die. (Note: I can only find thirteen children in any records, but according to everyone there are three more.)

Not only that, but she also saw three of her children and two of her grand children pass away, as well as both of her parents, Daddy's mother, and I don't know how many other relatives.

In one ten or twelve year period during the forties and early fifties, Mama lost eleven members of her immediate family. Eleven members. She lost both parents, two children, two grandchildren, and five brothers or sisters. That averages out to over one death per year, for over ten years.

Several of the deaths were exceptionally hard one's to deal with.

Mama and Daddy had four children, in this order.

William Norman was the first born, Carlos Odell, the one they called Kink, was born second, Shirley Ann, the only girl, was born third, and I was born last. Mama was 42 when I came along, and over the years many a joke was made about either Mama or Daddy, or maybe both, being middle aged crazy.

The way her children died must have been almost unbearable, and more than any parents should have to undergo.

Shirley Ann was the first of the children to die. She was a precious little baby girl, not quite three, and was Mama's pride and joy.

Shirley Ann had a penny. An Indian head penny. She kept it under the tablecloth on the corner of the eating table. Two or three times a day, someone would say something about her penny and she would go and check to be sure it was still there.

And it always was.

Shirley Ann died in Mama's arms as they crossed the bridge over the Cumberland River heading into Nashville. Shirley Ann had developed pneumonia and the doctor in Springfield had done all he could do. Their only hope was to get her to Vanderbilt Hospital in Nashville immediately. Willard drove Mama and Daddy and Shirley as quickly as he could, but they didn't quite make it. Mama once told me that she was holding Shirley as tightly against her breast as she could, and that she felt it when the life left her tiny body.

Mama kept the penny in a little bag that she had in her small mantle cedar chest. Now and then she would take out the penny and sit and hold it. Most of the time she'd cry. She didn't know I watched, but sometimes I did.

I have the penny now. Sometimes I take it out and hold it, and sometimes I cry. I have a feeling that Mama knows I still have it, and how much it means to me.

It's a 1907 Indian head penny.

Oh yes, I have the small cedar chest too.

Carlos was fated to be the next to leave her.

Carlos was seventeen when he got into some trouble in Springfield, and rather than see him go to jail, Mama signed the papers for him to join the army. She regretted it the rest of her life.

Carlos was killed in a country half way around the world from Springfield, and Mama never forgave herself for signing the papers that sent him there.

Later, and more than once, she told me that if she had it to do over, she'd rather see him prison than dead.

The way he died was heartbreaking.

According to the story, he was assigned to a chemical division and had been on the front line for over thirty days without getting a scratch, laying down smoke screens between our troops and the enemy.

On the thirty-first day they were relieved, and the next day, while they were back at their base camp, one of his buddies was cleaning his pistol and it went off and Kink was hit with the bullet. He was eighteen at the time.

Mama got the first letter from an army Chaplin telling her about the accident;

Dear Mrs. Harp,

Your son has been shot, it read.

He is in bad shape, but improving.

The second letter was from the same Chaplin, about six weeks later.

Your son is much better, and is being sent home. He is on the way at this time, and should arrive soon.

The third letter came a few days later.

Dear Mrs. Harp, it said. We regret to inform you your son had died en-route.

Cold regrets on formal Army stationary, with only a few words of explanation.

That's a pretty cruel way to receive that kind of news, wouldn't you say?

I still have the small military style letters that told the story of his death. The army said Mama was supposed to receive the Silver Star, but they never sent her one. She did get a Purple Heart medal, and she kept it and the flag the casket was draped in, but she never got over the fact that she was supposed to get the Silver Star and didn't. I'm sure you know that I still have the flag and the Purple Heart.

Norman was the last of Mama's children to die. He wasn't yet thirty. When he died, it was also a under a particularly bad set of circumstances.

Norman was married to Eva Mai, and they had already lost their first child, a daughter named Vera Mai. They had a second baby girl named Mary Evelyn, and in 1947 she got sick. When they took her to the doctor she was diagnosed with tuberculosis. She only lived a short time after that, passing away in 1948. After the funeral the doctor decided to test the other members of the family.

Norman was found to have the same disease, in a very advanced stage, and died in 1948. He was 28 years old.

So Mama and Daddy lost a son and a grandchild, and Eva Mai lost a husband and a daughter, all in the same year.

In 1969, Mama also was diagnosed with TB, and spent over nine months in the tuberculosis hospital in Nashville. She got well and came home in 1970, and it wasn't long after that that a vaccine or medicine was found to treat TB. With the new vaccine you could stay at home, and not nearly as many people died from it.

Mama's brother Paul was killed during World War II while serving on the USS Birmingham. The way we heard it, the Birmingham went to the aid of another ship and took a hit herself from a Japanese Kamikaze plane, and suffered an explosion during the rescue operation. They said the decks ran deep with blood, and that most of the sailors never knew what hit them.

Her brother Boyd had a heart attack one day while laying concrete blocks. They took him to the doctor and the doctor told him he'd have to take it easy for a while.

He did.

He took it easy for about two or three days, then he went back to laying blocks. Said his family had to eat.

He never finished the job. Had a massive heart attack and collapsed on the job, some say with a concrete block in each hand, and there was nothing they could do to save him. He was in his forties.

Of course Daddy was going through all of this too, and I imagine it was the hard times and heartaches as much as anything else that turned him to drink. And did he ever drink. Daddy loved his beer, and he drank a lot of it. But he was one of those rare persons whose bodily composition was such that beer didn't seem to bother him at all. He could drink beer for hours on end, and almost never showed any signs of having had a drink at all.

Whiskey was another story. Whiskey made Daddy drunk, and you could tell it. But he didn't drink very much whiskey. He would now and then, but mostly he drank beer. He knew Mama wouldn't say very much about beer, and he also knew she hated to see him drunk.

I've seen Daddy drunk on many occasions though.

THE LAST OF THE SOUTH TOWN RINKY DINKS
THE EXTENDED VOLUME

I remember we went to town one Saturday afternoon and Daddy parked the car down on Richard Street, which is two blocks from Main Street. We went to the Midway Cafe for chili and then went to the show, and somewhere along the way Daddy got hold of a pint of whiskey. He drank most of it at the show, I guess, and by the time the movie was over, he couldn't remember where he'd parked the car.

Mama wouldn't tell him. She didn't want to ride with him when he was drunk, and she surely didn't want me in the car. So we walked home. It was only about a mile, the weather was warm, and no one would bother us, so we walked home.

Daddy walked back to town the next day and found the car and drove it home, and never mentioned it again.

Daddy chewed tobacco, but he didn't smoke. He worked in the tobacco factories in the fall, stripping it and grading it, getting it ready to sell. Now and then, he'd bring home a few large leaves of tobacco and twist it into home made twists. He kept the twists hanging in the back room at the house, and now and then he'd take one down and cut off a piece and stick it in the top pocket of his bib overalls. That was some of the strongest tobacco you could ever imagine. If some of the kids today who take delight in Copenhagen or Skoal could cut a big old chaw off of one of Daddy's home made twists and stick it in their mouth, it might change their minds about using tobacco.

Daddy was born Birtle Odell Harp on August 8th, 1901, and passed away on Valentines day, February 14th, 1978. He always told us that he was a direct descendant of the infamous Harp Brothers who raised so much cain and killed so many people in Southern Kentucky and Northern Tennessee in the late 1700's. I've traced the connection and the names seem to bear out his story, so I have no reason to doubt that he was correct when he said the Harp family had some very bad blood.

I know there were a few strange things about Daddy, and one of the strangest came some thirteen years after he died.

For most of my life, whenever I did anything that particularly pleased Daddy, his only response was "Well, alright son." He always said the same thing.

In 1981, Helen and my fourth child was born.

Derek Andrew Harp, named in part after my grandfather, was born September 9, 1981 at Jesse Holman Jones Hospital in Springfield.

Helen and I were at the hospital, and Helen's sister Magdalene was staying at our house with our daughter Nikki. The only other person at the house was Mama, so that meant that the only people at home were women.

At about ten minutes before midnight, I called home to let them know that we had a beautiful baby boy.

I dialed the phone and listened as it rang at the house.

It was then something really strange happened.

A male voice answered.

Hello, the heavy male voice said.

Not thinking, I happily replied;

It's a boy, we have a boy.

And the voice answered;

Well, alright son.

Then I heard another receiver picked up.

It was Mama.

Mama, we've got a baby boy, I said.

That's wonderful, Honey, I'll see you soon.

Mama, who answered the other phone?

Why no one answered it, Honey, she said, Everyone is asleep.

But...

I went back into Helen's room, where she was just now beginning to come out from under the influence of the medication.

I stood at the foot of her bed as she began to wake up, and her first words were;

Donald, Pappy knows we have a baby boy.

Helen, like some others in the family, always called Daddy "Pappy."

And those were her very words. Still half asleep from the medication, she somehow came to with Daddy on her mind.

Later I told her the story of the telephone.

Mama smoked a pack of cigarettes a day. And later, sometimes she smoked two packs. She smoked for over fifty years, and they never seemed to hurt her at all. I guess cigarettes, like most bad habits, affect different people in different ways.

Once, when Mama was eighty-one, she got sick and had to go to the hospital. When she drifted off to sleep, the nurse came in and took away her pack of cigarettes.

When Mama woke up, the first thing she did was reach for a cigarette. Not finding the pack where she'd left it, she quietly got out of bed, put on her robe, and went out into the hall. Slowly she made her way to the nurse's desk, stopped long enough to spot her pack of cigarettes lying on the table behind the desk, and then walked behind the desk and picked them up.

I think these are mine, she said, and walked back to her room.

Later the doctor came in.

Mrs. Harp, he said, you've got to quit smoking. They're very bad for your health. It's been proven that smoking will kill you.

Doctor, I'm eighty-one years old, I've been smoking over fifty years, and I don't expect to live forever. Got a light?

The next year, she went into the hospital again.

This time with a circulation problem in her right leg.

It was February.

After two days of examination, the same doctor gave her his diagnosis.

Mrs. Harp, you have almost no circulation in your right leg. I'm afraid it's going to set up blood poisoning.

What are you telling me, doctor? she asked.

Mrs. Harp, I think we're going to have to take off your right leg just below the knee, or you may die from the infection.

Doctor, would have the nurse get my clothes?

Didn't you hear me? Mrs. Harp, he inquired. If we don't remove your leg, you may die.

I am going to die, Doctor, one day, all of us are. But I'm not going to die right now, and not from blood poisoning. And you're not going to cut off my leg. I was born with two legs, when I die, I'll die with two legs. Whether it's tonight or next week, or next year. But Doctor, I know that in about a month the weather will change. We'll get a few nice warm days and then my circulation will be fine. We'll just have to doctor it till then.

And that's what they did.

A homebound nurse came by the house three times a week and gave Mama therapy for her circulation, and when the weather broke, her circulation got just fine. She didn't die that year, or the next, and when Mama finally died, it wasn't from blood poisoning, and she still had both legs.

Mama had only completed either the ninth or tenth grade in school, but she was one of the smartest persons I ever knew. She had an appetite for reading that never diminished. She read anything and everything she could get her hands on, and remembered almost everything she ever read. She worked the daily newspaper crossword every day for years, right up until the time she had her stroke.

And she passed that love of reading on to me. We didn't have television, and instead of listening to the radio, Mama would hold me on her lap and read to me. Mostly she read the daily newspaper. In fact the first word I said was "Popeye."

Mama swears I knew my letters before I was three, and could already read two or three word sentences. She took great delight in holding me up to the window of the bus on our way back from Detroit and having me read highway signs to the other passengers. I was somewhere in the neighborhood of twenty-eight months old.

Mama also liked to write. I used to have a few little stories she wrote, but the last time I looked they weren't with the rest of the things I've managed to keep. I don't understand why, because I never throw away anything like that. I guess I inherited my love of writing from her as well, and I only wish she could have read this book.

THE LAST OF THE SOUTH TOWN RINKY DINKS
THE EXTENDED VOLUME

Mama dearly loved Elmer Hinton, a columnist who wrote for the Tennessean, the daily Nashville newspaper, and she wrote to his column on a semi-regular basis.

Once when Mister Hinton went on vacation Mama missed his column, and wrote him a poem upon his return. He published Mama's poem in his column on Thursday, October 10, 1963. The poem follows.

"I want to say I'm glad you're back,

I liked your fill-in but he seemed to lack

Your brand of corn, and corn I dig,

From the hill to the still

To the very last swig.

About hootenanny...

It makes me long for a gun that will shoot

For that kind of stuff, I don't give a hoot."

Mama also won five dollars once by writing a letter to Mister Hinton's column explaining her feelings on war.

I think it's safe to say that 21st.Avenue wouldn't have been the same without Mama.

She was the one the kids talked to when no one else would listen, and the one who talked to them when no one else paid them any attention. She always made time for people, regardless of how little time she had to call her own, and she never condemned folks for bad habits or bad judgment.

She fed people, she let people sleep on her floor, and she took them in out of the cold when they had no place to warm up.

And she was loved for these things.

I could write about Mama for months and never say all I wanted to, and probably never capture her spirit at all. She was such a multi-faceted person that to try to categorize her would be a pretty stupid thing for me to do. I'll leave you with one more story of Mama, and let you draw your own conclusions.

All of us always depended on Mama, and she was there each time she was needed. At the most heartbreaking times, she held us together, and she always held us close to her heart. Shirley Ann was resting in Mama's lap when she died. Kink's last letter was to Mama, and Norman was lying in Mama's bed when he drew his last breath. Mama held Daddy's hand right up to the last, and they would have been married for 59 years the year that Daddy passed away.

She lived her life for all of us, and never, not once, asked for anything at all from any of us.

Mama was born Lena Viola Walker on February 19, 1899, and died June 12, 1985, at the age of 86. She always joked about being "one year older than time" because, being born in 1899, she was always a year ahead of whatever year it was.

She died in the same way as she lived, watching after one of her kids.

This time it was me.

As I've explained several times, it was typical of many in Mama's family to develop heart problems early, and I'm sure she spent many hours hoping that it wouldn't catch up with me, but it did.

On January 14th, 1985, at about 9:30 AM, at the age of 43, I suffered a heart attack. It was bad enough to send me to the hospital for twelve days, and it was along around the first of February when I finally got back home.

Mama was waiting.

She walked the floor, and she stood by my bed, and she held my hand, and sometimes she cried.

One day, in mid February, her tiny body finally gave in to the temptation to shut down. She stood by the couch in the living room, in plain sight of the bed where I lay, and took one look at me, turned toward the couch and collapsed. She had suffered a massive stroke.

We had always said that we would never put Mama in a nursing home, but her condition was such that there was no way we could care for her at home.

During the next few months, I suffered several more, less serious, heart attacks, and Mama remained unconscious.

THE LAST OF THE SOUTH TOWN RINKY DINKS
THE EXTENDED VOLUME

In early June, I had another, more serious attack, and had to go back into the hospital. On June 5th, the doctors at Centennial Medical Center in Nashville performed an angioplasty on my heart, which nearly cost me my life.

I went into the operating room knowing that the procedure was potentially dangerous, but that almost everyone made it with very few complications.

An angioplasty is where they insert a tiny balloon type device into an artery of your heart and then inflate the balloon, thereby opening the artery and allowing the blood to circulate better.

It should have been rather simple.

But not this time.

When the doctor inflated the balloon the first time, the artery opened just fine. When he went to the second blockage and inflated the balloon, the first place he had worked on collapsed.

I actually heard the nurse say;

He's fibrillating.

Sometimes it doesn't pay to understand what people are talking about. But I did.

I felt, rather that saw, some one lean over me and pound on my chest, trying to re-start my heart.

They had to use the electric de-fibrillaters and shock me three or four times before my heart finally picked up the beat and kept going on its own.

This was sometime between eight and nine o'clock AM.

At exactly that same time, in the nursing home in Springfield, Mama had a relapse, and had to be rushed to the hospital.

I lay in the hospital in Nashville until June 12, and Mama lay in the hospital in Springfield the entire time.

When I was released, I didn't even stop at home, I went straight to the Springfield hospital and to Mama's side. I sat there with her for several hours, until finally I had to go home to rest.

The strangest thing happened at the hospital.

For the first time since she'd had the stroke, Mama woke up that evening. I sat there holding her hand, and unbelievably her blue eyes opened and stared up at me. Her eyes were clear and filled with much more emotion than mere words can ever say.

Donald? Honey, are you all right? Softly and tenderly she whispered the words.

Yes Mama, I'm fine. How do you feel.

I feel just fine now, Honey, just fine.

Her eyes closed again. Those few words and she was satisfied.

At about eleven thirty that night, they called from the hospital to tell me that Mama had died.

I wished it were me instead.

There is one thing of which I am totally convinced.

Mama was only waiting for me to get over the worst of my illness before she turned loose of the fragile hold she still held on life. She knew what was going on with me, every step of the way. Her love transcended the physical aspects of the stroke, and somehow she stood watch on the last of her children until she knew everything was all right. Then, reassured and ready to go, she turned loose.

I once had a dream that Daddy came to get Mama, and she was hiding from him. The night she died, I swear they were both standing at the foot of my bed, watching me sleep.

I'm reasonably sure that they're together again, and she's watching over her family from whatever home God prepared for her.

My mind, my imagination, and most of my personality was shaped by Mama, and there isn't a day that passes that I don't stop and look at her picture, and know that she is still with me, and always will be.

Mama, this book is for you. I know you're reading over my shoulder as I write, and if these words please you as much as I want them to, then I'll be satisfied.

More than anything else, Mama, I love you and I miss you. I'm sure you know that all of us that are still here miss you just as much. Helen talks about you often, and I sometimes catch Shelly, when she visits with us, staring at your picture, and I know she is remembering. Jason hardly ever says anything about the past, but when he does it's always about you and Daddy. Nikki and Derek also remember you, although they didn't know Daddy, and now and then they ask me some little thing and I find myself parroting words you spoke to me at some time or other. And so you see, your influence lives on, and always will, in our hearts and in our actions, and the things you taught us are passed on time and time again.

One thing you will find typical.

When Nikki's baby girl was born in 2000, she was a 7 month baby and only weighed 4 pounds. She is named Braxten, and she and Nikki live with us.

When Brax was first learning to walk and talk, I once told her a story about her "Nenie" and later that day I found her looking at your picture.

I walked over.

What are you doing, baby.

Nenie, she said, pointing at the picture.

We hadn't told her which one was you.

I suppose your love is never far removed from our home, and I think even the children, or maybe especially the children, understand that.

Goober (Please forgive me just one more time Ray) has read much of this book as I was writing it, and there is no doubt in my mind that he and Pat miss you and Daddy as much as anyone does. Eva Mai is and always will be his mother, but first, last, and always, he still calls you Mama.

As the last of your natural born children, and as one of the last of the South Town Rinky Dink's, I dedicate the stories, the memories, the laughter, the tears, and all the rest to you.

If I know you, I'm sure you'll enjoy my small effort at telling about the things you loved so much.

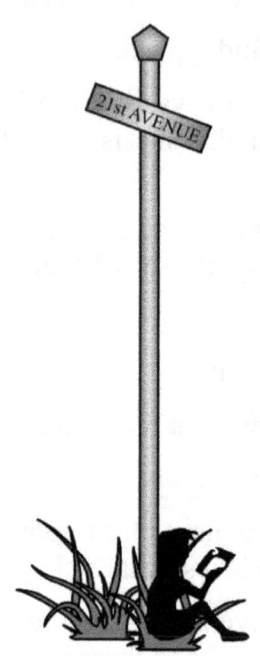

THE LAST OF THE SOUTH TOWN RINKY DINKS

SUPLEMENTS

This book has been an ongoing experience for me, and in the years I've compiled it and written it, I've been asked to recall another few things. I've placed three stories here at the end of the book, but I think they are as much a part of the Rinky Dink legend as any of the others.

SUPLEMENT 1
THE SOUTH TOWN WOODS

The South Town Woods was a place that was almost magical to many of the kids in South Town. On occasion when we didn't have anything else to do or sometimes if we just felt like a little adventure we took a hike to the woods and spent a few hours in a world all our own.

The woods were across 22nd Avenue from Woodland Street School, just behind the row of houses that lined the street. A quick run of a hundred yards or so from the street and we could put civilization behind us and pretend we were anything or anyone we wanted to be.

The woods brought up images of Tarzan and the great apes, and jungle rivers where danger lurked behind every bush and tree. There were lions and elephants and rhinos in the clearing just over the next hill, and in our minds they were as real as the trees, the green grass, and the rolling hills of the woods.

There was an old saw mill at the edge of the woods on Highway 431, which was later closed down, but I remember walking by and watching the lumber being trimmed into boards when I was younger.

There was also an old log house close to the sawmill, but I don't remember anyone ever living there. It was also torn down a few years later in the name of progress.

There was an old barn on top of one of the hills in the woods, and we spent many hours looking into the open window of the hay loft, imagining what might have happened there over the years.

Someone had told us that the barn had been used as a stop on the road North when they were taking slaves out of the South, and that one or two slaves had actually been hung from a beam in the top of the hay loft. I don't know if any of this was true or not, but after we had heard that sometimes at night you could see a ghostly figure gently swinging in the wind, suspended from a rope high in the barn, we tended to not get too close to the barn after dark.

None of us ever actually saw anything at all in the barn, but most of the time we pretended that we did, and it was a great tale to tell the younger kids.

There was also an old cemetery in the woods, back a little closer to Woodland Street, and once or twice we cleaned off a few of the tombstones and tried to figure out who was buried there, and when they had been buried. Most of the tombstones were too worn to read any of the letters, and I don't recall if we ever found out even one name. I also don't know what happened to the cemetery when they cleared the area in order to build a shopping center on the property.

It was in these woods that I tried to fly on my large kite, in fact it was from the same hill where the haunted barn stood, but perhaps the second most memorable event that happened in the South Town woods was the afternoon Wesley Birdwell and I had a run in with the large bull who roamed one of the fields.

We knew the bull was there, and we knew we had been told he was mean, but for some reason we still took a walk directly across his territory, and almost paid a huge price for it.

The wire fence around the field was four and a half to five feet tall, and about forty or fifty yards out in the field there was a large haystack. Playing on the haystack was what lured us out there, but spending a few minutes lying on our backs in the sun on top of the hay just wasn't worth the run we had a few minutes later.

THE LAST OF THE SOUTH TOWN RINKY DINKS
THE EXTENDED VOLUME

We had climbed the fence, walked across the field to the haystack, and had settled in to just do nothing. We were watching the skies for airplanes, talking about ball games and just passing the time, when all at once we noticed that the big black bull had noticed us.

He was standing across the field, staring directly at us, and you can believe we were staring back at him.

It was only a matter of a few minutes before he got curious enough to come on over and see if we were something he could either run out of his field or maybe just kill

He started over, but he was walking, and I took a quick look at the fence, and wouldn't you know it, it was now three or four miles away from us. Well. maybe not, but when a large angry bull is headed in your direction, a few yards seems a heck of a lot farther.

Uh, Wesley, you think we might be able to make it to the fence, I asked? Wesley? But I was talking to where Wesley had been. By the time I saw him, he was scrambling down off the hay, and eying the fence. I immediately knew he was going to make a run for it.

I knew the bull was faster than either of us, but in a moment of extreme clarity, I realized I didn't have to out run the bull to the fence. I just had to out run Wesley. And I knew for a fact that I could do that. I was a swift little rascal, and with the fear of the bull lending wings to my feet, I was pretty sure I had a better than average chance of getting to the fence before either Wesley or the bull.

I've already said that with me to think is to act, and I hit the ground at full speed only a few steps behind Wesley, and a few yards ahead of the bull.

We weren't half way to the fence when I passed Wesley, but I sure didn't look back to see where the bull was.

I didn't hesitate when I reached the fence, and while I don't know exactly how high is was, I've written elsewhere in this book that I had won a ribbon in the high jump at the field day down at the high school, and I cleared the fence with room to spare.

There were a few small sapling trees along the fence line, and one fairly large Maple tree with a branch some ten or twelve feet off the ground.

When I hit the ground on the other side of the fence I could hear the bulls huge paws pounding the ground, headed for us as fast as he could come. I knew he'd stop at the fence, so I wasn't worried about myself, but I couldn't see Wesley. He wasn't on the ground, and the bull wasn't goring him to death in the field, and in fact, he was nowhere to be seen.

Until I looked up, that is.

He was dangling from the lowest limb of the Maple tree, scrambling as quickly as he could to get his legs locked around the limb and then on up into the tree. Once in the tree, it would be simple to go out on a larger limb and jump over the fence to safety.

Which is what he did.

Now, I thought I had made a pretty good high jump by clearing the fence, but when we looked back at the limb Wesley had jumped to, we saw that he had to have gotten his hands at least as high as a basket ball goal in order to grab the limb. I'd say that was also a pretty good jump for a small kid.

We never told our parents about the encounter with the bull, but you can bet that was one area, and one field in the South Town woods we never visited again.

THE LAST OF THE SOUTH TOWN RINKY DINKS
THE EXTENDED VOLUME
SUPLEMENT 2

THE CARR'S CREEK CRITTER

1966 was the year the infamous Carr's Creek Critter made the local news and had the people of Springfield and the surrounding communities up in arms. And I mean that quite literally. We really were up in arms for a month or so that spring and summer.

Late spring and through the early days of July brought such traffic through a couple of the back roads of Robertson County that by the 4th of July, the police were cruising the narrow gravel roads trying to make sure no one actually got hurt. I always suspected they were trying to catch a glimpse of the critter itself, although I'm sure they would have denied it.

Shelly was a baby that spring, having been born on March 9, and Mama kept her anytime we wanted to go look for the critter, which was almost every night.

But I'm getting ahead of myself.

The Carr's Creek Critter is a story worth telling, but you have to remember that we are talking about the Rinky Dinks here, and not a bunch of sophisticated men who actually had a clue about whatever was going on.

To the best of my knowledge, Charles Lee Hutton and his girlfriend Brenda Taylor were the first people in town to actually come in contact with the critter, and I was there when they first told their story.

It was sometime in mid April, and Charles and Brenda were on a date, and, as so many of us did back then, they rode out in the country to park for a while. They chose the dark, tree lined country back road called M. Etta Lahr's road. I'm not sure if that's how it's spelled or not, but if you're from Springfield, once you say the name you'll know exactly where I'm talking about.

The old gravel road called M. Etta Lahr's road was a favorite parking place for most of us, and the area around Flat Rock was one of the most popular on the road. The road is mostly single lane, covered in gravel, and twists and turns up and down hills for a couple of miles down by Carr's Creek. Carr's Creek had been a favorite swimming hole for generations of folks from Springfield, and somewhere in my collection I even have a picture of Mama in a bathing suit sitting in the cool water.

The road traverses the distance between Highway 431 and Highway 49, and once you get on the road, there are only those two ways to get off it. There was one other road that branched off the main road, but it was a dead end, and you couldn't get out of the area by going that way.

A mile or so into the road from the Highway 431 side you come to a steep and curving hill that seems to go down forever, especially if it's dark when you're there. At the bottom of the hill the road crosses Carr's Creek, and when I was younger, before the events in this story take place, you had to ford the creek, but by the time of the Critter, they had built a new concrete bridge over the creek, which made it much easier to travel the length of the road.

On the first night the Critter made its presence known, Charles and Brenda had driven past Flat Rock and parked at the bottom of the hill, in a small cleared area to the side of the road just before you crossed the bridge.

I was there when they came back to town that night, and like the others I pretty much laughed at the story they had to tell.

The story was strange sure enough, but Charles swore it was true, and Brenda backed him up. They told us that they were sitting in the car when something suddenly caused the car to rock back and forth, exactly like there was someone in the back of the car rocking it. We laughed and said it wasn't hard to figure out why the car was rocking, but they just went right on with their story. Charles said the car was rocking so hard that it would have taken two or three people to make it move like that, but he swore that when he looked in his rear view mirror he saw no one at all.

He said they were afraid to get out of the car, because they didn't know what was out there, but in a minute or so the car stopped shaking and they heard something crossing the fence off to the right of where they were parked.

Charles and Brenda got out of the car and looked in the field across the fence, and both saw a huge something, some very large white or silver gray *thing*, walking across the field.

They couldn't tell if the thing was animal, human, or what, but it was huge and was walking upright. It didn't seem to be in any hurry, and they watched it until it disappeared in the darkness.

THE LAST OF THE SOUTH TOWN RINKY DINKS
THE EXTENDED VOLUME

It was then that they came back into town to tell the story.

Of course, they came by Mama's house first, knowing they would find several of us there, and sure enough they were right.

I don't recall for sure who was there, but I do remember the reaction of those of us who heard the story. Laughter.

Sure you saw something out there, Charles, sure you did.

I did, Donald, I swear I did.

We saw something big and white walking across the field, Donald, Brenda said, and we were scared of it, so we came back to get some of y'all to go back out there with us.

Ok, I said, I'll tell you what we'll do. We'll go out there tomorrow after work and see if we can see anything. But I doubt it.

Well, we didn't get to go out the next day, in fact we didn't go back out there for about a week, and we only went back after we had heard reports of a few more people seeing some large white creature walking in the night woods.

It was about this time that the story took a really big turn.

Something, large and white, got into a goat pen and killed a couple of goats. Of course the farmer lived on Carr's Creek, and he swore he saw the critter, and took a shot at it. But either he didn't hit it or the shot didn't hurt it.

A night or so later, something got into a fight with another farmer's dogs, and killed one of them.

It was about this time that we remembered Charles and Brenda's story, and began to think of it in a "do you think they really saw something out there?" kind of way.

So we did what any red blooded, hotheaded bunch of sixties kind of guys would have done, especially if they were Rinky Dinks. We grabbed up all the guns and knives we had, jumped into our cars, and headed for M. Etta Lahr's road and our date with the Carr's Creek Critter.

We drove up and down the old gravel road twenty or thirty times, leaning out of the car windows and peering into the woods. We even looked up in the trees, but I never was sure exactly why that was. Not one report had ever said the critter might climb a tree, but what the heck, it was a possibility. We hunted the critter the next night, and the night after that, and every night for the next few weeks, but each night brought the same results. No critter.

By this time the story had spread until there were literally a couple of hundred fully armed men and women walking around in the woods, many of them with a drink or two under their belts, and more than one of them ready to shoot at anything that even resembled a critter.

I began to get worried that one or another of the hunters might actually look like the critter if one of the guys was drunk enough, and by now the rumor had also spread that there was a three hundred dollar reward for the thing, dead or alive.

Son, for three hundred dollars, we were pretty sure something was going to get killed.

I sure hope this fine couple remembers it this way, because I'm pretty sure it was them, and I'm pretty sure of the story. Anyway, one of the people who lived in the area was a young man named Johnny Haun and his wife Joyce, and one night we came up to their place and Joyce swore that something had been in her front yard and had moved the gas tank a few inches. As this was about a five hundred gallon tank, and really heavy, we knew that it had to be the critter that moved it. Hot dang, we were finally getting close.

Sure we were.

The next couple of weeks weren't much better, and by now there were so many heavily armed half drunk guys in the woods every night that a lot of us paid more attention to keeping out of the sights of their guns than we did in actually looking for the critter.

The Springfield newspaper had begun to write a few articles about the Critter, and that of course brought a flurry of hunting activity throughout a lot of June.

The last night we hunted it was sometime near the end of June, and marked about two solid months of vigilant night activity. By now, people were hearing screeching noises and various sounds, but by now, what with all the publicity, they could have been most anything, including man made.

That particular night we were riding the road on the other side of the bridge, coming back toward the creek and I was leaning out of the front window of the car with a 12 gauge shotgun when I suddenly saw two large glowing eyes directly in my line of fire. I had already begun to squeeze the trigger when the cars lights swung far enough around that I could see the huge, very scary, very ugly, great big Carr's Creek black angus cow that I was about to kill. Wow, I thought, I never would have gotten that cow paid for.

Getting ourselves back together, we slowly pulled about a mile on up the road, got out of the car, took a few long pulls on whatever bottles we had with us, and were just about to head for the house when we heard gunfire.

Somebody's found it, one of us yelled, and we jumped in the car as fast as we could and headed in the direction of the shots.

We slid to a halt in the gravel at a spot that was close to where the shots were fired, jumped out of the car and ran up a small hill, wondering if we'd finally get the chance to see this thing that had become an obsession with us over the past few weeks.

We could hear very little as we moved down the other side of the hill toward a small pond, but as we got closer we could see a man standing there, his rifle pointing in the direction of the water, and as we came to a stop he fired again.

I carefully brought my flashlight out across the water, and sure enough, we could see the dead creature lying half in and half out of the pond. In fact, there were several critters lying about on the muddy bank. But they weren't large, or white, of furry, or any of the things we were expecting. They were rather small, and green, had long hind legs and looked exactly like a bunch of…frogs.

It was Bud Bollinger standing there with the smoking gun, and a Camel cigarette dangling from the corner of his mouth.

Think Miss Lena will mind cooking up a mess of frog legs, Donald, he asked, as he drew a bead on another of the tasty little critters?

Nope, Bud, I don't think she'll mind at all.

We loaded up and went on home, and to the best of my knowledge the frogs were the only victims of the famous Carr's Creek Critter hunt.

About a week later, on the Fourth of July, the local radio station placed a car at both ends of M. Etta Lahr's road to count the traffic, and they say they counted over eleven hundred cars that drove the infamous route that night.

We weren't among them.

The Carr's Creek Critter never did get caught or killed, and the Rinky Dinks moved on to bigger and better things, but I don't think any of us ever parked down by the bridge on M. Etta Lahr's road again.

THE LAST OF THE SOUTH TOWN RINKY DINKS
THE EXTENDED VOLUME
SUPLEMENT 3

THE RINKY DINKS TAKE THE PLUNGE
(THE OLE SWIMMING HOLE)

Most of the South Town Rinky Dinks swam in Carr's Creek or Sulfur Fork Creek one of the swimming holes at Red River, and spent many a Sunday afternoon swinging from a rope into the cool water of Hill's Mill. The millpond was a deep hole that was perfect for the swing, and we swam there for years. I seem to remember that we only stopped going there when the creek area become overrun with snakes.

We also loved to go to the rock quarry just outside Adams, Tennessee, because there were high cliffs that we could jump or dive off of. I was never quite up to jumping form the tallest cliff, which was about 100 feet high, but I did manage to go off of a spot about 30 – 40 feet high quite often.

The rock quarry was a favorite swimming hole for many of the paratroopers stationed at nearby Fort Campbell, Kentucky, and some of them would occasionally jump from the 100-foot high cliff, yelling their famous "Geronimo" cry as they fell toward the water.

I don't recall ever seeing anyone get hurt diving off the high rock cliffs, but the story was that one soldier was killed when he dove off the 100-foot high side and hit the water wrong. I have no idea if this was true or not, it could have been, or it may have just been a story told to try and prevent us from diving off the high cliff.

The rock quarry was very deep and very cold, as it had filled from an underground spring the workers had hit while excavating rock. There was supposed to be a bulldozer at the bottom that the workers had to abandon as the hole filled up so quickly. There were several old cars at the bottom of the quarry as well, most of them stolen and pushed off the cliff to hide. You could see dark objects somewhere deep in the water, and we always thought they were the stolen cars.

The strange thing is that we also quit going to the rock quarry to swim because of snakes. The hot rocks made it an ideal breeding ground for the snakes, and there were simply too many to kill to make it worthwhile. Not to mention that we never knew when we would be lying on a towel getting a little sun and find that we had a copperhead lying beside us. I suppose they were getting a little sun also, and we didn't want to intrude upon their space.

As we grew older we started to leave the creeks and rock quarries behind and began to go to the Springfield Swimming Pool. As I recall, at that time it only cost a quarter to get in, and while there was no rope swing, there were also no rocks to bruise your feet on, and you didn't have to share your space with a 5-foot long snake. These two features made the pool an acceptable alternative to Carr's Creek, and from the time I was in about the 10th grade I spent a lot of time in the water.

We went everyday that we could scrape together enough money, and if we were ever concerned about the effect the hot Tennessee sun was having on our bodies, I don't remember it. We were all as tanned as hickory nuts, and no one thought anything about skin cancer or what we were doing to ourselves.

Although we swam there most days, the best times I remember at the pool was after we grew older, and discovered the joys of night swimming.

I remember going to the pool just as the sun went down, when the hot summer weather made night swimming delightful. I also recall that there were nights when the weather was not quite so hot, and those nights we stayed in the water so that only the top half of our body or maybe just our shoulders were exposed, and that's all that would be shivering from the cool night breeze that blew through the hollow where the pool was located.

I remember moving as close to my girlfriend as I could to capture a bit more warmth, and of course just to feel her smooth skin next to my own in the water as we listened to the music floating on the air as effortlessly as the lifeguard sometimes floated in the water. I remember holding hands underwater as we sang along with the songs, and a long kiss or two, first stolen and then reciprocated.

I remember myself, Kenneth Carroll, Bobby Dean Pentecost, Porter Henderson, Melvin Tanner and Wayne Wilson running the mile from uptown Springfield to the pool, and then creeping through the trees as we approached the pool from the back side, finally climbing over the fence and sneaking into the pool in the hours after midnight. As we cooled down after our efforts, we could feel the tension in the air as we tried to be as quiet as possible, hoping that no one would catch us.

THE LAST OF THE SOUTH TOWN RINKY DINKS
THE EXTENDED VOLUME

We swam with one eye on the water and the other watching for the police patrol car that made its rounds every night, shining its long beamed searchlight across the dark waters, trying to catch just such juvenile delinquents as we in the act of swimming. But of course, as we were waiting for the patrol, each time we saw them coming we sank into the water until only our noses were above the water line, and we were never caught.

We didn't think of a little bit of night swimming as stealing anything, and we never once broke into the pool building or took anything that happened to be lying around. We went for the cool water and the hot rush we got just waiting for the patrol, knowing that if we were seen we would have to try and grab a few clothes and our shoes and try to make it over the back fence and through the trees to safety. We were pretty sure that even if we were caught the worst that would happen would be that our parents would be called, or we would have to go explain ourselves to Coach Smith or Mr. Koss the next day.

In my opinion there have never been two finer men in Springfield than Coach Smith and Peter Koss, and I'd like to add a third to that list. I don't recall if he was associated with the pool or not, but Jimmy Suter was as good a man and as good a teacher as ever graced the halls of a high school anywhere.

I remember Jerry and Jimbo Pearson swimming at the pool, and was there the day Jerry dived off the high board and collided head first with Joe Brown, who happened to be swimming almost directly under the board.

Blood was everywhere, and for a few minutes I thought that one or maybe both of them were dead, but other than a fine scar or so, neither of them suffered any lasting repercussions, at least none that I know of.

In less than an hour Jerry was back on the board, but this time he made sure Joe was swimming somewhere else.

I remember the first time I ever tried to do a one and a half summersault dive off the high board. I misjudged the amount of energy the dive would take, and actually did two complete summersaults, ending up flat out and face down and headed at the water with a great amount of speed. I think they call what I accomplished a belly buster, and I'm pretty sure it would have qualified me for the Olympics had they been holding a tryout that night, and of course, if there were a belly buster division in the Olympics swimming events.

The redness wore off in a while, and later that night I tried again, with much better results. I was never a great diver, but I could do a few basic dives, like a one and a half, a tuck away, and a backward dive. Most of the time I preferred just swimming to diving, and left the really tricky moves to the more accomplished folks.

I recall that someone once told us a story that if you laid a sheet of newspaper on the top of the water and jumped on it before it got soaked and sank, that it would be just like jumping onto flat concrete.

Of course, after hearing that, we had no choice. We had to try it. We patiently waited until the lifeguard wasn't looking, quickly laid the sheet of newspaper down and I jumped off the high board, aiming at a spot just below the center of the headline. This time I went in feet first, never thinking that if the story was true, I stood a good chance of breaking an ankle or a leg. I hit the paper, but not as solidly in the center as I would have liked, and the only thing it did was wrap around my head as I sank. I didn't break anything, but for a minute or two I was pretty sure I was going to drown. I still don't know if the story is true, but we never tried it again. Hmmm, maybe … nah, maybe not.

There were other lifeguards at the pool that I can remember, with one being a young man named Sam Traughber. Sam spent many a night watching over the kids in the pool, and although he was not as heralded as some of the more popular life guards that worked the pool, Sam did as good a job or maybe better than any of them. Sam could swim like a fish and was also a pretty good diver, and most of the time he had better form in his dives than many of the other kids, but he was never one for showing off, so most of the time he only practiced his diving after most of the kids left.

Patty Summers was also lifeguard certified and taught many of the girls at summer camp their first basic swimming strokes. My wife was one of those kids, and still remembers great summers at camp and in the pool.

As I grew older and started working in Nashville, I went to the pool less often, and had started going to other pools such as Pleasant Green Plunge or Rawlins, but the affection I and so many others had with the

THE LAST OF THE SOUTH TOWN RINKY DINKS
THE EXTENDED VOLUME

Springfield Swimming Pool will always be first in my heart, as I'm sure it will be in theirs.

That's all folks. For now.

My thanks, my admiration and my lifelong friendship is reflected in every page of this book. It has been a labor of love for me, as I recalled all those days, all those old stories, and, most of all,

THE SOUTH TOWN RINKY DINKS

You know who you are. But on the next couple of pages there's a list that I call the Rinky Dink Honor Roll, just in case you might want to take a look

THE LAST OF THE SOUTH TOWN RINKY DINKS
THE EXTENDED VOLUME

RINKY DINK HONOR ROLL

Besides the author, Don Harp, a partial listing of the South Town Rinky Dinks of the late 1940's and 1950's includes the following people. I have tried to remember as many kids as I can that lived in South Town when we were growing up, and I publicly apologize because I know I will more than likely leave some out. Please believe that it is not intentional, and that the names are in no particular order.

William Ray Harp
*Betty Mayes
*John Wesley Wilson
*Larry Wayne Wilson
Wesley Birdwell
Wayne Birdwell
Juanita Faye Birdwell
*Lawrence Thaxton
*Wanda Thaxton
*Betty Thaxton
*Billy Gragg
Helen Faye Gregory
*Patricia Parker
*David "Bill" Bollinger
*Jimmy Bollinger
Debbie Bollinger
Jerry Pearson
*Jimbo Pearson
*Jerome P. Ellis
James Walker
Virginia Gainous
Josie Walker
Tom Walker
Eddie Walker
Buford Walker
*Rodney Walker
James Bilyeu
*Jerry Mantlo
Faye Mantlo
Marjorie Fryer
*Charles Fryer
*Virginia James

THE LAST OF THE SOUTH TOWN RINKY DINKS
THE EXTENDED VOLUME

*Yvonne Davidson
*Brenda Davidson
M.L. Knight
*Michael Hayes
*Donald (Duck) Starks
*Charles Rippy
*Jerry Rippy
Harold Dean Binkley
 Faye Eden
*David Woody
*Betty Ann Woody
Joyce Woody
Danny Woody
Charles Hutton
Roger Hutton
*Anita Hutton
Spencer Hutton
Larry Evilcizer
John L. Evilcizer
*Sue Anne Evilcizer
*Betty Lynn Evilcizer
*Gary Evilcizer
Ray Harris
*Charles Harris
*Jackie Harris
*Brenda Harris
Melvin Tanner
*Carolyn Tanner
Larry Browning
Kay Wooden
Doug Wooden

Judy Tanner
*John Tanner
*Ralph Tanner
*Buddy Roland
*Mary Sue Birdwell
*Dorothy Birdwell
*Thomas Lee Birdwell
Beverly Jane Birdwell
*Junior Trogland
Sandra Fulps
Mary Sue Fulps
Patsy Smith
Edna Lois Smith
Charlie Buddy Smith
*Richard Bolton
*Joe Brown
*Leon Leftrick
*Ray Leftrick
*Faye Leftrick
*Bobby D. Pentecost
*Joyce Henderson
Betty Henderson
David Dean
*Mack Rigsby
Barbara Nell Dorris
Rachel Dorris
Winifred Croslin
Christine Croslin
The Poole sisters
Edna Blackburn
Elizabeth Blackburn
Jimmy Evans

THE LAST OF THE SOUTH TOWN RINKY DINKS
THE EXTENDED VOLUME

*Billy Hulsey
*Bobby Hulsey
*Buddy Whiting
*Tommy Lemons
*Martha Gezley
*Thomas Sircey
*Mabel Daniels
*Jerry Daniels
*Wayne Heatherly
*Ducky Heatherly
Pat Hutcherson
*Terry Hutcherson
*Jimmy Hutcherson
*Mona Raye Freeman
Patty Moats
Jimmy Carter
*Jackie Wilkison
*Bobby Wilkison
Paul Wilkison
Charles Wilkison
Linda Kay Whiting
James Blackburn
*Ricky Hutcherson
*Junior Tanner
*Terry Tanner
*Diane Tanner
*Hillis Walton
*Hank Walton
*Julius Walton
Eunice Walton
*Robert Fuqua

Stella Moss
*Mary Lee Harp
Jacqueline Harp
Wanda Harp
*Sam Harp
Walter Harp
Shirley "Bogie" Harp
Jerry Turns
*Donald Ridge
*Larry Ridge
Terry Black
Donnie Adkins
Beth Adkins
*Bobby Lee Jones
*Hix Watson
*Wayne Watson
*Ronnie Crabtree
*Bobby Pendleton
Martin Pendleton
*Marvin Pendleton
*Sue Anne Bilyeu
Charlie Bilyeu
*Jackie Flatt
*Bobby Flatt
John Wayne Allen
*Hickey McEwing
*Donald McEwing
*John Wayne Eden
Johnny Conquest
Jerry Gann
*Shadrick Dean
*Raymond Bugg

THE LAST OF THE SOUTH TOWN RINKY DINKS
THE EXTENDED VOLUME

*Rayburn Bugg
*Jerry Dozier
*Glenn Duffer
Jerry Sowell
*Faye Sowell
*Ray Sowell

* Deceased

MY THANKS

Thanks to all my friends, thanks to all of the Rinky Dinks who lived the life that inspired this book, thanks to those who contributed to it, and thanks to all of you who believed in this project. Without you it could never have happened.

E. Don Harpe

THE LAST OF THE SOUTH TOWN RINKY DINKS

EXTENDED VOLUME

E. DON HARPE

1

A RINKY DINKS FIRST LOVE
E. Don Harpe

I don't suppose there's ever been a small country town in the South, especially in the 40's and 50's, that didn't have a junkyard. The town where I was born and raised, was no exception. I used to love to go down to the corner of South Main and 20th Avenue and just wander around through all of the junked heaps and visualize them as they once were. No matter if they were rusted out, missing a door, or sitting at an odd angle with a wheel or so up on blocks, I always saw them as bright and shiny unpolished gems waiting for the touch of a master to bring them back to their former glory. When I was 14 or so I had no doubts that I could take any car on the lot and in a week or two it would be a souped up hot rod, ready to tear up gravel roads all over town.

A man named George Cox owned the local South Town junkyard, and he didn't mind if some of we kids roamed about the lot, looking at the cars and wishing, because he knew that there was at least an outside chance that one day we would come up with a few dollars and he'd be there to put us in the driver's seat.

Mister George had a garage building on the corner of the lot where a few local men could usually be found. Sometimes they drank a cold beer or two, and sometimes they shot dice. There were daily checkers games, and now and then one or two might even spend some time working on an old car. Mostly, however, they were killing time. Dressed in overalls and work shoes, they'd discuss the state of the country, talk about how hard it was to find a job in town, tell tall tales, lies, and old war stories, and just sit in the shade and let the hard scrabble days fade away.

There were cars scattered about on both sides of the street, taking up room that the large yellow sunflowers seemed determined to not let them have. The flowers dotted the empty spaces between most of the cars, and there was usually a stray dog or cat or two hanging around.

My first love, of the automobile variety of course, was an A Model Ford that someone had brushed painted white over its original black and then sold to Mister Cox when they needed a bit of money for something more pressing. The car would run, and now and then I'd talk one of the guys that worked there into starting it for me and letting me sit behind the wheel.

Now and then Mister George himself would walk over, spit a stream of brown tobacco juice, scratch his head, and say;

How's yer daddy doin', boy?

He's doin' fine, sir. Workin' fer Mister Rawls today.

How's Mz Lena?

She's good. Fixin' dinner I think.

Like that car, do ye?

Yessir, I like it a lot.

I'll let you have her cheap, son.

Yessir, wish I had the money to buy her.

Of course, cheap to him was an enormous amount to me, and I didn't have any way to come up with the cash that Mister Cox was asking for the car. Fact is, if I could have gotten my hands on the money, I'd have been driving that beautiful machine all over town the next day. I tried to save my money, but a quarter here and a nickel there didn't seem to mount up all that quickly. Besides, it was hard to keep money past Saturday afternoon, when the cowboy stars were featured at the picture show. I wanted the car, but I couldn't resist my weekly helping of Roy and Gene, and

THE LAST OF THE SOUTH TOWN RINKY DINKS
THE EXTENDED VOLUME

I might have wanted to ride Trigger as much as I wanted to drive that old Ford.

Most days I'd make the three or so blocks from our house to the junk yard just to visit with my new love. I always took the time to ask Mister Cox how he was and how his family was doing, and then I'd mosey on over to the car and just sit there for a while drinking it in. Summers in my part of the South are hot, but we didn't even know anyone who had air conditioning, so I thought nothing of spending my time outside in the sun. I've spent many pleasurable afternoons sipping on an RC Cola™, crunching a Butterfinger™ candy bar with my teeth, wiping the sweat off my forehead and swatting the gnats away, as I pictured myself waving at the girls as I peeled rubber and thundered down toward the creek. Did I mention that I was at just exactly the right age to be thinking about girls, maybe as much as I did about cars. I've always thought it was kind of unfair of God to make boys start wanting cars and girls at about the same time, but of course, I kept that opinion to myself. Neither my mother or Brother Mason, the local Baptist preacher, would have appreciated it. Perhaps God enjoys the irony, but to me having so much to want and so little chance of getting either the car or the girl is just unfair.

So, my dreams usually involved me in the car, with at least two and sometimes three of the neighborhood beauties in the seat beside me. Me driving, of course, and them smiling at me and waving at everybody we passed. Man, what a way to spend the afternoon.

I never did get that car, Mister Cox just wanted more money for it than I could get, but a year or so later I did manage to drive around with a couple of the girls. In another car, one that I got when I was a junior in high school. This one was a newer model, bright and shiny and fast, but somehow it didn't have the same power to turn my imagination on as the old A Model did.

I've thought about that old car a lot since I grew up, realizing that if I owned it now it would be worth its weight in gold. Not that it wasn't worth that back then, it was, but in some ways it was probably more valuable as a spur that kept me dreaming and setting some kind of goals. Another few years and most of us would be enlisting in the Army, or headed off to school, and before long we'd be married with kids of our own. I only hoped that in the future my kids would be able to find something like that A Model to dream about, because I know that childhood dreams can actually help shape our future, and as long as we can dream, we can accomplish anything.

I guess I might as well tell you that Mister Cox was asking $20 for the old white A Model. I turned 14 in the summer of 1955, and that was a princely sum to try and come up with, at least for a poor town kid. He sold it later to some guy I didn't know, and I'm glad I wasn't there to see him take it away.

But it sure would have been nice to hop into that old jalopy, shout *Get in*, to Faye and Wanda, and drive off down 21st with my hand on the wheel, whistling a happy little tune and grinning like a possum that's just eaten a green persimmon.

THE LAST OF THE SOUTH TOWN RINKY DINKS
THE EXTENDED VOLUME

RINKY DINK RECOLLECTIONS
James A. Walker

I was born after the original Rinky Dinks had moved from the vacinity of 21st Avenue, but I consider myself and my brothers and sisters Rinky Dinks just the same, because we have a long and colorful history with the rest of the people in this book. I wanted to share a few of my recollections about growing up Rinky Dink, and get them into print for posterity's sake. So here you go, hope you enjoy.

Lena Harp was a one of a kind woman and with the benefit of hindsight I now know that she has been the most important woman in my life. I had a special relationship with Aunt Lena but I suspect everyone that knew her feels the same way, she was like that. During the times in my young life that we lived in town it was never more than a few blocks away from her house so visiting was easy, happened frequently, and I don't ever recall having felt unwelcome. Aunt Lena was like that.

Aunt Lena was a wisp of a woman but she loomed large in our lives and her word was law. She had Uncle Birtle and all her brothers to back her up but it was never an issue because she was universally loved and respected. She used to tell me that when left her house that she never knew who would be there when she came home but in all her years no one had ever taken anything or said a cross word to her. She them smiled that little smirk of hers that she got when she was about to share a secret and said, "of course I don't if they love me or are scared to death of my brothers" I think it was the former.

I learned to read on her couch and front porch and over the years developed the habit of dropping by every Sunday and reading the paper with her. We would talk about what we were reading and she provided lots of insights, she was well read, well educated and had more common sense that anyone I knew. She had a consistent message to me from a young age which was to finish high school and leave Springfield. She explained the local caste system to me and how I would undoubtedly do better anywhere but there. She always stressed trying to get a college education and to learn how to make a living with my brain rather than my body like all our family. I heard the message so many times I guess it stuck. I left after high school and only returned briefly after my Army tour of duty.

Aunt Lena offered me so much advice and different ways of looking at things that I cannot remember many specifically. I do recall her lecture when she heard me using a racial slur that was common back in those days. She chastised me and told me to at least have the decency to get to know someone before you talk bad about them. She told me that once you know people I promise you that you will find better reasons to dislike them than the color of their skin, sexual preference or sex. She was right and of course she also knew that if I put that effort out I would probably learn to like more people than I learned to dislike. She was clever.

Aunt Lena's take on religion was one I think I adopted; I honestly don't know where else I would have come up with how I see religion except from her. I didn't know anyone else that even gave it a thought. They went to church, tried to live like the preacher said and gave a little change to the church if they could. They just accepted what they were told. She didn't operate like that. She thought about stuff and asked questions and read about it. She then decided for herself. I was at her house one night when a preacher dropped by, he was out going house to house looking for new church members. He was a well dressed young man, too well dressed for south town. She listened patiently then started asking questions that obviously took him by surprise. He went into the typical sales mode telling her she must have faith etc... She let him finish, walked him to the front door and on his way out she suggested that he might do better selling cars. She was very nice but clear.

I had been living in Chattanooga for several years when Aunt Lena passed away. I remember I was in Cocoa Beach, Florida on vacation when the word reached me. I jumped in my car and drove straight back to Springfield and then to Cross Plains to attend the funeral and to act as a pall bearer.

It was one of the saddest days of my life.

20+ years later I was in a deep depression that was brought on by the tragic death of my son Tyson. It was the low point of my life.

One Saturday morning, while out running errands I was driving through our neighborhood, and I had what can only be called a vision. It was if a portal into heaven opened in front of my very eyes and there stood Aunt Lena and Tyson, as clear as day and obviously very happy. The feeling of warmth and love that poured over me was unlike anything I had ever experienced and I spontaneously starting smiling ear to ear, laughing like I was crazy and crying my eyes out. Thank goodness I was only going 15 miles an hour. I know that the mind can take two separate things and merge them together into an illusion, if you will. I also know that the mind cannot create from scratch very well; you must have experienced the feeling before. This event was the first and only time I have felt pure love and unrestrained joy. I just assume it was heaven that I saw for a few seconds and all because Aunt Lena knew my mental state and once again came to my aid. Aunt Lena may have saved my life that day.

####

In the fall of 1959/1960 Mama and Daddy, along with me and Virginia, lived on South Main at 15th Avenue, one door down from Mr. Baggett's Grocery and across from the ice plant.

I was 4 or 5 years old and was in the front yard watching daddy rake the leaves from our yard and from Jimmy Lee and Lillian Gray's yard, they were the next door neighbors. I remember him raking them out along the street and then setting them on fire. Well it wasn't long before someone in a fire department car pulled up and began getting on daddy about his actions. Daddy was giving him heck of course and was in the process of explaining how he was more of an expert with fire than this fellow.

Right in the middle of his dissertation he takes the big cigar he is smoking and sticks the hot end into his mouth and burned the heck out of his tongue. The fireman started laughing like crazy and just drove away and left daddy to finish burning his leaves.

While we lived at this same house you might remember daddy building this bench probably 10-15 feet long and bar height. He then started buying all those ice cold watermelons from across the street and just serving them to any one walking by. I ate until I threw up and 50 years later still have no taste for watermelon.

Of course Bill Bollinger and I were best friends more like brothers when we were young and spent a lot of time hanging around Aunt Lena's house. We both thought she hung the starts and moon and Don and Goober were good about keeping us occupied running errands etc. I earned plenty of free cokes and in process learned the right way to wash and wax a car. One summer night Bill and I decided to get 10-15 coke cans and stand them in a nice straight line across South Main. Then we hid up in the tree in Pat's front yard across the street just to see what would happen. The first few cars just hit them and drove on and we would climb down and set them up again. Kind of like bowling. Then someone came by and didn't see them until they were almost on them, didn't know what they were and swerved hard to not hit them, ending up on the sidewalk and pissed off. I don't know if me or Bill hit the ground first but I'm pretty sure I out ran him as we high tailed it away from there.

Bill Bollinger and I were typical boys although he was much braver or meaner or sneakier than I was, probably why I stuck by his side. He could be a bit of a bully on occasion and I generally just put up with it because it was not my nature to fight. (I know that is unheard of in the Walker clan) but one day I guess I had had enough and I just started fighting him. We were at Aunt Lena's house, of course we were, we always were.

We fought so long we mutually decided to take a break and we actually started again. Somewhere along the line Goober apparently got tired of it and decided he would break us up and Bill slugged him. He knew it was a bad idea when he did it and Goober drove that point home pretty well. I don't recall Bill or I ever fighting again and I think that may have been the last time he swung at Goober but I'm not sure.

When I was a senior in high school I started having a cold Budweiser every now and then and even some store bought wine (Boone's Farm). Daddy learned I was drinking that and seemed appalled not that I was drinking at 17 years old but that I was drinking crappy wine. He drove me to Nashville one Sunday afternoon to a house on Decarnucci Ave and bought me one gallon of homemade grape wine. Bobby Tanner and I decided the next Friday night to see how much we could drink. I dang near died of alcohol poisoning and had dry heaves for two days. Didn't drink wine again for 20 years, daddy was pretty smart sometimes.

We both know that the code of "ethics" we grew up with were kind of odd sometimes but still effective. Daddy once cut a guys throat over a half dollar bet, but would also can stuff and deliver it all over town to people in worse shape than us. Thinking back those folks must have been in sad ass shape since we were about as far down as you could be. Daddy really did believe that a man's word was all he had and once given must be kept.

I joined the army in the fall of 73 and in Jan 74 found myself in Fort Dix, NJ and colder than I had ever been and I didn't like it, so I decided I had to go and came up with some crazy scheme to get out of the army. I called home to run my plan by daddy.

He listened to me then told me he had some questions for me. He said when I went in the army I swore an oath, did you? Yes sir I answered. When I went in the army I had to sign a contract, did you? Yes sir I replied. He said my last question is the hardest one. Is your word any good?

I served the entire 3 years, every day in NJ. I couldn't risk him thinking less of me.

Man, I miss him.

3

IMPORTED RINKY DINK
Christine Vaden Brown

School in Smith County where I had attended my entire life was wonderful. Everyone, including the teachers were either family or friend, but eleven days before 4th grade was over, Daddy took a job in Springfield, Tennessee, with Williams Jewelers as watchmaker. He had lost his job in Carthage, so we had little choice other than to move. He would be making $70.00 a week which in the 50s was a pretty good salary, and as my mother had some very serious health problems, we needed every cent of it.

Which of course meant we were classified as poor folks, so it made perfect sense that daddy found a house in New Town on 17th Avenue. He rented it from his boss, Mister Williams, and we thought we were lucky to get it.

I had already taken all of my final 4th grade exams and had passed so it turned out I didn't have to attend school the last eleven days in Springfield. Well, other than the fact that Daddy insisted it would be good for me since it would give time to become adjusted and get to know everyone. Besides, nothing too bad could happen in just eleven days...

Without any of my family realizing it, moving to a neighborhood South of the tracks had already placed me in a particular category with in the Springfield hierarchy of town folk. Moving there automatically made me "a South Town Rinky Dink," and looking back, I realize how lucky that made me.

I braced myself for school and tried to have a positive outlook. The teacher was suffering with terminal cancer and she was finishing up the year with as little effort as possible, and as it turned out, I didn't really help her outlook all that much. With only 8 days left in the school year, she was summing up what we had learned and was asking questions to which the class volunteered an answer. The biggest mistake I ever made was to volunteer to answer her question, *What is fog made of?* I answered, *a low-hanging cloud.* This brought a very unfavorable response from the teacher but the truth is I have never learned what fog is made of. She just didn't want to hear about anything that I had learned in my old school in Carthage. As far as I was concerned, I missed my old school and wished I could go back. The result was that I cried like a baby, which of course brought more unfavorable response from her. She ordered me to go to the restroom and wash my face and to not waste any time in returning to the classroom.

With only 7 days left before the end of the year, I made another mistake, this one even worse than the other one. We had a "Show and Tell" one day, and for some reason that I don't even understand, I volunteered to sing a song. Without even thinking of her health problem, I stood in front of the class and sang an old Hank Williams' "May You Never Be Alone Like Me." About mid-way through the song, I heard a loud sobbing sound behind me that I didn't understand, but I finally figured out it was the teacher, unable to handle the lyrics. Of course I didn't know why until one of my classmates finally told me. I suppose you could call this a pretty good example of "poetic justice."

I went on to graduate from Springfield High School with the class of 1959, and made some friends there that will remain close to me for the rest of my live.

BILYEU SKIES FOR THE RINKY DINKS
Wanda Bilyeu Keith

I come from one of the largest families that ever lived in south town...the Bilyeu's. Our family actually originated in France, and over there I think maybe the name is pronounced like it's spelled. Maybe "Bil...yeu."

That's not the way it's pronounced in the South though, at least not in Springfield where we grew up. The fact is we have our own way of talking. It's a combination of old fashioned southern and town kid poor, and we never paid a lot of attention to how the name is supposed to be pronounced, we just always talked kind of slowly, and over the years we've always said our name was Blue. Like the sky, or the color, or maybe what a lot of our lives were like living in South Town. Now, pronouncing it this way wasn't all bad, so long as we were in the company of people that are already familiar with the pronunciation.

The problem always started when someone new come in. Such as one of the new teachers we always seemed to be getting. When a new teacher came to town that had not previously taught one of my two brothers, or my four sisters...or any of my millions of cousins...all of the name things could get quite comical. After all, they DID have a degree in teaching, and they came to this little hillbilly town to teach us how to *speak* correctly. But, in the end, they would give up on proper speech, and say the name like the rest of us Rinky Dinks did...Blue.

For all of us, and all of our friends, that was fine. Well, unless your middle name is LOU...which mine is...so you can imagine the many fun times my friends and I, and especially the rest of our school mates had with Lou Blue. Actually, now that I'm well past the grown age, I realize that all of that just added to the fun we had of growing up with an unusual name.

I have to say, though, that I come from a great family that I am very proud of. I am blessed that God decided to put me in this family.

But, He could have, maybe, just maybe, given us an easier to spell name… and one that was a bit easier for everyone to pronounce. Just saying….

My family lived in south town for many years. My earliest memory goes back to when we lived on Park Street and I was still small enough to be in a stroller,

When I close my eyes, it was almost like it happened yesterday.

I was on the front porch with my sister, Louise, more commonly known to all the family as Mutt and several other grownups. For some reason, they all decided to go into the house, and left me on the porch alone, except for some kid around 4-5 yrs old.

I can actually remember feeling something that probably meant *Oh No* when I saw the other child was walking over toward me. Looking back, and drawing on my early television watching days, I can only describe this as a Dennis The Menace moment.

I recall pushing with my little feet in the stroller, trying to get away, but of course I didn't make it. She was just too old, too big for me to escape from. Dang them 5 year old kids anyway.

I finally began to move, but it was too late. Without much effort she grabbed hold of the handles on the stroller and before I knew what was happening, we were headed directly for the one place I didn't want to go. The edge of the porch.

Our porch was some 3 – 4 feet high, and to a kid in a stroller, that's like approaching the edge of the Grand Canyon. And we headed in that direction as fast as the kid could run, pushing me in the stroller of course.

We were probably only inches away from tumbling into the South Town dirt of our front yard when suddenly my sister Mutt came back out on the porch, and immediately ran to help.

Too late.

My television watching kicks in again here, and it seems that I did my own version of Buzz Lightyear soaring thru the air, for at least a few feet. Out and down, that's the way one always tumbles off the front porch.

Luckily I wasn't hurt, and my sister packed me around for hours, babying me. So, I survived. Turned out to be the first of several times I've taken a fall, and somehow I've always managed to survive. But of course, you could say I learned my survival skills early. Hmmm, comes to me that many kids that grew up in South Town have those same skills.

Not long afterward, our family moved away from South Town into a tiny, 3 room house in another part of town. There was no indoor plumbing, maybe not even any electricity, and at times there were as many as 9 of us living there. I remember loving that old house, but not a lot about that it, and maybe that's just as well

I do remember a lot more about the next place we lived.

When I was about 11 years old, Daddy announced one day that we were moving back to South Town, and that's just what we did. We packed up, picked up, and moved into a very nice brick house back on the other side of the tracks. This house had four – count 'em – four bedrooms and two bathrooms. Yea for indoor plumbing. Up till then I didn't know what I'd been missing.

I also didn't know it at the time, but this new home was going to change my life forever. And change it for the better.

What a change it was. We now lived in a "real" neighborhood, and not in a little three or four room shotgun house. This was a brand new brick house that no one had ever lived in before. It had a nice big yard, very nice neighbors, and for the first time I lived in a named community.

The Projects.

All of the homes there were new brick house — duplexes — which meant that we had another family living in the same house with us, just on the other side of the wall. How neat was that?

Actually, it was pretty neat, because it wasn't long until we were all kind of one big extended family, and we built relationships that have lasted until today.

Our back yards seemed to go on forever, as there was no division between one house and another, except for narrow little sidewalks. And, in the middle of the wide-open space that all the houses' back yards connected to, was a huge, steel swing set and basketball goal. This particular spot was "the" meeting place for my generation of Rinky Dinks. And this is where our friend Chester Frazier, and his loyal side-kick Herschel Dickerson, would serenade us for hours at a time, singing their own rendition of all of Elvis Presley's hits. And they had all of Elvis' moves down to a science. These two were hilarious together. Too bad someone didn't bring out the old 8MM camera.

One night I was spending the night with my friend, Patricia Johnson. Actually, during this time period, I practically lived at her house. Her parents, "Bubber" and Oberlin, were two of the best people I have ever known. They loved me and treated me almost as if I was their own. On this night, me, Patricia, and another friend, Joyce Rawls, wanted to go riding around with some more friends of ours. But her parents told us that we couldn't go because they didn't know these other friends of ours. So we did the only thing we could do, we hatched a plan. We got word to them to wait for us at a place not too far from Patricia's house, and as soon as her parents were asleep, we would sneak out and meet them. So, we quietly raised her bedroom window (but left the venetian blinds down) and jumped into bed, fully clothed, even with our shoes on. Her mother came in the bedroom, talked with us for a few minutes, and then turned out the lights. We lay there…giggling …like girls do, when they think they have just pulled the wool over their parent's eyes…then jumped out of bed. We quietly moved over to the window, jerked the venetian blind up, and there leaning on the window seal was Patricia's oldest brother, Johnny Ray. He smiled very wickedly at us and said; *GOING SOMEWHERE, LADIES?* Gotta love big brothers.

One night, Bubber let his middle son, Joey, use the family car to take his girlfriend, Wanda Oliver, out on a date. So, of course, in reality that meant "lets see how many people we can squeeze into the car." And then someone had a brilliant idea. Lets get some beer. And since none of us were old enough to buy it, we had to find a "grown-up" that would purchase it for us. I was nervous about doing this, because I had never had beer before, and the very smell of it would literally almost make me throw up. But I didn't want my friends to think that I was a "sissy" by any means. So, when it looked like we weren't going to be able to find a way to get the beer, I was probably the loudest one "complaining" because we didn't have any beer. But secretly I was thrilled.

And then Joey thought of one more person who might be willing to buy it, and, sure enough, he got it for us. Papst Blue Ribbon tall-boys at that. So, they passed the beer around, and everyone except me turned it up. I tried, but every time I brought it close to my nose, I would gag. So I came up with a plan (always have a plan). When no one was looking, I splashed a little bit of beer on my face around my lips and even a little on my blouse so I would "smell" like I was drinking. Then I tossed the very full tall boy out the window, while saying *Gimme another one.* But when the can hit the pavement it made the un-mistakable THUNK sound that only a full can of beer can do. Joey looked around real quick and said *Who just threw out a full can of beer?* To which everyone in unison said *WANDA did.* Needless to say, I was cut off for the rest of the night.

Fast forward to the present day. None of us became alcoholics and we are all still great friends. Joey and Wanda have been married for over 40 years, and Bubber got his car back in one piece. Well, at least THAT night.

One of my biggest partners in crime from south town was Patsy Hilliard. She was another friend that we took turns jumping from each other's houses. At the time I was the only one of us to have in my house that wonderful thing called the telephone. And I LOVED to pull pranks on people with it. Remember, this was long before caller ID. We would spend hours calling stores, asking them silly things like; *Do you have Olive Oil in a jar?* And, when they said *yes*, we would say *Well, you'd better let her out, cause Popeye is on his way, and he's really MAD.* And, then we would just die laughing. Kids today just don't know what they are missing.

I think our very favorite phone joke was to call a cab and send it to someone's house down the street, and then laugh hysterically when no one came to the door. One night I got really creative. I called the Dairy Queen and ordered 2 of their largest hamburgers, French fries, and milkshakes. Then, I called the cab station and told them to pick up the order and deliver it to a home on Carter Street. which was right in front of my house on 21st Ave. That was so could see all the action. The way it worked was that when a cab picked up an order to be delivered, the driver would pay for the food, and be reimbursed when they delivered it. One night Patsy and I are sitting under the double windows in my bedroom...peaking up every few seconds to see if the cab is coming...and then we see the lights on the cab coming down the street. Pure adrenaline was pumping through our veins like we had just won the lottery. The cab drove past my house, turned onto Carter Street, and pulled up to the address we'd given. The driver took food and drinks to the door and knocks. By this time, we are laughing so hard we are almost crying. Then this little lady of about 80 or so comes to the door and obviously tells him it is not her order. We could tell by the way he got back into his cab that he was definitely NOT a happy camper. All of a sudden, I jumped up and started to turn the lights on, but Patsy grabbed me and said *What are you doing?* I said *I've got an idea. We'll stop him and tell him that since he went to the wrong address and has already paid for the food, we would take it.* To which she said, *IDIOT. And just HOW are you going to explain to him that we even KNOW about the food?* To which I answered; *Oh yeah*, as I quickly took my hand away from the cord that turned on the light.

Throughout our 45 years and counting friendship, Patsy has proven to be a MUCH NEEDED voice of reasoning for me.

I have to say that I truly enjoyed growing up Rinky Dink.

E. DON HARPE

5

SPRINGFIELD HIGH SCHOOL DAZE
A RINKY DINK AT SHS
E. Don Harpe

Our high school days are some of the best of our lives, but we don't always realize that until we have been out for several years. Springfield High School, SHS, held many memories for me and for the rest of the Rinky Dinks. And, speaking of dear old SHS, as I have a couple of times in this book, let me put in a couple of stories from my high school years that I find kind of funny, but very telling of the times and the people.

There were some things that could be done back then that would be entirely forbidden now, and yet they were harmless little things that nobody thought anything of.

I'll relate a few, but this time I'll keep it personal, involving only myself and a few close friends, and a few teachers that I thought a lot of. By keeping it personal nobody can find reason to say I told something they didn't want told, or that they don't remember it the same I do.

I was a junior in the 1957/58 year, and one day I was in the old gym shooting a few baskets when the rear end of my pants ripped in half. Anyone who has ever experienced that knows the feeling. You're afraid someone might see something they shouldn't, and it kind of embarrasses you. At the same time you're a little excited, because you don't know what your next move will be.

To tell the truth, I knew exactly what my next move would

be, and I didn't hesitate at all in getting started on it.

With both hands covering the read of my pants, I headed for Mrs. Bell's Home Ec classroom. Now I knew there'd be nothing but girls in the class, probably Patty and Faye, maybe Barbara and Hollis, hell, there was telling who'd be in there, but it was the only place I knew to get what I needed.

I knocked on the door, ever so politely, and Mrs. Bell opened it in her own time.

Hello Mrs. Bell, I said, and of course she replied with

Hello and what can I do for you?

If I could, ma'am, I'd like to borrow a needle and thread.

A needle and thread?

Yes, ma'am. I kind of ripped the seat of my pants, and I need to sew them up.

She thought a minute.

Turn around, she said.

I turned around and stood still as she checked out the damage.

Well, she said, keep your back to the wall and not to the class and go over to my desk.

I did as she instructed, and she had me bend over her desk and stand still while she deftly stitched up the rip in my pants.

As I recall, the entire episode took place with the background sound of high pitched giggles and even some hearty laughter.

But I got my pants sewed up, and got back to class, and to this day I remember thinking that I wished that had been the day when the class was baking ice cream cakes.

####

And then there was Mrs. Padfield.

I was in Mrs. Padfield's home room for two years in a row, and she was a very good, very dedicated, teacher. I really liked her, but even so, I was never above being a little bit, shall we say rambunctious, now and then, and there were several times she had to call me on whatever it was that I was doing.

My hair was pretty long for a lot of my high school days, and when I pulled it forward and down it covered most of my face. I wore it in a wave and a large curl that came down over my forehead, and at the time I thought it looked pretty good. Mrs. Padfield used to like to bring me up in front of the class during homeroom, sit me down in a chair, and give me a new hairdo. She'd comb it and style and we'd all get a big laugh out of it. There was nothing whatsoever wrong with this, but can you imagine a teacher doing it now? The parents would protest, the authorities would be called, and her job might even be on the line. I'm not sure just when it was we let our common sense take a back seat to political correctness, but we certainly did just that.

####

I was in the 9th grade in 1955/56, and the craze that fall was small, metal water guns. They held about 2 shots of water, and we had a great time, right up until we got caught.

Mrs. Blankship was another teacher that everyone really liked, and she decided to take up all of the water guns, so she asked us to turn them in. I was a good student so I stood up, walked to the front of the room, and laid my on her desk. I neglected to tell her that it was one of 2 of the little guns I had in my pocket, but that didn't seem really important, at the time.

After that class was over, I went to the bathroom and filled up the second of my water guns, and right back in the hall I went.

Just as I pulled the trigger to spray someone, Mrs. B (as she was called) walked out of her room and saw me. She walked up to me and politely took the gun from my hand.

Another one, I see.

Yes, ma'am.

Well, I hope this is the last one.

Yes, ma'am, it is.

Donald, now I don't want to catch you with another one. (At this point I was still doing pretty well with her. I should have let the subject drop.)

No, you won't, I replied, but I didn't mean for you to catch me with this one.

Open mouth, insert foot.

Mrs. B was not pleased with that reply. So much so, in fact, that she had me write off a hundred times that I would not bring another water gun to school.

By the way, Mrs. B was also the teacher who dubbed me the *Poet Laureate* of Springfield High School, and had me write a poem celebrating the graduating class of 1956, which was the very first thing I ever had published anywhere. It was published in the local newspaper, and all I can remember are the first two lines.

Lo we present, with good intent, the class of '56

For four long years of smiles and tears with them we did mix...

# # # #

I had started smoking an occasional cigarette by the time I was a senior, and under the bleachers at the football field was the favorite place for us to slip off and light up. And this story might have turned out a little differently had I actually chosen under the bleachers to sneak a couple of drags one day a week or so after the senior year had started. But I didn't. Kenneth Carroll and I walked out to the bleachers, intending to get in a few quick puffs, but then one of us had to go to the bathroom, so we headed for the old gym where there was a little used bathroom in the basement.

As it was the main bathroom used during football games. the bathroom had one of those extra long troughs that could be used by a lot of men at once, and Kenny and I had just lit up our cigarettes when all at once Coach Smith walked in.

THE LAST OF THE SOUTH TOWN RINKY DINKS
THE EXTENDED VOLUME

He walked up to the trough and just stood there for a moment.

You boys planning on playing basketball this year? He asked.

Yessir, we replied in unison.

Then you might want to put those cigarettes out, he said, and finished his business and then left us standing there.

Needless to say we put out the cigarettes and if I remember it correctly, that was the last one I smoked during my senior year.

Coach had a way of getting things done that I think a lot of teachers could benefit by today.

Oh, and Kenny and I did play basketball on the SHS team our senior year.

As I've written elsewhere in the book, I've always loved music. It was no different when I was in high school. I had already started my love affair with singing, had already tasted a bit of how it felt to be paid for doing it, and I was already pretty sure that I wanted to be around it for as long as I lived.

Remember, this was the mid to late fifties, and we had some of the very best music the world has ever, or will ever, see. And let me tell you something DaddyO, it wasn't just country for me back then either.

These were the years of the Platters, with songs like *The Great Pretender, Smoke Gets In Your Eyes,* and one of the most beautiful songs ever recorded, *Only You*. We were already getting a taste of pre rock and roll, with artists like Fats Domino singing *Blueberry Hill,* Bill Haley and the Comets with *Rock Around The Clock,* and the many truly legendary songs of the one and only Chuck Berry.

And then there was the King, Elvis Presley. Who didn't want to be him, back in the day? They say Elvis ushered in the age of rock and roll, but I don't that he ushered it in so much as he caught the tidal wave just as it started to break and rode it better than anyone before or since.

By then I was singing a mixture of songs, from the fledgling rock and roll tunes to the high lonesome Hank Williams songs I'd cut my musical teeth on. I had joined with a couple of friends, Sam Traughber and Ralph Leftrick, and we were performing on talent shows and in schools around the county. Not really making much noise, and not winning any of the talent contests, but getting to know what it felt like to be on stage, singing in front of an audience that might or might not like us, and getting to understand first hand how to tell what the people wanted to hear, and how to modify our set list to give them the music they enjoyed the most. I played in a couple of small honky tonks about that time, even though I wasn't old enough, and gained even more valuable experience about how to please the crowd. And even though I never went on to become the recording artist or the award winning songwriter that I dreamed of being, I found that all that really mattered was the music, and that I could be very happy without the fame and fortune.

But school was a different matter. All we really had in high school was the glee club, and so I gave that a try. I think back then they put me in the baritone section, and of course that was fine with me, as I just loved the music and being a part of the group. I recall we had a very fine pianist, a girl in my class named Hollis Shannon, who was also part of a singing trio, or maybe it was a quartet, and they were very good. Hollis went on to become an extraordinarily fine musician, making a name for herself everywhere she played, and earning a well deserved reputation with everyone who ever heard her play.

Thinking back I can't remember the songs we sang with the glee club, or even performing with them, but I still get a good feeling when I let myself go back to those years, and those times.

High school is truly some of the best years of our lives, but I kind of feel like the guy who said; *"Youth is a wonderful thing,*

THE LAST OF THE SOUTH TOWN RINKY DINKS
THE EXTENDED VOLUME

it's a shame we waste it on kids." I know exactly what he meant by that. I can't say youth is really wasted on kids, but how many times have we heard someone say; *I wish I was a kid again, and know what I know now?* Well, I don't really want to be a kid again, because today's kids are under entirely too much pressure and have too much going on in the world around them. But I might like to try being maybe 35 or so again. Oh, and knowing what I know now.

####

One of the highest compliments I ever had in high school was from Mrs. Johnston, our very strict English teacher, and at the time I didn't even realize it was a compliment. That came several years later, in fact, when I ran across a poem I'd submitted in her class in my senior year.

The poem was entitled *FROM WHENCE THE CHANGE*, and it talked about the changing of the seasons, one to another, and how ours lives could be compared to they way they changed. In it, I asked the question, *From Whence Cometh The Change.*

Mrs. J (yeah, we seemed to call a lot of our teachers with just the initial of their last names) handed me the paper back, and had marked it with a "U" for unsatisfactory. I couldn't understand the grade, as I was pretty certain it was a good poem, and I was expecting an "A." I walked up to her desk, paper in hand, and asked for an explanation.

Mrs. J, why did I get a failing grade on this poem?

Because I think you copied it out of some old poetry book from the library.

What? I didn't copy the poem. Why would I do that? I write pretty good poetry by myself.

Can you tell me the meaning of the word "whence?" she said.

Yes ma'am, I can, and I proceeded to tell her the meaning of the word.

She looked at me for a moment.

I thought you had copied the poem, but I can see now I was mistaken. Let me change that grade.

She took the paper, crossed out the "U" and wrote an "A+" on it. This was a highly unusual grade for Mrs. J to give on poems, but I just smiled and walked back to my desk

Many years later, after I had started writing a lot of fiction, I came across the poem, and remembered that day as if it were right then. It was then that it occurred to me how much of a compliment that was. She'd actually thought I'd copied the poem from an old book, which meant she thought it was that good. That told me a lot about my writing ability, and gave me the understanding that perhaps I might be able to write things that could be published, and that people would like.

One thing I know for sure. I'd certainly like to be able to take Ms Grace Youngblood, Mrs. Johnston, Mrs. Padfield and Mrs. Blankenship a copy of this book, and tell them this all came about because of them, and because they encouraged a little ragged Rinky Dink to follow a dream, and to put his thoughts on paper, and to never give up.

DANCE HALLS, BEER JOINTS, HONKY TONKS, & SKULL ORCHARDS

I've been lucky in that I got to work in and around the country music business in Nashville for a good many years. I've been a studio manager, a publishing company manager, and I've managed to get quite a few of my songs published and recorded. I've never had the really big hit by a major artist that would have allowed me to make a living writing songs, but I've had more success than many people who try.

I've played shows in Nashville, performed at writer's night, and became friends with some truly great people. I even wrote a couple of songs with Charlie Louvin, and I've performed on stage with Tresa Street and her Street Talk Band. I've met Willie Nelson, Garth Brooks, Brooks and Dunn, Patty Loveless, Freddie Hart, Ray Price, Patsy Cline, Roy Acuff and the list goes on and on.

But I don't do much in the business anymore, other than playing a local senior citizens center now and then, and I have to say I don't regret a minute of it.

But here's the way it started.

####

There is a tradition in many rural areas around the part of the country where I grew up that scores of people used to indulge in on a regular basis. Sometimes it involved hopping around and waving your arms, making outlandish faces and grinning like a possum who had bit into a wild persimmon before the first frost. At other times it meant moving about with your eyes closed and your mouth forming unspoken words as you slowed down and moved to the rhythm of the music, slowly sliding your feet around in uneven circles across a slick hardwood floor. It involved laughter, sweat, unreleased inhibitions, and, more often than not, a good helping of cold beer.

The tradition is that of you and your wife or best girl, or you and your husband or best boyfriend, visiting a local dance hall on a Friday or Saturday night.

If it's all right with you, why don't we go back in time a few years, and visit one of the places that had a weekend hold on so many people. If you get there early, say 7:30 PM or so, you can usually find a parking spot pretty close to the door. That might be important later on, especially if you've had a few too many ice cold beverages between opening and closing time. Walk inside the door, and usually there will be someone sitting at a table near the entrance, they're there to collect the door charge, which is generally the money that will go to pay the band. You walk into the dim lit room, grab a table as near the dance floor as you can, order a couple of frosty cold beers, and get set to listen to your favorite local band play all your favorite country music songs.

It's called honky tonkin', and there was a time when it was enjoyed by a large number of country folk nearly every weekend. The buildings usually weren't all that large, and during the week they served as a watering hole where the local farmers could grab a sandwich or a cold drink during the day. Most of the places had names like The Blue Angel, The Cadillac Club, The Hideaway, or Miami Gardens. The buildings usually had at least two rooms, with a bar and maybe a pool table in the front room, and a large dance floor complete with tables and a corner bandstand in the other room. They were smoky for the most part, as the majority of the patrons used tobacco, and they were loud, and sometimes they were borderline dangerous. But the fact is when they came alive on Saturday night as the high lonesome, honey sweet sounds of Hank Williams, Lefty Frizzell, or Carl Smith filled the air, they were fun. In fact, they were a lot of fun, and they were a good way for a hard working man to shed the worry about bills and everyday life for an hour or so, and just lose himself in the arms of the one he loved on the dance floor.

A lot of people didn't earn very much money back in those days, back in the 50's and 60's and early 70s when the era of the honky tonk was at its zenith, which made the local honky tonks the number one choice for a little weekend recreation. Most of the time the door charge was $2 a person, and beer was about $1 a bottle, and back then bands played for four full hours, usually from 8 PM till midnight. Combined, this meant you could have a lot of fun, and still get enough sleep to make it to church the next morning, where you knew you would see several of the people you were laughing and dancing with last night. You could let off a lot of steam, have a weeks worth of laughs, get excited when you did a little slow dancin', and not do anything that might be harmful to another living soul. Well, discounting the few who always insisted on engaging in a fist fight or two at some point in time during the night.

The bands were made up of local guys, boys who worked on the assembly line or the service stations or in the fields during the day, and transformed into guitar pickin', rakish young devils when the sun went down on the weekend. As singers, some of them were bad, some were good, and some were really good. Some bands built up a local following of folks that went to whatever club that band was playing; folks who knew what songs they were going to sing, which singer was going to sing them, and how long they were going to last. The ladies loved the bands; there's something about a guy singing to them that gives them a feeling that nothing else does. And for the most part, the men loved the bands too. They liked the music, and a lot of them could do a bit of pickin' themselves, and they liked to get a little loud and sing along, knowing that when they did, the ladies would be sure to give them a little sideways look too.

If you could live with the preacher telling you it was not a good thing to do, a honky tonk was a great way to have four hours of fun and glitter now and again on the weekend. For years I was one of the guys in the bands who played music in all of the little hole in the wall honky tonks and skull orchards on the Tennessee/Kentucky state line, and I don't think I'd change one minute of that time even if I could. We played honest country music for honest country people, and when I look back on it, the only thing that runs through my mind is that I'd like to play just one more show. See one more dance floor filled with people who loved what I was singing, see one more waitress moving to the music as she moved around the tables with cold beers in her hand, and yes, even see one more knock down drag out fight. In fact, off the top of my head I can recall three memorable fights from those years, and if you have the time …

I suppose we've played for just about as many fights as we have dances. Back in the late 50's and through most of the 60's, bar fights were pretty much expected to break out when folks were out drinking and dancing. Back then, men and women went to honky tonks for the same reasons. To have a few drinks, dance a few belly rubbing numbers with somebody of the opposite sex, and maybe, just maybe to experience the rush that comes when a few words are tossed about, and then a few fists start flying. We used to say that on some Saturday nights we went to a fight and a dance broke out. Men will stand face to face and slug it out, and laugh as noses are bloodied and teeth are broken. Women, on the other hand, are much more vicious. Men will usually quit a fight when they win or when they lose, but women almost never want to stop. They're like that little pink bunny, they just keep going and going and going.

Back in those days, the little clubs once seemed to grow almost like weeds along the Tennessee/Kentucky state line. There were several country towns close enough to produce a good audience, and most of the clubs were just a short drive away from

THE LAST OF THE SOUTH TOWN RINKY DINKS
THE EXTENDED VOLUME

Fort Campbell, Kentucky, home of the 101st Airborne, a group of the greatest guys this country has ever produced. Although some of the clubs were off limits to the soldiers, you could still count on seeing a few Screaming Eagles every weekend. I'm proud that our band attracted a following of paratroopers, and over the years I've seen a lot of strange fights break out with some of them.

One old grizzled veteran, being in a helpful kind of mood, decided one night to break up a fight between a young soldier and a local man. He didn't count on the local boy's wife getting in on the action, however, and when he grabbed the man to pull him off the soldier, the wife cleaned his clock with a very large, very heavy purse she was carrying. I suspect she had some heavy object in the purse just for that reason, and I know for a fact that the Sarge never knew what hit him. When he grabbed the woman's husband, she stepped up behind him, and knocked him out cold with her purse. So much for being a good Samaritan. That turned out to be one of the wildest fights we ever played for. The players are numbered seven. There was the soldier, the Sarge, the husband, the wife, the mother and the waitress, and then, closing the show, was the club owner.

The owner of the Food Bar was a small man, maybe 5'6" or so, who'd had polio as a child, and walked with a limp. He knew there were gonna be a lot of fights in his place, and he carried a very large pair of brass knuckles in his pocket as a way of crowd control.

This particular night, when the woman knocked out the Sarge, the owner knocked out the woman. Through it all, we played "Wipeout" and the faster the drummer made his rolls, the quicker the action on the fight floor became. We knew if we played faster, they'd fight faster, and it would be over quicker. The waitress worked at a club about two miles down the highway from where we were playing but they had closed early because all of the customers were at the club where we were playing listening to us. The waitress and a couple of friends came down to do the same. The mother, for some reason, thought that the waitress was looking at her man, and she called her a name or two and then took it to the next level. In less than a minute the two of them were on the floor, scratching and clawing, with the waitress getting the best end of the deal.

The daughter, seeing the commotion from the other side of the room, began yelling; "That's my mama, that's my mama," and trying to push her way through the crowd. Her husband got there first and began trying to separate the two ladies, and then the young soldier grabbed the husband. That's when the Sarge grabbed the husband's arm to try and break up the fight. By that time the daughter had made it through the crowd and saw the Sarge grabbing her husband. So she unloaded on him with her purse. She swung the heavy purse like it was a ball bat and when it connected with the Sarge's head, it slammed it into the wooden beam that held the ceiling up. He went out like a 20 watt bulb when 240 volts hits it. Before anyone could stop her, she had jumped into the fray, and had grabbed the hem of the waitress' dress. Without a thought she ripped the dress from the waitress, and then the two undergarments as well.

When the owner, remember the little guy who once had polio, got through the crowd, the Sarge was knocked out, the waitress was stripped bare, the mother was crying, the daughter was screaming and yelling, swinging at everything that moved, and shouting words that would make sailors blush. She was getting ready to leap at the soldier, who was still holding the husband to keep him out of the fight.

Now it wasn't very sportsmanlike, and it wasn't very nice, but the owner appraised the situation, stepped in close, and clipped the daughter on the chin with his brass knuckles. She lost all of her inclination for further fighting, and in a moment or so all of them were escorted out the door. Meanwhile, back on the bandstand, we had launched into "Wooly Bully" another good old song with a fast paced frenzied rhythm. Great for dancin' or fightin'. We never missed a beat, not even when the clothes came off. We played that same club for a couple more years, and I don't think we ever saw any of those people back in there again.

THE LAST OF THE SOUTH TOWN RINKY DINKS
THE EXTENDED VOLUME

Fort Campbell put the club off limits, and while some of the guys came anyway, a lot of them stopped coming after that night. There is another memorable scrap that happened one night that may have a bit of merit. We were playing a little club one Friday night, down on the river in Clarksville, and one of our regulars had come out for a little dancing and fun. Of course it was Lawrence Thaxton, and he was a country boy who loved to fight. He'd rather be in the middle of a good brawl than just about anything, and while he seldom started a fight, he ended many of them. Lawrence went with us a lot of weekends, and much of the time he sat at a small table near the door, collecting the money from the folks when they entered. We knew he wouldn't let anyone in that didn't pay, and he wouldn't let anything happen to even $1 of the door money. He was as honest as the day is long, and at the end of the night there was no doubt that all of the money that was supposed to be in the box would be in the box.

It was winter, January or February I think, and this particular night had went off without a hitch, read that fight, and by midnight-thirty we were packed up and headed for the cars, another great show behind us, and some breakfast waiting when we got back to Springfield. The parking lot was just about empty by the time we got outside, but there was some noise coming from around the side of the building.

Lawrence took off ahead of us, but we were pretty close behind him, and the scene was a strange one, to say the least. There were three guys lying scattered about in the parking lot, and two more were fighting beside a parked car. Well, fighting isn't exactly what both of them were doing. One was hitting the other one about the face and head, and he was just kind of beginning to slump. It was a sure bet that he'd join his friends on the pavement in a couple of seconds. I took a quick look at the guy who was still standing, and saw he was someone I didn't know. I didn't recall him being on the dance floor, and I'm pretty sure I'd remember him if I'd seen him. He was enormous. The man looked to be 6'7" or more, and if he weighted 10 pounds, he weighed 300.

He'd taken on all four assailants and left all four lying in the parking lot, and he hadn't even worked up a sweat. He had a bottle of beer sitting on the hood of a nearby car, and when the last guy fell he picked it up and took a long swallow, draining the bottle, and then threw it over into the weeds at the back of the lot. I noticed some movement out of the corner of my eye, and turned just in time to see Lawrence hurriedly removing his coat. I had just a moment to think that him getting into this scrap might not be such a great idea. Lawrence could hold his own with about anyone, and loved to fight, but, did I mention the other guy was a damn giant? I shouldn't have worried. Lawrence might have loved to fight, but he was pretty smart, and without hesitation he rushed over to the big guy, looked around at the bodies on the asphalt, and then looked dead into the man's eyes and what he said was pure magic. "Need some help," Lawrence asked him. The big guy laughed. "Nah, I think I've got it covered," he said. "Well, if they bother you anymore…" "Thanks, but I don't think they will."

Laughing, we walked back to our cars and got them fired up to leave. A police car, with lights flashing, was pulling into the lot as we were leaving, but we didn't stop. We had nothing to tell him. I saw the big guy was pulling out of the lot at the same time we were, so I was sure nobody was going to jail. Well, not unless it was the guys on the ground who were just starting to move about a bit. I often wondered if they got hauled off to jail for public drunkenness that night. I think that might have been the icing on the cake, after getting their butts whipped so soundly. By one man. One huge, gigantic, freaking hulk of a man.

The other fight that I recall vividly, with a bit of humor, happened one night up on Highway 31-W, near White House, Tennessee, in a small club called the Blue Angel. We'd been playing there for about two months, and usually attracted a good crowd. But this was a Friday night, and one of the few nights we played to less than a full house. But it was high school football night in Tennessee, and back then most people were going to a ball game before they came out to a club.

THE LAST OF THE SOUTH TOWN RINKY DINKS
THE EXTENDED VOLUME

There were two guys sitting together at a table in the back right hand corner of the room, and had been alone all night. They were there to drink, look at the women, and not much else. I noticed them when they stood up, and nodded to the guys when I saw one of them shove the other one. "Let's go outside," the other one yelled, and so they did. We were right behind them. They had a few words, and then one of the guys reached into his back pocket. I knew that meant he was going for a knife, but there wasn't much to be done about it. Hell, it was their fight. Again, I shouldn't have worried. When his hand touched his back pocket, the other guy knocked him down. He scrambled back to his feet, reached into his pocket again, and got knocked down again. He got up a lot slower this time. Reached for his pocket again. Same result. Got knocked on his butt in the gravel. This time the other guy knelt down beside him, grabbed him by the hand, and lifted him to his feet. They stood there a minute or two, then the one who'd kept getting knocked down kind of shook his head and walked back toward the club.

We went back inside, got back on the bandstand, and I started singing "Cold, Cold Heart," an old Hank Williams tune. The two guys sat back down at the table, ordered another round of Carling Black Label, and acted as if nothing had happened. When we were leaving that night I saw they were leaving too, both in the same car. I can't help but think they were best friends, and this wasn't the first time something like this had happened. I can honestly say I don't think it would have ended this way, had it happened the weekend before that, instead of one cold football Friday in 1964, at the Blue Angel Inn on Highway 31-W, just outside White House, Tennessee.

I've mentioned elsewhere in this book that I played my first "paying gig" when I was 14, when a buddy of mine and I went with his dad out to the home of an old black man who sold barbecue and beer. His customers were mostly the farmers who worked the fields about Adams, Tennessee, but that one day we went out and sang old Hank Williams songs and he gave us hot barbecue and a cold beer or two. And that was pretty much what hooked me on picking and grinning.

There was some pretty talented people among the Rinky Dinks, and one of the first honky tonk bands we put together was me and Charles Rippy, with Ralph Leftrick playing rhythm guitar, and I don't recall who was on drums or bass. There were 5 of us, and we figured that was just exactly the right number. We didn't have a lot of equipment, and if a microphone went out, then we just sang louder. We carried a couple of extra strings, and faced the crowd with a confidence that I somehow managed to hold on to for the rest of my life.

The first night we played the Blue Angel there were 5 people there. At $2 a person that means we made $10 for the night. $2 for each of us. I'd put in $2 worth of gas to get there, bought a little E string for .10 cents, and played 4 hours for 5 people. That means I went .10 cents in the hole for the night.

Four weeks later the club was packed. Turns out the people liked us, and from that night on we had a good crowd in every place we played, and that was just about every club in the vicinity.

We later spent most of our playing time down around the state line, quite often in Clarksville or Fort Campbell. The clubs on the state line were skull orchards for sure, and not many nights passed that there wasn't at least one or two fights. That never really bothered us that much, because most of the time we weren't involved in the fisticuffs. There were a few times we had to fight out way off the band stand, or physically toss some would be singer off the stage. Didn't happen very often though. We became friends with some of the paratroopers from Ft. Campbell, and most of the time they'd sit up near the band stand, and that usually discouraged any would be brawler who'd decided one of us had been looking at his woman a little too much.

Truth is, sometimes that really happened. But if you're standing on the stage and singing a song like Marty Robbin's "Love Me," or Don Gibson's "I Can't Stop Loving You," it's a fact that just about every night you'd get some pretty strange offers.

THE LAST OF THE SOUTH TOWN RINKY DINKS
THE EXTENDED VOLUME

And when that happened sometimes a husband or boyfriend wanted to take it personally. Hell, we were on a stage in front of a room full of people, just what did they think we were going to do?

We played a few clubs in Clarksville back in the early 60s, and it is a fact that a black guy, who was later to be an extremely famous star, was stationed at Ft. Campbell. If I recall it right, he was out there in a few of the clubs now and then, doing much the same thing we were doing, learning the craft and playing his music for the people. I don't think you'll find much about those clubs in his biography, and I'm not going to call any names, but I still get a kick out of knowing that at least once or twice I shared a stage with him.

Our manager back then tells the story how this guy once offered him $5 to let him sit in with us for our second set. And then the manager offered him $10 if he'd sit in the third and fourth. Knowing the way our manager thought, I have no doubt this is a true story.

This same manager booked us into a club in Hopkinsville, Kentucky, one Friday night, and as a couple of our regular guys were already booked, we took two other musicians with us. Both were black. One played bass, the other sax. We were still sitting up when I noticed a large group of local rednecks eying us with a few streaks of lightning in the gaze. I knew when those boys got drunk, there was going to be a huge fight, and as this was a very touchy time in our county, it might evolve into even more. Like a hanging. We'd heard there had been hanging or two in Hopkinsville, and to be honest I wasn't quite ready for a necktie party.

I told the guys what I was thinking, they took one look at the boys in the back and agreed. So I stepped up to the mike, informed them that our drummer had busted the head on one of this drums, and we were going to have to get our back up set out of the station wagon. Ha. Like we carried a back up set of drums. In a few minutes we were headed back toward Springfield, and a little talk with our manager about which clubs he was going to book us in from then on.

Sometime around 1964 or '65 we got booked into a club in Printer's Alley in downtown Nashville. Even though we'd opened a local show or two for some country stars, the Printer's Alley gig was by far the best booking we'd ever had. This was the big time for a local band, and I remember that we all wore black pants and white shirts, with a little black string tie. Trying to look the part, don't you know.

We got set up and our lead guitar player, who also sang all of the "rock" style songs, said we were going to have to go with the Elvis and Chuck Berry music, and maybe a few Jerry Lee songs thrown in for good measure. So that's what we did. The first set we didn't have one single person on the dance floor, and the manager had already started giving us the eye. When we took our first break, I told them we were going to change the play list just a bit.

When we cranked up the amps for the second set, I opened up with "Don't Worry," backed up with "Begging To You." Two Marty Robbins songs. The dance floor filled, and we learned a lesson. Many of the people still preferred plain old good country songs to any of the floor shaking rock n' roll things we could do. We finished the night with the rest of our country songs, and got asked back to play again. I can't help but think we might not have been booked again if we'd continued to play what we started with. I learned a lesson that night, and it stuck with me the rest of the days I played music. Always try to figure out what the crowd wants to hear, and then play that as much as possible. The club owners likes bands that the crowd likes, and if he sells beer and food, there's a good chance you'll get asked to come back.

After that, we got pretty good at playing music that made people dance, which made them buy beer, and kept the owners happy. By the way. if you were looking for a club to play, and when you went in to talk to the owner and saw there was chicken wire around the band stand, you knew immediately what kind of club it was, what kind of crowd it drew, and if you played it

THE LAST OF THE SOUTH TOWN RINKY DINKS
THE EXTENDED VOLUME

anyway, you had nobody except yourself to blame if a fight or seven just happened to break out every night you were there. Dance halls, beer joints, honky tonks, and skull orchards. We played them all, and I don't regret a minute of it.

Man, if I were only 25 again…

E. DON HARPE

THE LIFE AND TIMES OF
JOHN WESLEY WILSON
July, 1939   June 23, 2019

My Last words in this book are for a true friend, a man who was a credit to his family, his community, and to everyone that knew him. The world is richer because he was in it.

I turned 79 years old in May of 2020, and that is pushing 8 decades pretty hard. There are times when my body feels every second of all the years, and more times when my mind is tired. It's not great to know what I used to do, and now not be able to do any of it. Too many miles and too many illnesses, and too much water under the bridge.

One of the very hardest things we learn about growing older, and I'm talking about the late 70s and into the 80s, is that we begin to lose so many of our long time friends. It seems almost every month brings another obituary, another friend that I was once so close too. In the past I've had some losses that were extra hard to take. Sam Traughber, Ralph Leftrick, and Kenneth Carroll were very hard on those who loved them. They were great friends and my life was better because they were in it. I still miss them a lot, and think about them often. We shared some really good memories over the years, and I miss them more than I can tell.

And then there are a few that are in a kind of different class.

Friends, but more like family, and my heart aches to think they are gone. The ones I grew up with, and knew from before the first grade, and came to think so much of over the years. Lawrence Thaxton was one of those. So many memories, so much in common we shared. And then a few years ago, we lost Larry Wayne Wilson. We played cards together, went to dinner together, laughed and talked and shared books and old memories of comics and ball games. God, I still miss him.

And today comes news of another one lost, another South Town Rinky Dink, who has always said he was proud of where he was raised. He was a man who was much like a brother to me for all of my life. John Wesley Wilson, Wayne's older brother, was a man who stood taller than many of us, in many ways. I knew him as long as I can remember. We played on the same ball teams, I got my driver's license in his car, he was responsible for getting me a great job in Nashville about 1961, and we've spent countless hours just riding around and talking. Hell, we even dated the same girl back in those days. On a side note, after we had both broken up with her, one night we bought a fifth of whiskey and a couple of cokes, and drove out by Wartrace Lake to talk and drink her out our lives. Girlfriends come and go, lifelong friends are just that, life long. That night though we hadn't taken over a couple of small drinks when a car came driving down the road, and we soon saw it was the police. They used to cruise the back roads, trying to catch guys, or gals, or who knows out there, maybe … drinking. His window was down and mine was up and he tossed his glass, along with the bottle, out the window just as the police cruiser stopped beside us, I started rolling my window down to talk to them, and kind of slid my drink over to him, and he tossed it out also. We talked to the two cops for a few minutes, convinced them we'd just stopped to take a leak, and they left us alone. We talked about getting and looking for the bottle, but we didn't. They might come back, and our luck might run out.

For those that don't know, or have never heard, or might not believe, Wesley was much better than average roller skater when we were in our late teens and early twenties. He could skate as well as just about anyone I've ever seen. I've seen him hold a match between his teeth, and spread his legs out until the skates were wide apart, and then get close enough to the floor of the rink to strike the match. I did it once or twice, but he could do it every time he tried. Another trick with a match you might not believe, but he could fasten a kitchen match to the trunk of a tree, and light it with a bullet from a .22 rifle. If you don't think that's hard, remember, if you hit the match head it will just be blown away. To strike it you have to shoot close enough that the friction of the bullet will strike the match, without actually hitting the match. There's another kind of funny story about Wesley and a gun. When we were kids, he spent many, or most of his summers with his grandpa on the farm in Coopertown, and I suppose that's where he learned his work ethic. He also learned to hunt, usually with a 12 gauge shotgun. He and I went rabbit hunting a couple of times when we were bigger, him with the 12 gauge, me with a .22. One day he shot a rabbit and it didn't kill it. We went up to it and the little thing was just screaming in pain, and to be merciful he had to go ahead and kill it to put it out of its pain. I never forgot the way the rabbit was screaming, and I never went hunting again. And I won't even try to eat any kind of wild game.

Some years later, 1962 or '63 maybe, we were all at a friend's house one Saturday and we decided take the friend's 30.06 hunting rifle out behind the house and fire it a couple of times. Phillip, our friend, and I had fired the rifle several times before, but this was a first for Wesley. He held the big rifle up and squinted through the scope, and got ready to fire. I stopped him. "Wesley," I said, "you're got to hold this rifle really tight, and keep the scope away from your face. It kicks like a mule." He kind of laughed, "Well, damn, Donald, you know I've been shooting a 12 gauge shotgun all my life, and this is just a rifle. Can't kick like the 12 gauge." Hmmm. OK. He put the big gun back to his shoulder, aimed at the target in the gully, and gently pulled the trigger. The rifled fired with a loud pop, plastering itself back into his shoulder, and the scope hit him square between the eyes, just about his nose. He sat down pretty hard on the ground, but we never did say the gun did that. Blood was running dawn his face, and he looked up at me. "Damn, that thing kicks like a mule." I grinned, "yep, and it's not a 12 gauge mule. Wesley carried a little half horseshoe scar just about his nose for most, or all, of his life. It wasn't quite as noticeable the last few times I saw him, but if you knew where to look, you could still see the faint outline of the 30.06 rifle's scope, you know, the one that didn't kick too hard.

I recall once he bought a beautiful pearl colored 1957 Chevrolet, and we drove that dang thing everywhere. We went to the bowling alley one night, parked on the street, and went in and bowled a couple of games, which he was pretty good at, by the way, and when we came out, the car was gone. Stolen. Turns out it was stolen by a guy we'd known for years, and it turned up a day or so later in one of the small towns in Kentucky that's close to the state line.

A few years ago, when I was writing the Rinky Dink book, I'd tell him I was still working on it. "Ah, you'll never get that thing done, Donald," he used to say. I was very proud when I finished the book, and sent him a manuscript copy, before it was even published. He said he really enjoyed it.

Wesley was always a man with a lot of common sense, always with an eye to what he thought was best, and I don't recall him failing at anything he ever tried to do. He was a hard worker, and an astute businessman, owning a very successful wire manufacturing business in Nashville for many years. He was there for us when Daddy died, and again when we lost Mama, and when we buried Eva Mai. He showed up at our 50th wedding anniversary, and we've talked on the phone once every few months for a long time. In fact, we spoke just a few weeks ago, and he told me then he was in very bad shape, and said he's never live to see the end of this year, but that he was ready. I have to believe he was.

I've dreaded to check the news from home for the last few days, and yesterday, he was proven right. He left us on June 23, 2019, a date not far removed from his birthday, which in mid July.

THE LAST OF THE SOUTH TOWN RINKY DINKS
THE EXTENDED VOLUME

Wayne's was in June, and I always got them mixed up. He has gone on to once again be with Wayne, and with his wife Shirley, whom he loved and was married to for many years. He's with his mother Cotton, and his dad Whit, (Yes, I know it's Rose and Marvin, but I knew them all my life as Cotton and Whit) and to be joined once more with so many more of our dear old friends.

I will miss our phone conversations, and the few visits we had over the last few years, but I know he is no longer in pain, no longer living under the cloud of cancer, and is in a better place today. He's reunited with Wayne and their parents, and his true love Shirley. The sun is shining, he's laughing, and reliving so many old memories. My tears will fall today, and I will once again raise a toast to one of the finest men I've ever known, a man I will miss till the end of my own days.

I have been fortunate to have some friends that I truly loved, and Wesley was one of them. Rest in peaceful slumber, my dear old friend, and know that we shall meet again one day, in a land much fairer than this one we leave behind.

E. DON HARPE

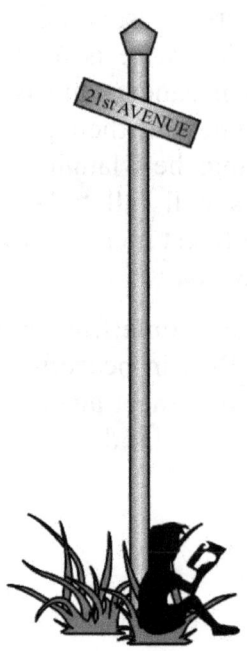

THE LAST OF THE SOUTH TOWN RINKY DINKS
THE EXTENDED VOLUME

PUBLIC DISCLAIMER CONCERNING THE USE OF THE NAMES OF ACTUAL PEOPLE IN THIS BOOK

In this book I have used the real names of family members and friends that I grew up with, all of whom I recall with nothing but the fondest of memories. I do not believe that I written one word that is detrimental to anyone. I was not certain about the spelling of some names, but I have tried to do my best to be sure the names I use are correct.

As work was progressing on *The Last of the South Town Rinky Dinks*, I looked up and managed to let quite a few of the people mentioned in the book read the initial stories, and I have had absolutely no unfavorable reaction at all from any of them.

Some of the family and friends that have had the opportunity to read *The Last of the South Town Rinky Dinks* are: John Wesley Wilson, Faye Birdwell Ellis, Ray Harris and Mary Alley, Billy Gregg, Patty Summers Evilcizer, Lola Bollinger, Clayton Bollinger, and Sam Traughber. My cousins Betty Mayes, Juanita Draughn, Lulu "Doodle" Walker, Billy Walker, as well as friends John Cassell, Ron Rentchler, Delilah Reed, Joe and Christine Brown, and Edith Scott. They have let others read parts of the book, and none of these have expressed anything other than delight that the stories were being told, and all have said they enjoyed the book very much. No one has asked not to be mentioned, nor has anyone asked to have their name removed from the book. However, I will be more than willing to remove any name should that person request it be removed.

I have endeavored not to invade anyone's privacy, and have intentionally excluded any private or embarrassing fact of legitimate public concern.

The Last of the South Town Rinky Dinks was written as, and is meant to be, a tribute to those people I loved so much, and no harm is intended in any fashion whatsoever, either intentional or unintentional.

E. DON HARPE

The Last of the South Town Rinky Dinks is autobiographical in nature, and as many of the incidents took place some 50 years ago, finding every person mentioned in the book is an impossibility.

This disclaimer is intended to show that the stories are true to the best of my recollection, and to proclaim to the public at large that I have intended no harm to anyone mentioned in the book.

Ernest D. Harp
© Ernest D. Harp .
September 2008 & 2021. First Edition Published by Purple Iris Publishing, a subsidiary of RJB Publishing. Second Edition - The Extended Volume, is published by Flint River Press. All rights reserved. No part of this book shall be copied, either manually or by any electronic means, either existing or invented in the future, without the written consent of the author and/or publisher.

THE LAST OF THE SOUTH TOWN RINKY DINKS
THE EXTENDED VOLUME

Award winning author *E. DON HARPE* is a direct descendant of the Harpe Brothers, and for years his branch of the family is the only one that could be found that never denied their connection to the brothers.

E. DON HARPE has had a varied career, from *military service* in the 60's to years spent as an *industrial engineer* for a major appliance firm. Harpe is a *Nashville songwriter* who has had many recorded, and who for years ran his own music publishing company. While in Nashville Harpe was the *office manager of a publishing company* that had several number one country music hits, and was also the *Creative Director* for one of the most successful syndicated radio programs of the early 90's. During this time he won the coveted *Silver Pen Award* from the Nashville Banner daily newspaper.

Since retiring from public work in 2004, Harpe has concentrated on writing novels, and 2021 finds him working on yet another action/adventure novel, which will be his 11th published book He also has more than 30 short stories available on line, including two in an anthology called Twisted Tails II, published by Double Dragon Publishing, which won the *EPPIE AWARD* for best science fiction anthology of 2007.

Now retired and living in Georgia, Harpe devotes his time to Helen, his wife of more than 50 years, to his children, grandchildren, great grandchildren, and to his writing.

"I'm pretty satisfied in my own skin right now," Harpe says, *"and I just want to continue to write things that will entertain and hold the readers interest."*

Connect with Harpe on the Internet at his website, as well as on Facebook and other social media.

Facebook - http://www.facebook.com/home.php?
Books and shorts available on Amazon and Smashwords.

E. DON HARPE

THE LAST OF THE SOUTH TOWN RINKY DINKS
THE EXTENDED VOLUME

ALSO BY E. DON HARPE

DARKWOLF UNLEASHED
RESURRECTION: REBIRTH OF THE TERRIBLE HARPES
REDNECK UNIVERSE
STORMCHILDE
FULL CONTROL
UNDER THE INFLUENCE OF A FULL MOON
SUNDOWN TWO with PHIL WHITLEY
13 TWISTED TALES with EUGEN BACON

SHORT STORIES

THE HARPE'S LAST RAMPAGE
FIRE FROM HEAVEN
REDNECK RIVIERA - A REDNECK RIVIERA STORY
TALLEDEGA TWOSTEP - A REDNECK RIVIERA STORY
COTTONDALE CONFIRMATION - A REDNECK RIVIERA STORY
MUSIC CITY MOJO - A REDNECK RIVIERA STORY
STUBIAN SWAMPDEVILS - A REDNECK RIVIERA STORY
FLAMINGO FIASCO - A REDNECK RIVIERA STORY
REDNECK RASSLIN' - A REDNECK RIVIERA STORY
ANGEL IN AMBER
KILLING FROST
THE DEMON REGISTRATION ACT
CYPHONS
THE TROPICAL TABOO CAPER
MILLER'S LUCK
THE EDGE
THE SKY IS FALLING
WHAT GOES AROUND
THE BIG PICTURE
FEBRUARY
THE WEDDING HELMET
SLUGGER
THE FLAT ROCK KID

E. DON HARPE

THE LAST OF THE SOUTH TOWN RINKY DINKS
THE EXTENDED VOLUME

NEW FOR 2022
From E. Don Harpe

TEARS OF GOD

FABLES AND FABRICATIONS FROM HONEYSUCKLE HILL

www.ingramcontent.com/pod-product-compliance
Lightning Source LLC
Chambersburg PA
CBHW050854160426
43194CB00011B/2146